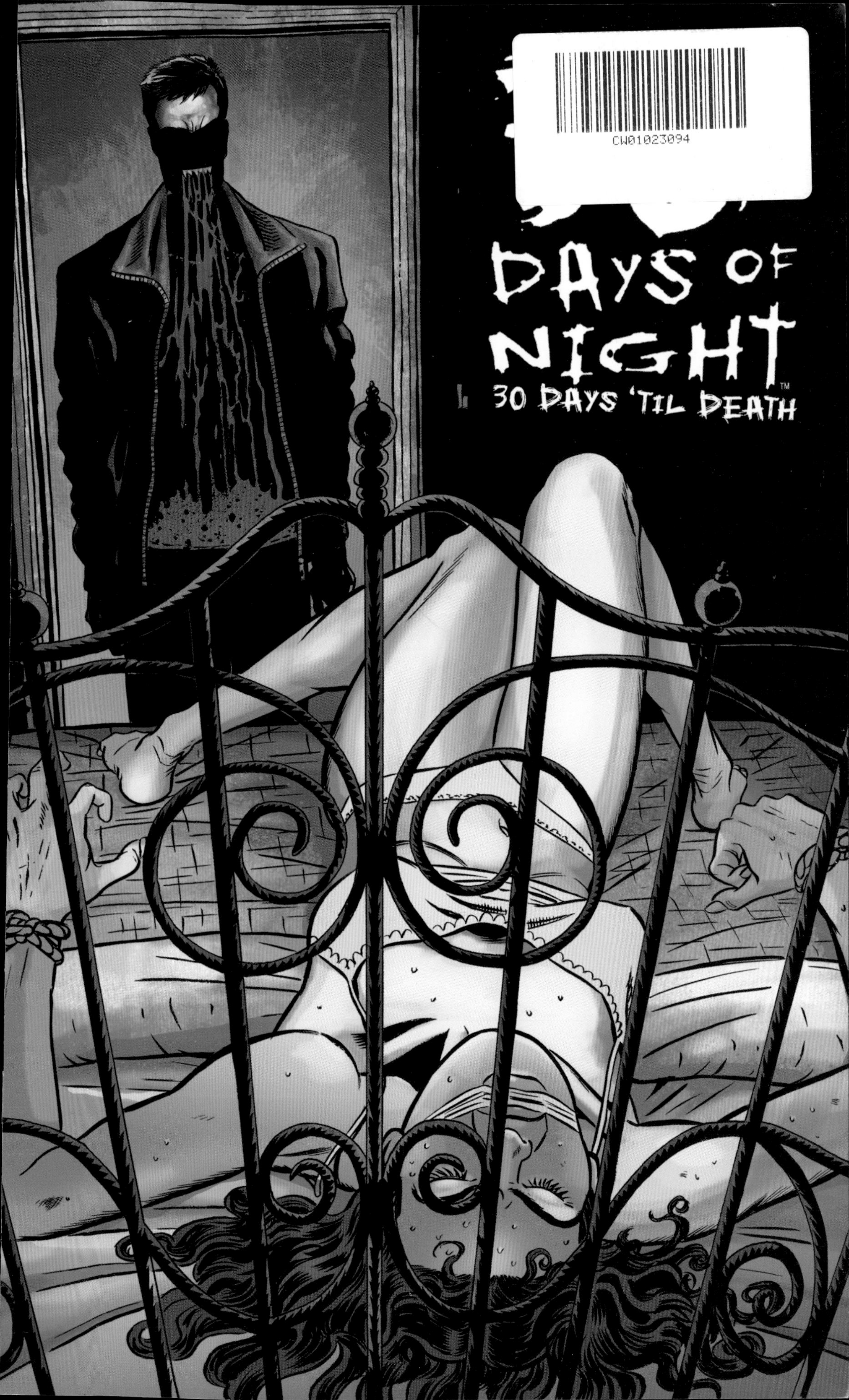
DAYS OF
NIGHT
30 DAYS 'TIL DEATH

30 DAYS OF NIGHT: 30 DAYS 'TIL DEATH

story and art: David Lapham

colors: Len O'Grady

letters: Neil Uyetake & Chris Mowry

original series edits: Scott Dunbier

collection edits: Justin Eisinger

collection design and production: Chris Mowry

ISBN: 978-1-60010-441-1
12 11 10 09   1 2 3 4

IDW Publishin
Operation
Ted Adams, Chief Executive Offic
Greg Goldstein, Chief Operating Offic
Matthew Ruzicka, CPA, Chief Financial Offic
Alan Payne, VP of Sale
Lorelei Bunjes, Dir. of Digital Service
AnnaMaria White, Marketing & PR Manag
Marci Hubbard, Executive Assistai
Alonzo Simon, Shipping Managc

Editoria
Chris Ryall, Publisher/Editor-in-Ch
Scott Dunbier, Editor, Special Proje
Andy Schmidt, Senior Edit
Justin Eisinger, Edit
Kris Oprisko, Editor/Foreign Li
Denton J. Tipton, Edit
Tom Waltz, Edit
Mariah Huehner, Associate Edit

Desi
Robbie Robbins, EVP/Sr. Graphic Art
Ben Templesmith, Artist/Design
Neil Uyetake, Art Direct
Chris Mowry, Graphic Art
Amauri Osorio, Graphic Art
Gilberto Lazcano, Production Assista

30

DAYS OF

NIGHT

30 DAYS 'TIL DEATH ™

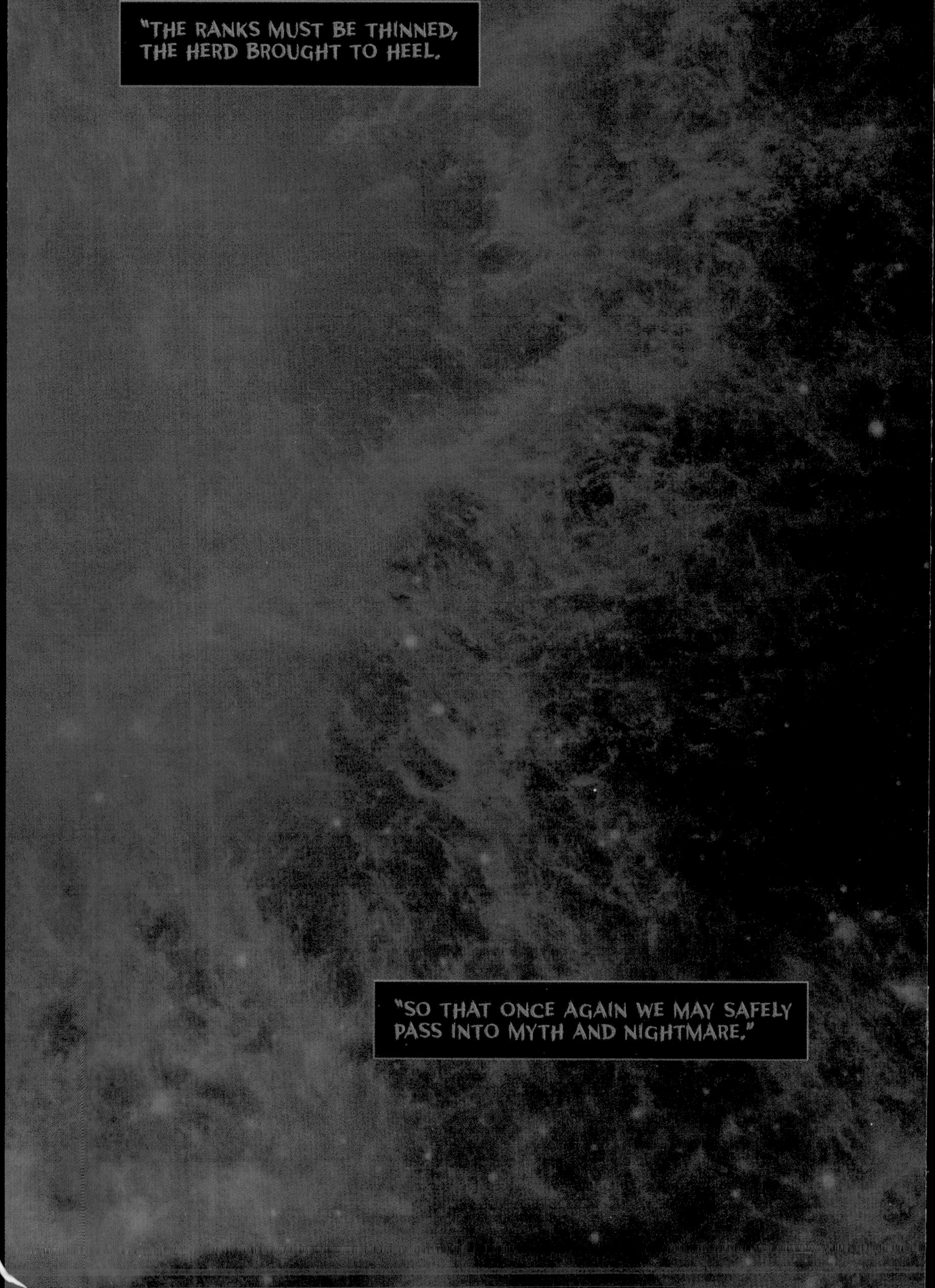
"THE RANKS MUST BE THINNED, THE HERD BROUGHT TO HEEL.
"SO THAT ONCE AGAIN WE MAY SAFELY PASS INTO MYTH AND NIGHTMARE."

CHAPTER ONE

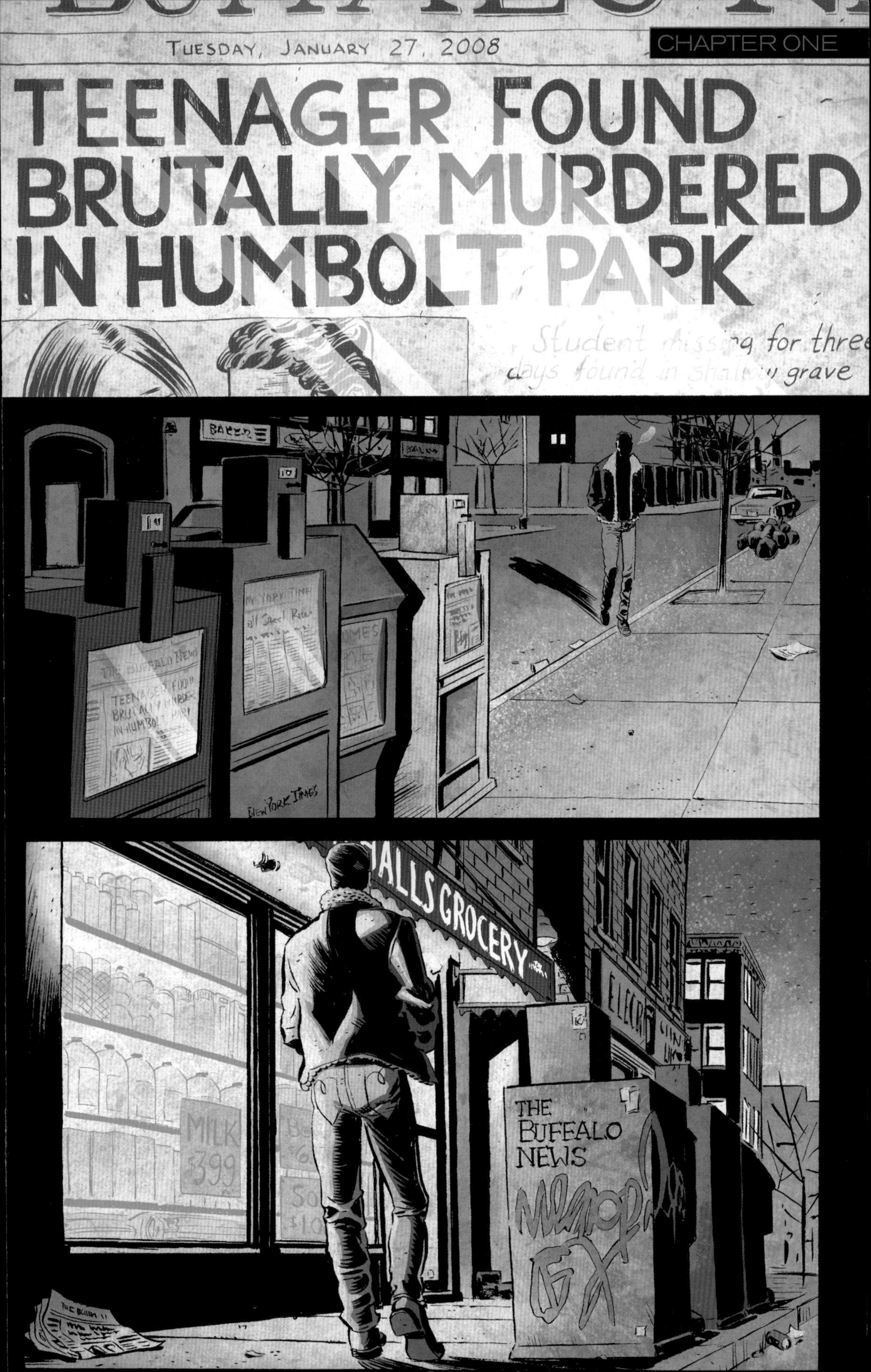
TUESDAY, JANUARY 27, 2008
TEENAGER FOUND BRUTALLY MURDERED IN HUMBOLT PARK
Student missing for three days found in shallow grave
THE BUFFALO NEWS
TEENAGER FOUND BRUTALLY MURDER IN HUMBOLT PARK
NEW YORK TIMES
HALLS GROCERY
MILK $3.99
THE BUFFALO NEWS

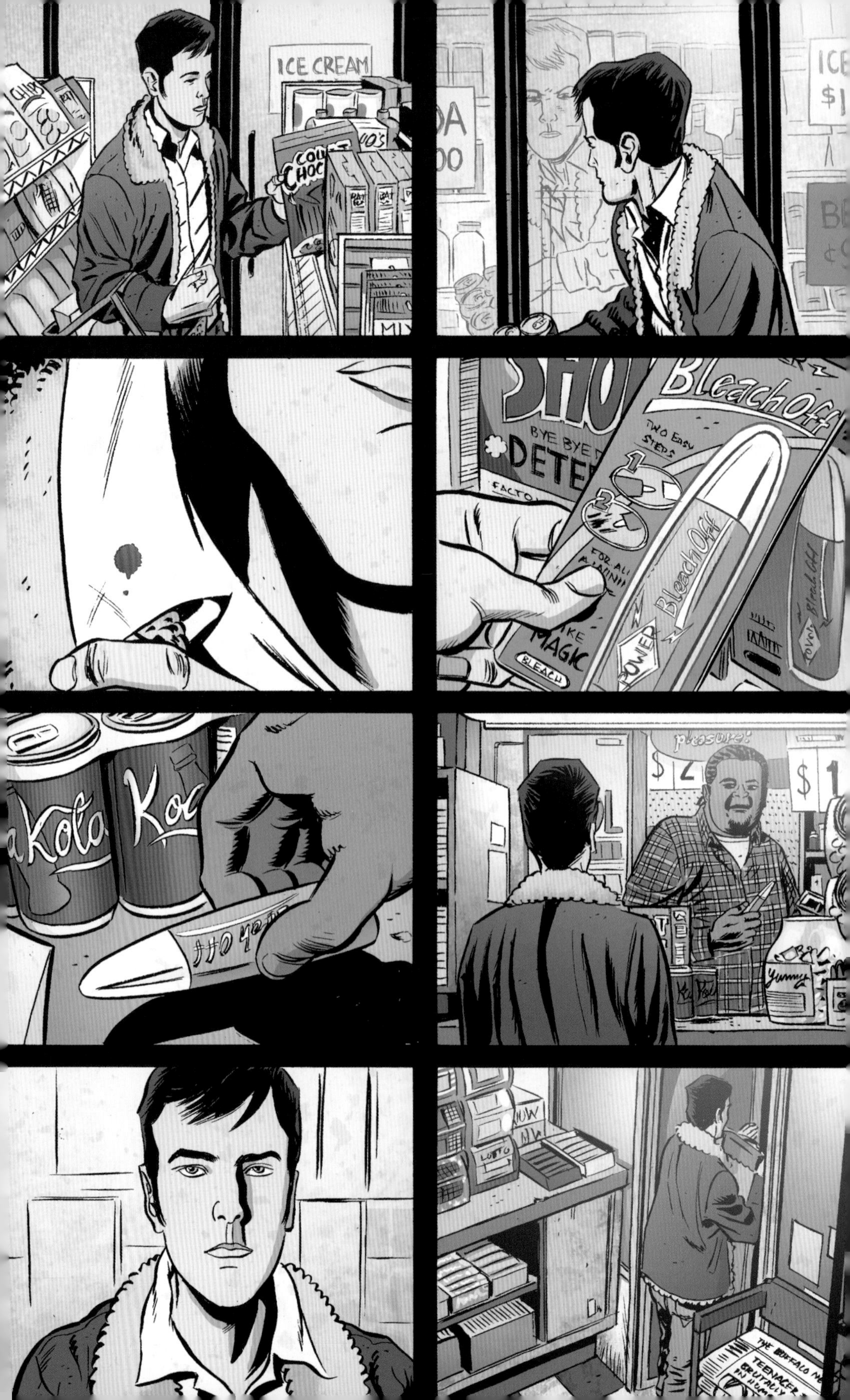
ICE CREAM
BleachOff
TWO Easy STEPS
BYE BYE
MAGIC
BLEACH
POWER
pleasure!
TEENAGER
BRUTALLY

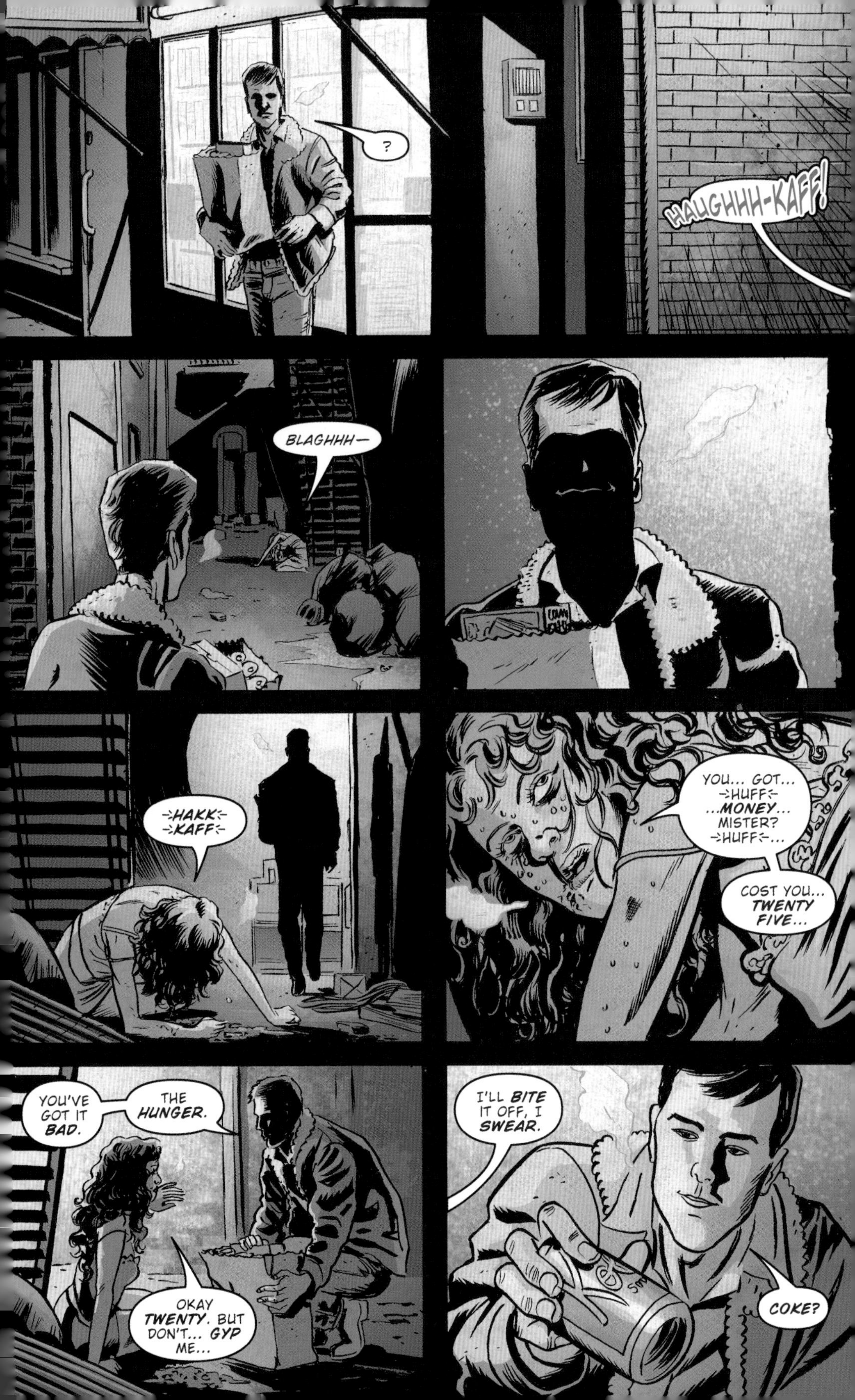
?
HAUGHHH-KAFF!
BLAGHHH—
HAKK
KAFF
YOU... GOT... HUFF ...MONEY... MISTER? HUFF...
COST YOU... TWENTY FIVE...
YOU'VE GOT IT BAD.
THE HUNGER.
OKAY TWENTY. BUT DON'T... GYP ME...
I'LL BITE IT OFF, I SWEAR.
COKE?

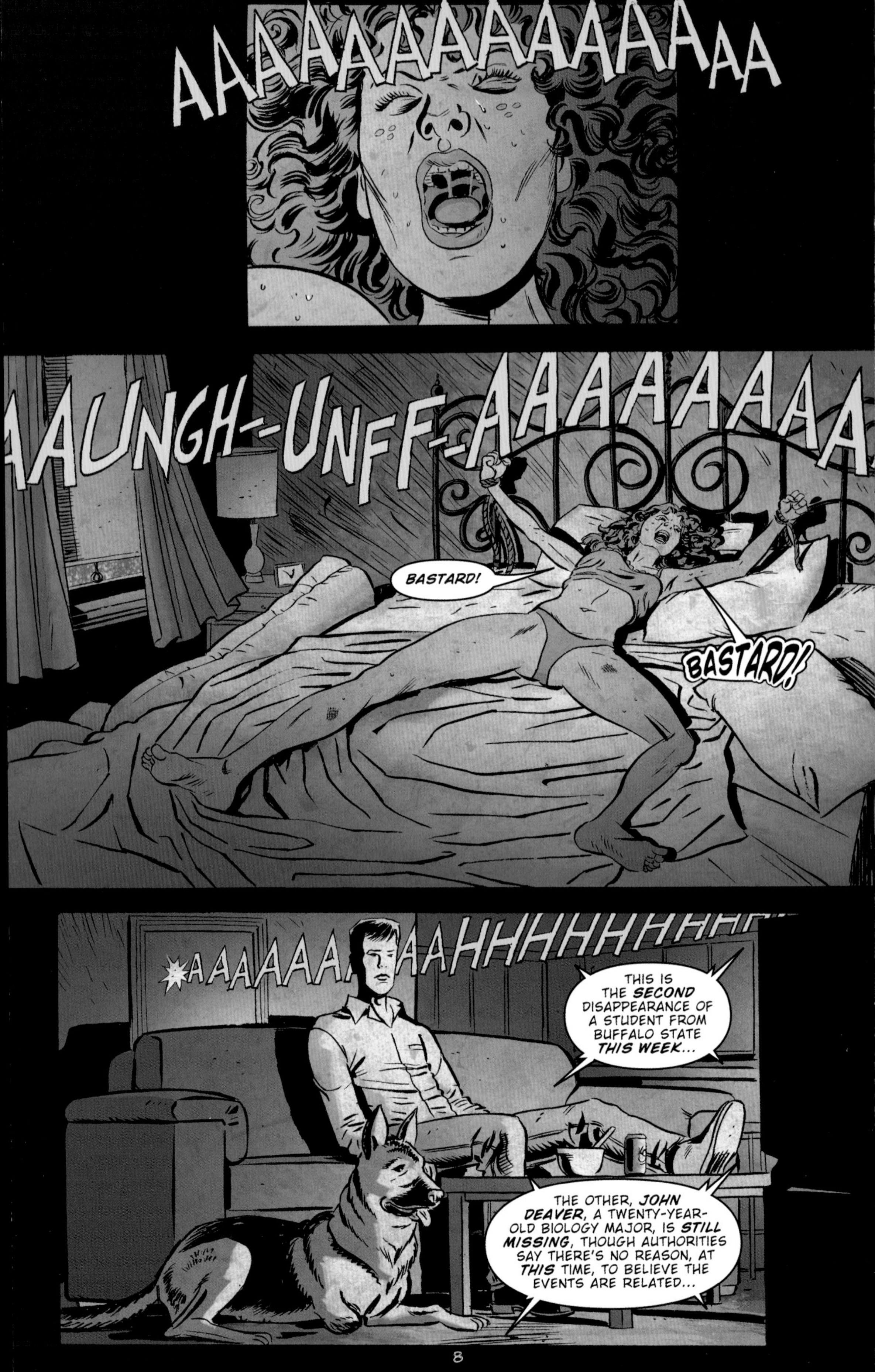
AAAAAAAAAAAAAA
AAUNGH--UNFF--AAAAAAA
BASTARD!
BASTARD!
AAAAAAAAHHHHHHHHHH
THIS IS THE SECOND DISAPPEARANCE OF A STUDENT FROM BUFFALO STATE THIS WEEK...
THE OTHER, JOHN DEAVER, A TWENTY-YEAR-OLD BIOLOGY MAJOR, IS STILL MISSING, THOUGH AUTHORITIES SAY THERE'S NO REASON, AT THIS TIME, TO BELIEVE THE EVENTS ARE RELATED...

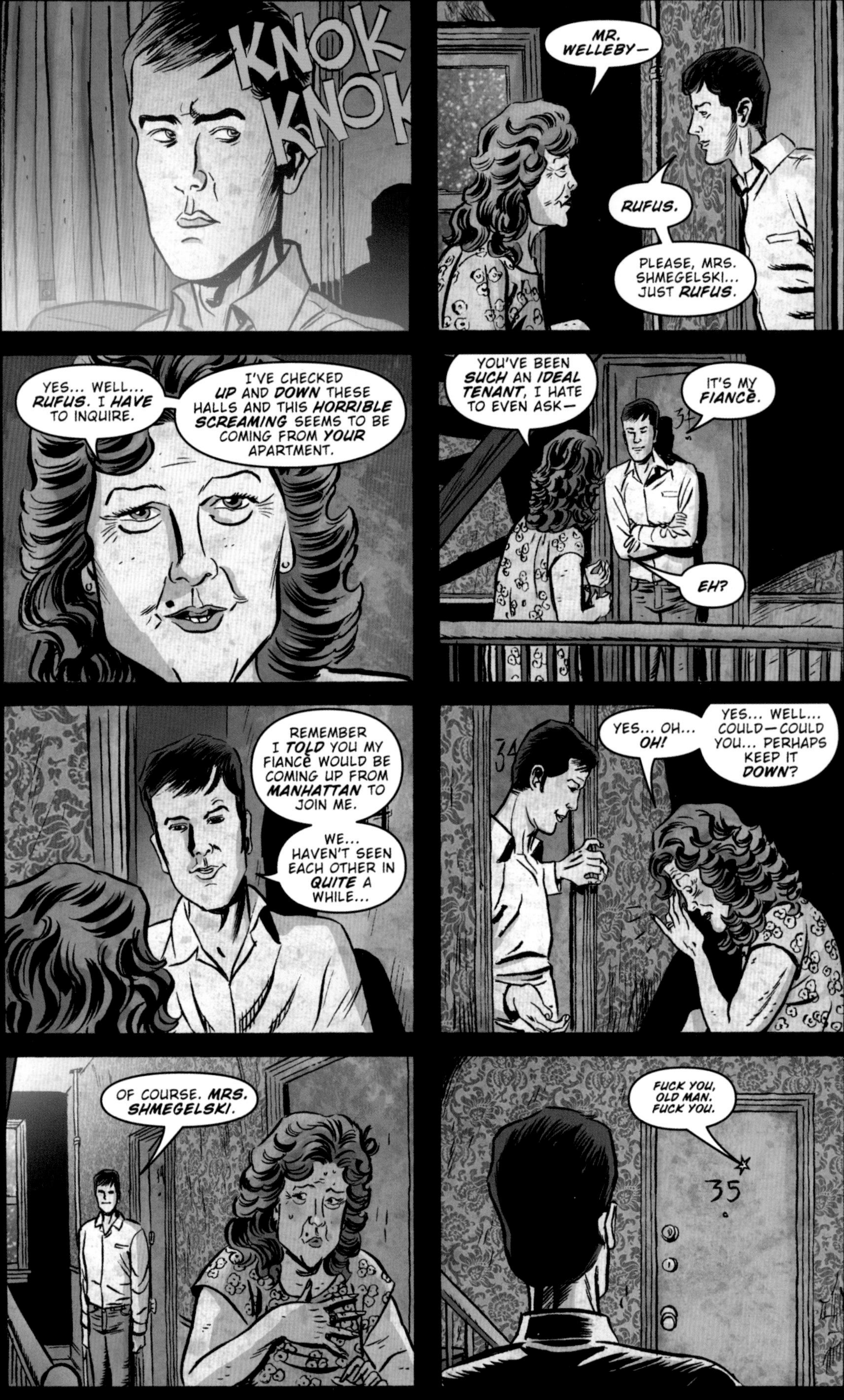
KNOK
KNOK
MR. WELLEBY—
RUFUS.
PLEASE, MRS. SHMEGELSKI... JUST RUFUS.
YES... WELL... RUFUS. I HAVE TO INQUIRE.
I'VE CHECKED UP AND DOWN THESE HALLS AND THIS HORRIBLE SCREAMING SEEMS TO BE COMING FROM YOUR APARTMENT.
YOU'VE BEEN SUCH AN IDEAL TENANT, I HATE TO EVEN ASK—
IT'S MY FIANCÉ.
EH?
REMEMBER I TOLD YOU MY FIANCÉ WOULD BE COMING UP FROM MANHATTAN TO JOIN ME.
WE... HAVEN'T SEEN EACH OTHER IN QUITE A WHILE...
YES... OH... OH!
YES... WELL... COULD—COULD YOU... PERHAPS KEEP IT DOWN?
OF COURSE. MRS. SHMEGELSKI.
FUCK YOU, OLD MAN. FUCK YOU.
35

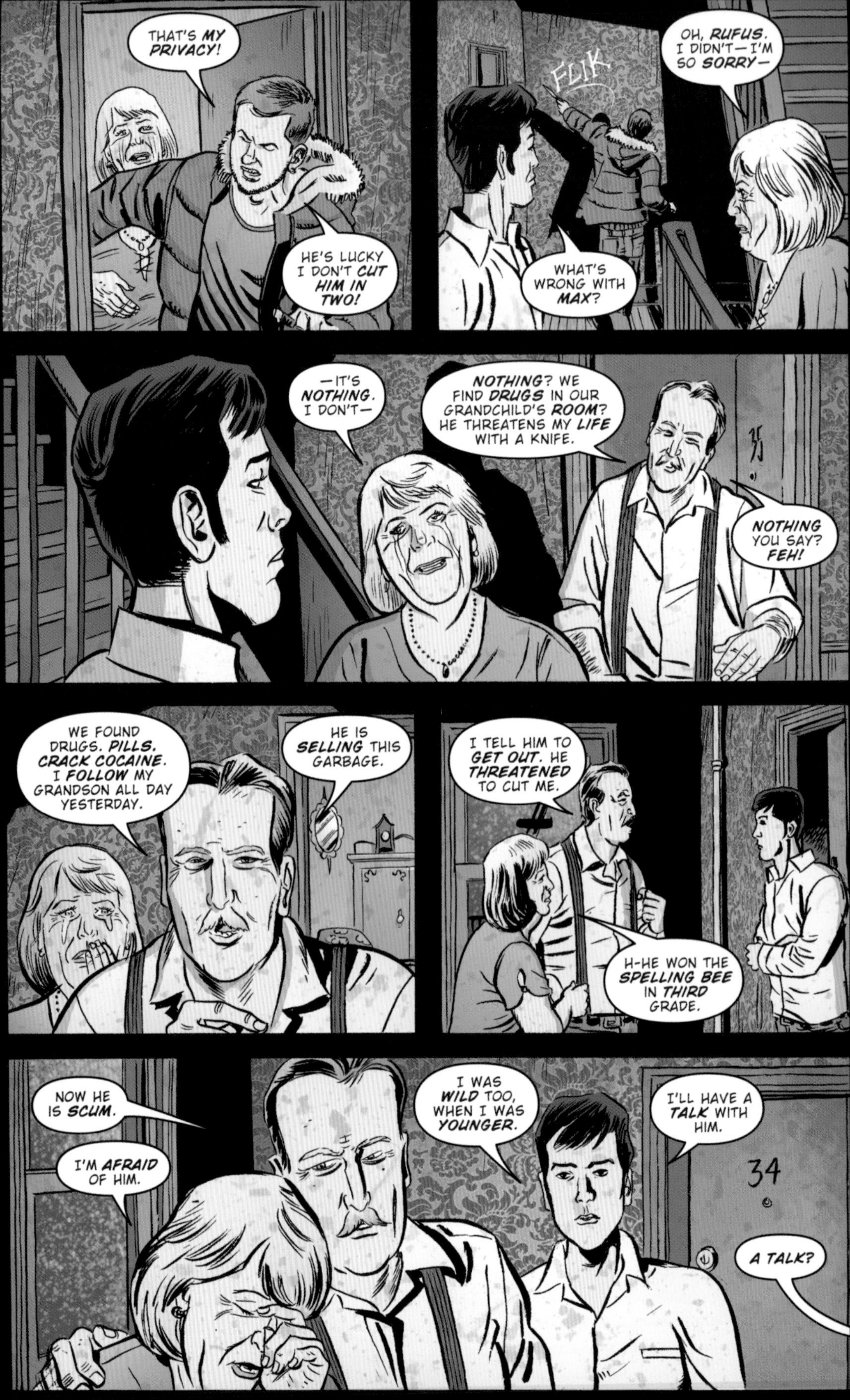

THAT'S MY PRIVACY!
HE'S LUCKY I DON'T CUT HIM IN TWO!
FLIK
OH, RUFUS. I DIDN'T—I'M SO SORRY—
WHAT'S WRONG WITH MAX?
—IT'S NOTHING. I DON'T—
NOTHING? WE FIND DRUGS IN OUR GRANDCHILD'S ROOM? HE THREATENS MY LIFE WITH A KNIFE.
NOTHING YOU SAY? FEH!
WE FOUND DRUGS. PILLS. CRACK COCAINE. I FOLLOW MY GRANDSON ALL DAY YESTERDAY.
HE IS SELLING THIS GARBAGE.
I TELL HIM TO GET OUT. HE THREATENED TO CUT ME.
H-HE WON THE SPELLING BEE IN THIRD GRADE.
NOW HE IS SCUM.
I'M AFRAID OF HIM.
I WAS WILD TOO, WHEN I WAS YOUNGER.
I'LL HAVE A TALK WITH HIM.
34
A TALK?

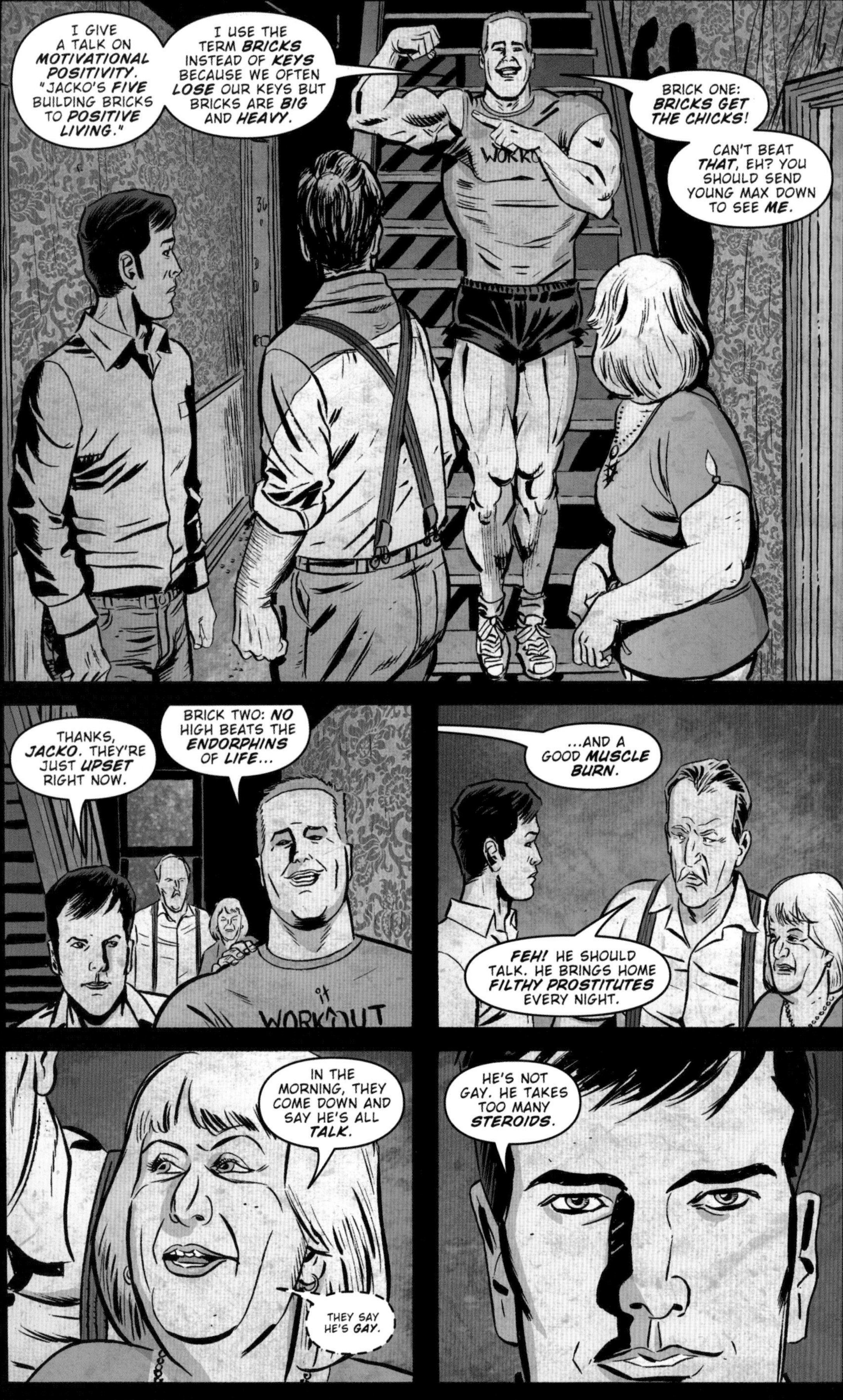
I GIVE A TALK ON MOTIVATIONAL POSITIVITY. "JACKO'S FIVE BUILDING BRICKS TO POSITIVE LIVING."
I USE THE TERM BRICKS INSTEAD OF KEYS BECAUSE WE OFTEN LOSE OUR KEYS BUT BRICKS ARE BIG AND HEAVY.
BRICK ONE: BRICKS GET THE CHICKS!
CAN'T BEAT THAT, EH? YOU SHOULD SEND YOUNG MAX DOWN TO SEE ME.
THANKS, JACKO. THEY'RE JUST UPSET RIGHT NOW.
BRICK TWO: NO HIGH BEATS THE ENDORPHINS OF LIFE...
WORKOUT
...AND A GOOD MUSCLE BURN.
FEH! HE SHOULD TALK. HE BRINGS HOME FILTHY PROSTITUTES EVERY NIGHT.
IN THE MORNING, THEY COME DOWN AND SAY HE'S ALL TALK.
THEY SAY HE'S GAY.
HE'S NOT GAY. HE TAKES TOO MANY STEROIDS.

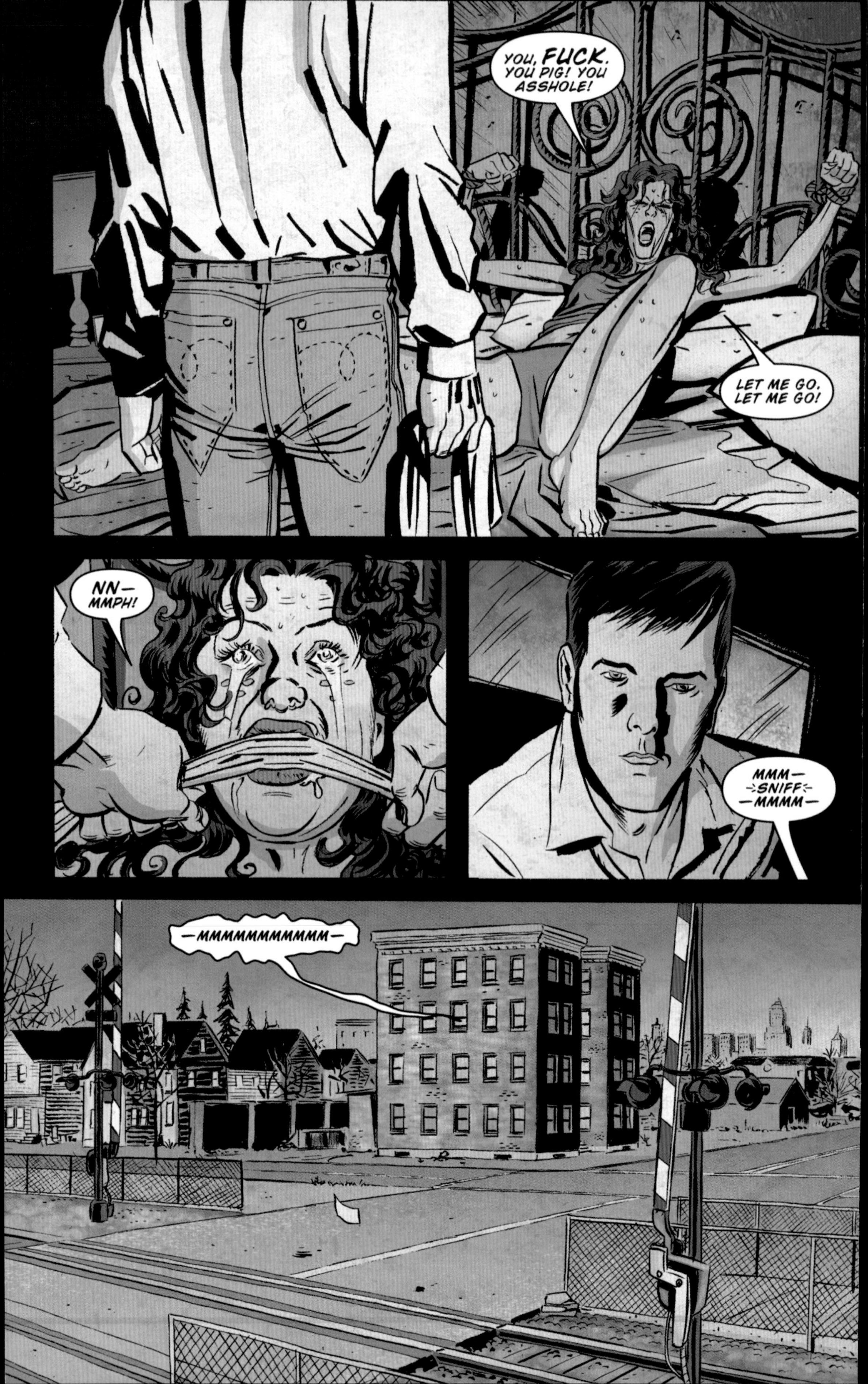
YOU, FUCK. YOU PIG! YOU ASSHOLE!
LET ME GO. LET ME GO!
NN—MMPH!
MMM— -SNIFF- —MMMM—
—MMMMMMMMMM—

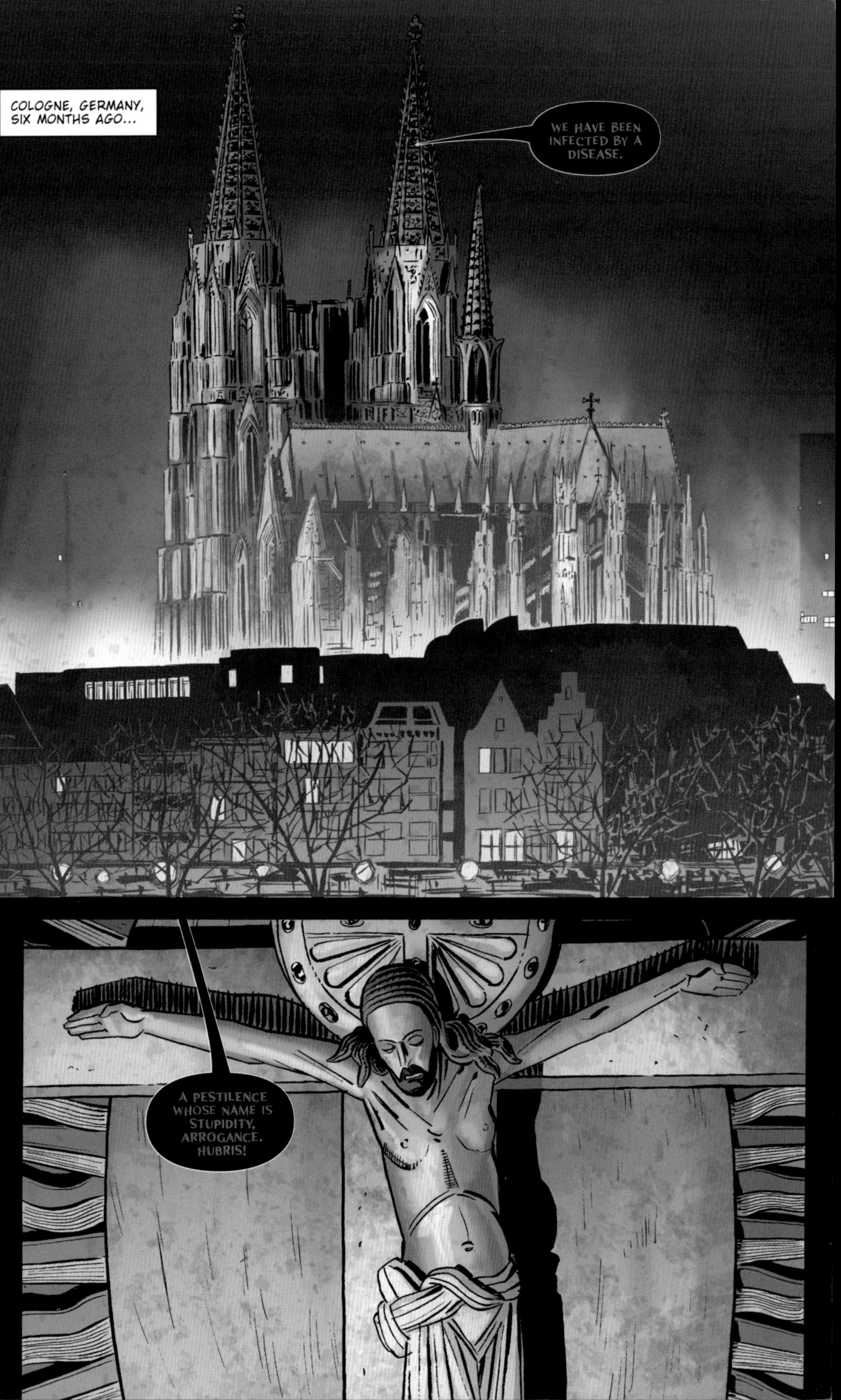
COLOGNE, GERMANY, SIX MONTHS AGO...
WE HAVE BEEN INFECTED BY A DISEASE.
A PESTILENCE WHOSE NAME IS STUPIDITY, ARROGANCE, HUBRIS!

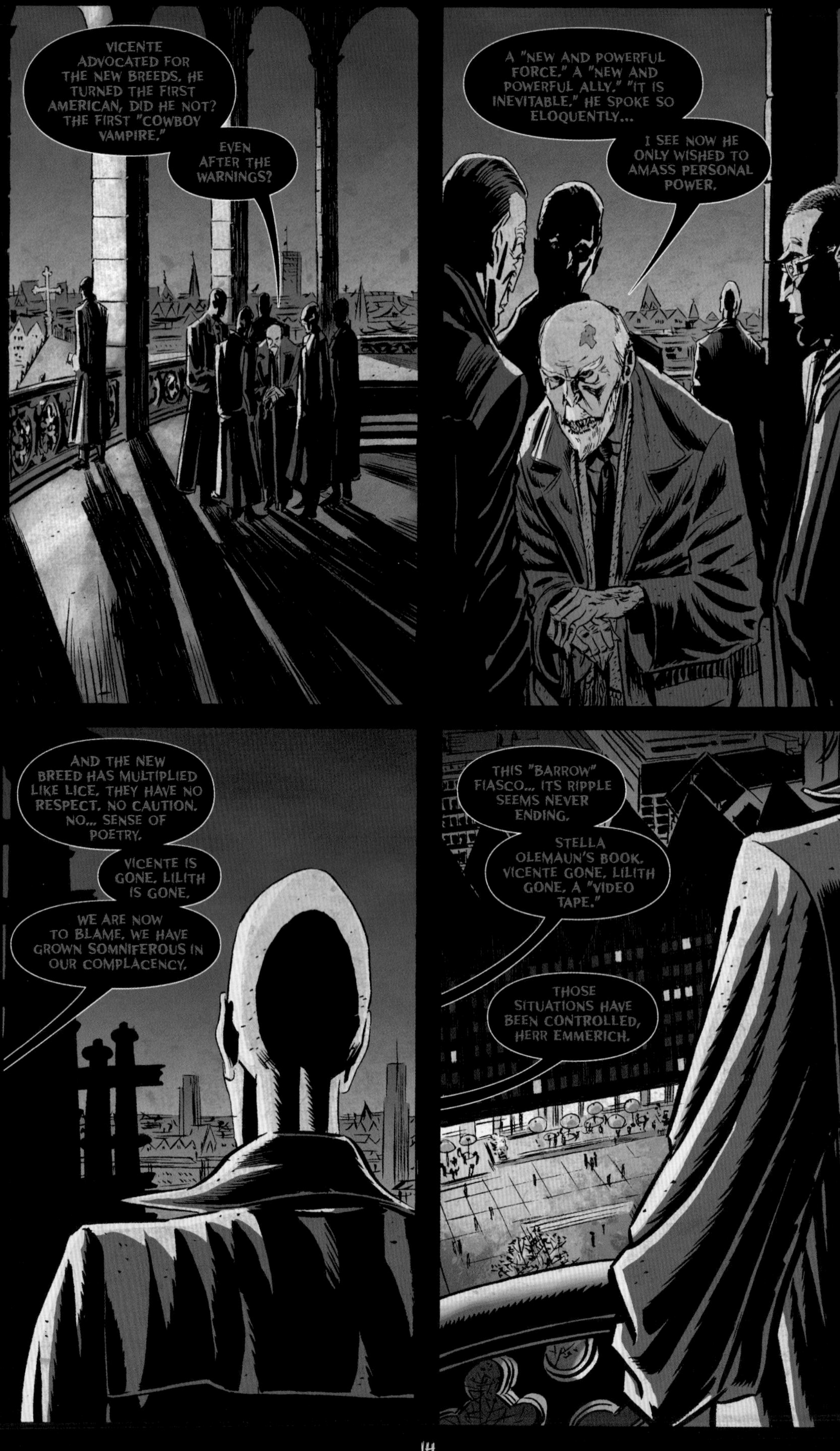
VICENTE ADVOCATED FOR THE NEW BREEDS. HE TURNED THE FIRST AMERICAN, DID HE NOT? THE FIRST "COWBOY VAMPIRE."
EVEN AFTER THE WARNINGS?
A "NEW AND POWERFUL FORCE." A "NEW AND POWERFUL ALLY." "IT IS INEVITABLE." HE SPOKE SO ELOQUENTLY...
I SEE NOW HE ONLY WISHED TO AMASS PERSONAL POWER.
AND THE NEW BREED HAS MULTIPLIED LIKE LICE. THEY HAVE NO RESPECT, NO CAUTION. NO... SENSE OF POETRY.
VICENTE IS GONE. LILITH IS GONE.
WE ARE NOW TO BLAME. WE HAVE GROWN SOMNIFEROUS IN OUR COMPLACENCY.
THIS "BARROW" FIASCO... ITS RIPPLE SEEMS NEVER ENDING.
STELLA OLEMAUN'S BOOK. VICENTE GONE. LILITH GONE. A "VIDEO TAPE."
THOSE SITUATIONS HAVE BEEN CONTROLLED, HERR EMMERICH.

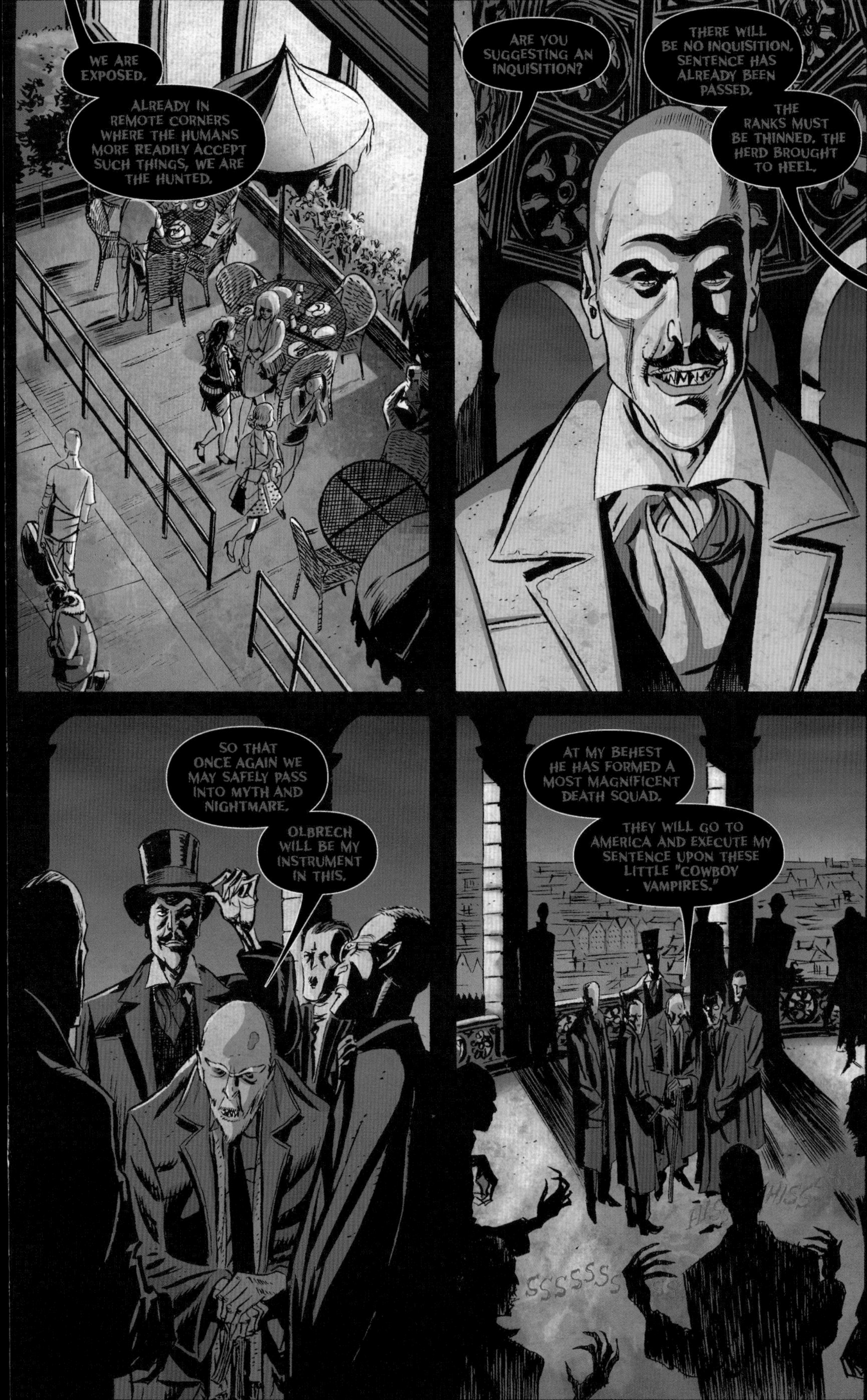

WE ARE EXPOSED.
ALREADY IN REMOTE CORNERS WHERE THE HUMANS MORE READILY ACCEPT SUCH THINGS, WE ARE THE HUNTED.
ARE YOU SUGGESTING AN INQUISITION?
THERE WILL BE NO INQUISITION. SENTENCE HAS ALREADY BEEN PASSED.
THE RANKS MUST BE THINNED. THE HERD BROUGHT TO HEEL.
SO THAT ONCE AGAIN WE MAY SAFELY PASS INTO MYTH AND NIGHTMARE.
OLBRECH WILL BE MY INSTRUMENT IN THIS.
AT MY BEHEST HE HAS FORMED A MOST MAGNIFICENT DEATH SQUAD.
THEY WILL GO TO AMERICA AND EXECUTE MY SENTENCE UPON THESE LITTLE "COWBOY VAMPIRES."
HISS
HISS
SSSSSSS

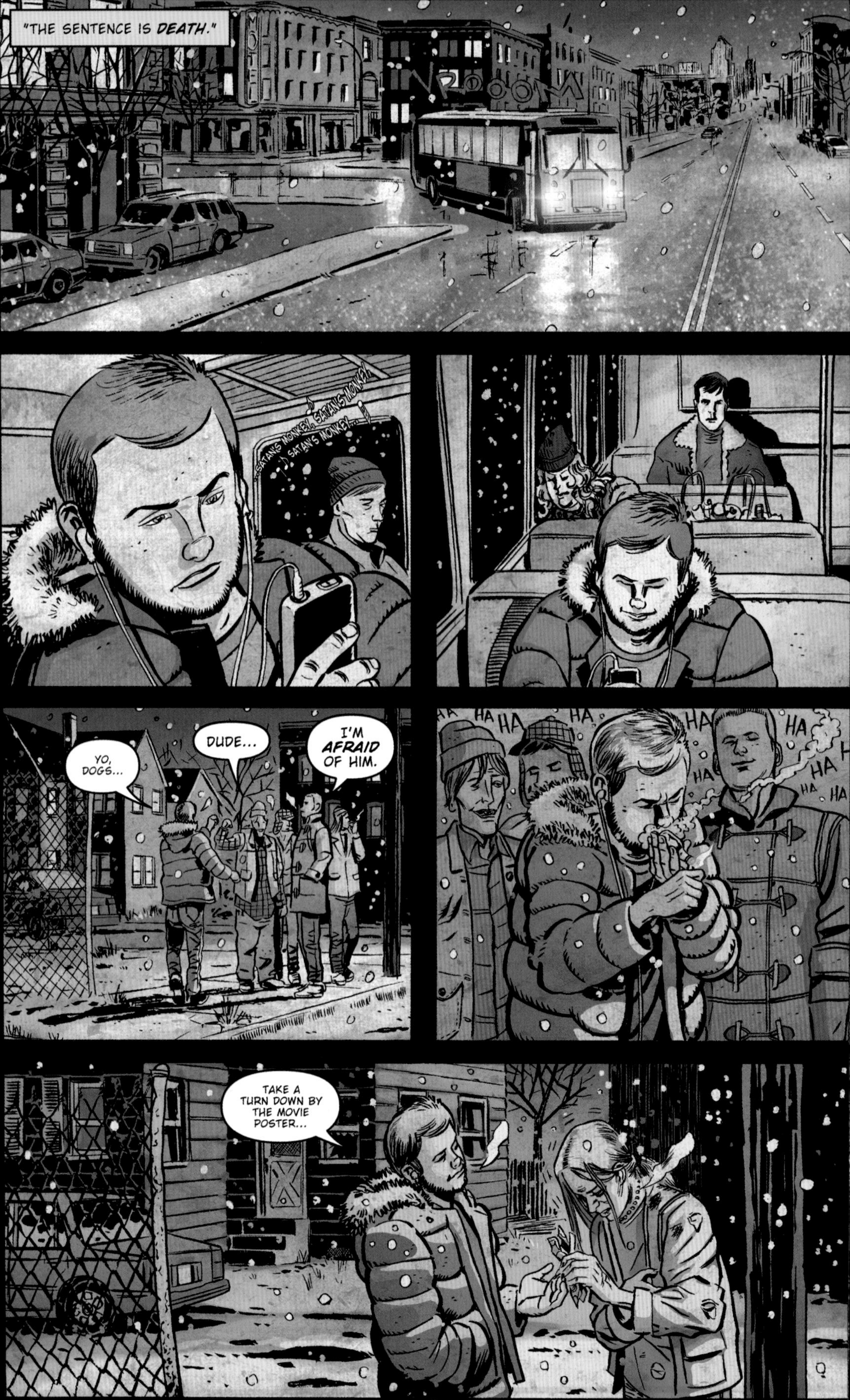
"THE SENTENCE IS *DEATH*."
...SATAN'S MONKEY, SATAN'S MONKEY, SATAN'S MONKEY,
SATAN'S MONKEY...
YO, DOGS...
DUDE...
I'M *AFRAID* OF HIM.
HA HA HA HA HA HA HA HA
TAKE A TURN DOWN BY THE MOVIE POSTER...

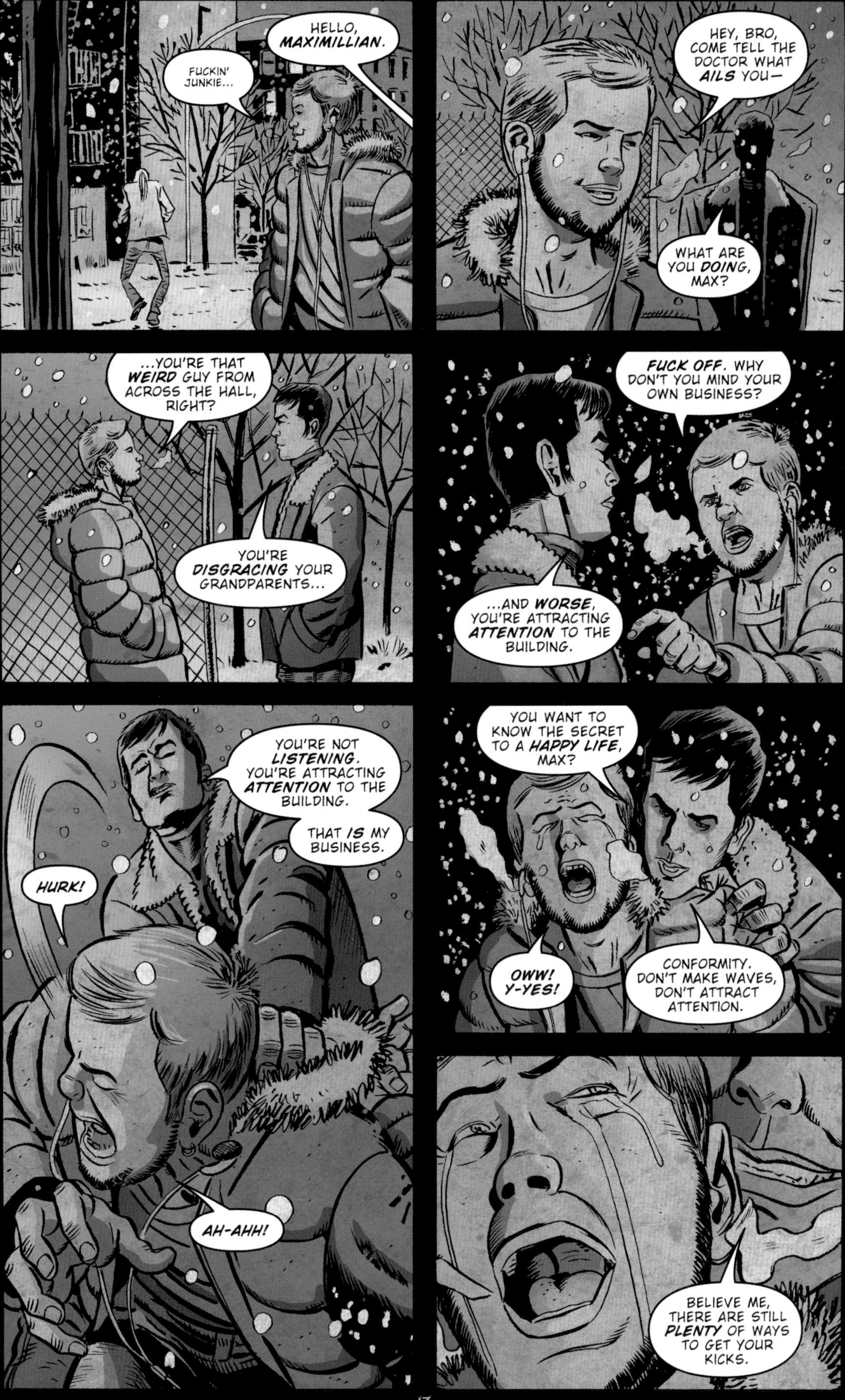
FUCKIN' JUNKIE...
HELLO, MAXIMILLIAN.
HEY, BRO, COME TELL THE DOCTOR WHAT AILS YOU—
WHAT ARE YOU DOING, MAX?
...YOU'RE THAT WEIRD GUY FROM ACROSS THE HALL, RIGHT?
YOU'RE DISGRACING YOUR GRANDPARENTS...
FUCK OFF. WHY DON'T YOU MIND YOUR OWN BUSINESS?
...AND WORSE, YOU'RE ATTRACTING ATTENTION TO THE BUILDING.
YOU'RE NOT LISTENING. YOU'RE ATTRACTING ATTENTION TO THE BUILDING.
THAT IS MY BUSINESS.
HURK!
AH-AHH!
YOU WANT TO KNOW THE SECRET TO A HAPPY LIFE, MAX?
OWW! Y-YES!
CONFORMITY. DON'T MAKE WAVES, DON'T ATTRACT ATTENTION.
BELIEVE ME, THERE ARE STILL PLENTY OF WAYS TO GET YOUR KICKS.

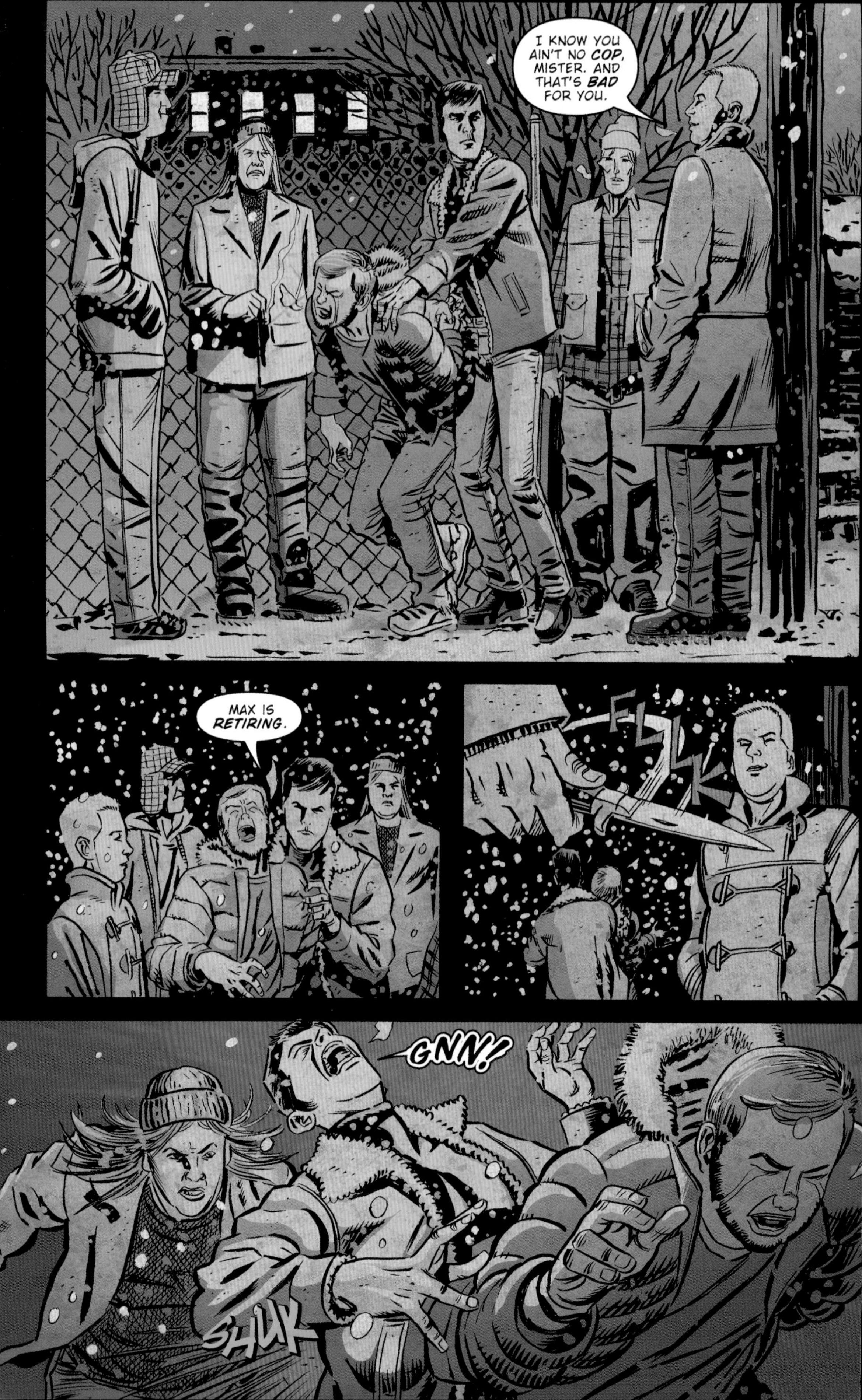
I KNOW YOU AIN'T NO COP, MISTER. AND THAT'S BAD FOR YOU.
MAX IS RETIRING.
FLIK
GNN!
SHUK

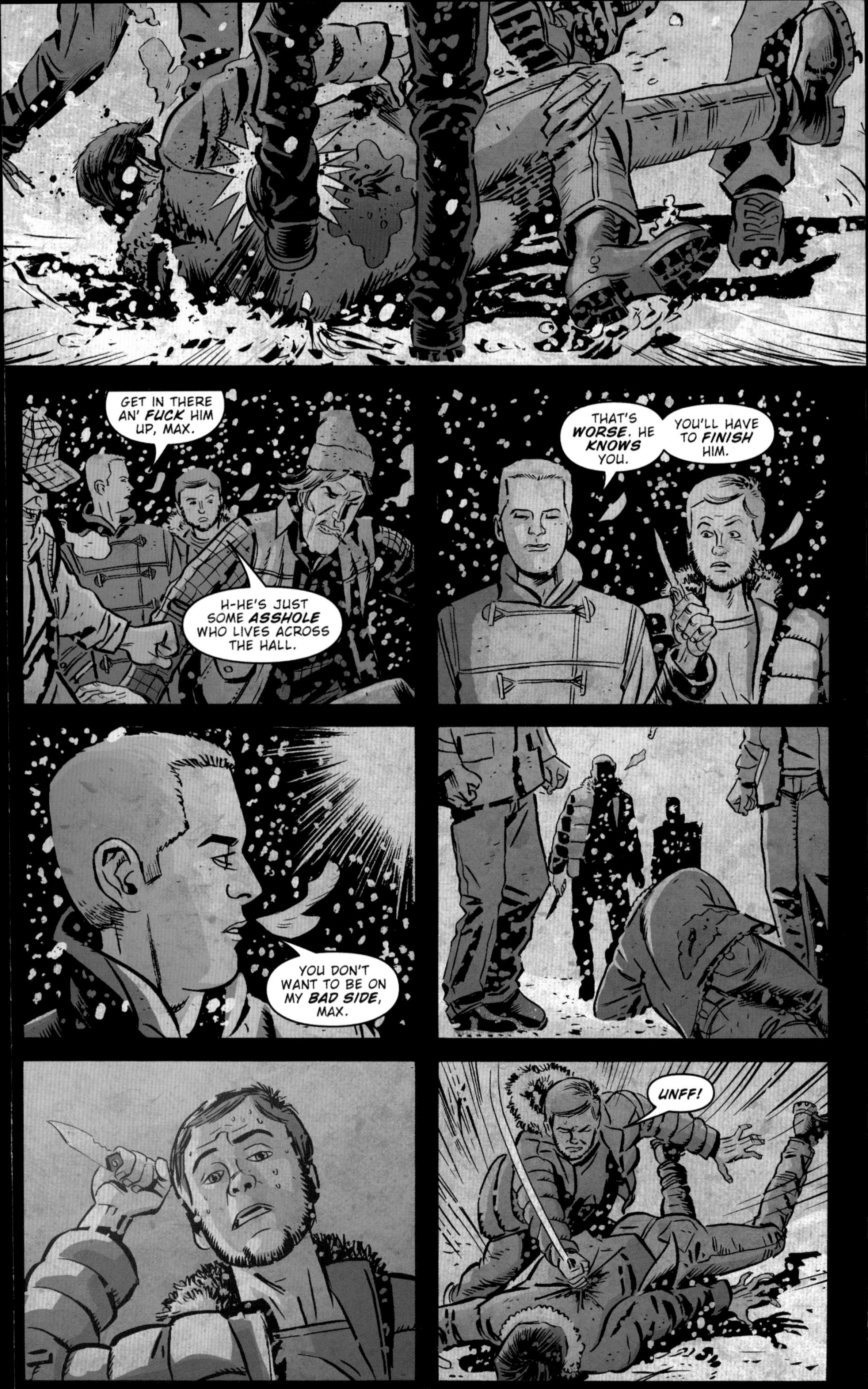
GET IN THERE AN' FUCK HIM UP, MAX.
H-HE'S JUST SOME ASSHOLE WHO LIVES ACROSS THE HALL.
THAT'S WORSE. HE KNOWS YOU.
YOU'LL HAVE TO FINISH HIM.
YOU DON'T WANT TO BE ON MY BAD SIDE, MAX.
UNFF!

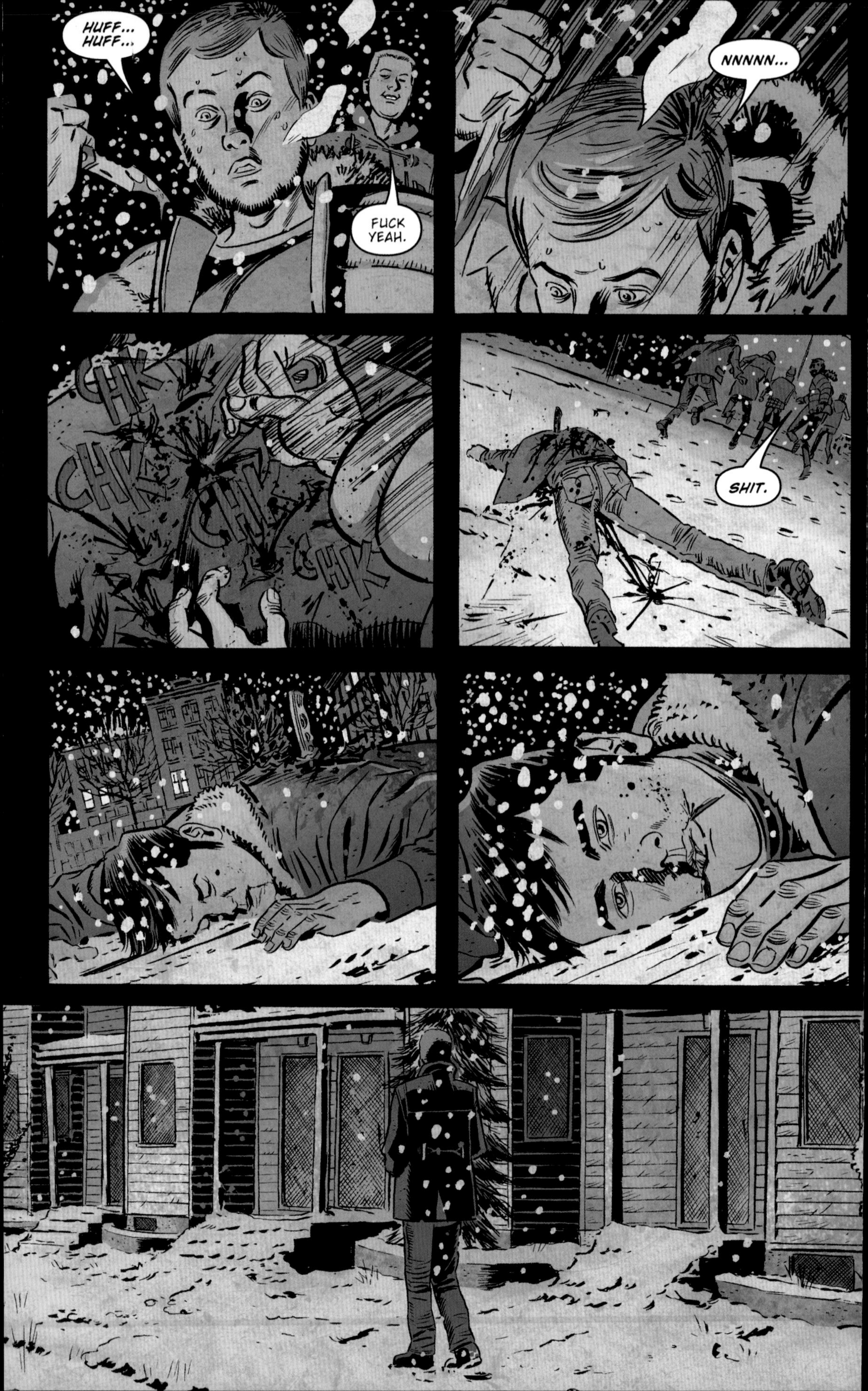
HUFF... HUFF...
FUCK YEAH.
NNNNN...
CHK CHK CHK CHK CHK
SHIT.

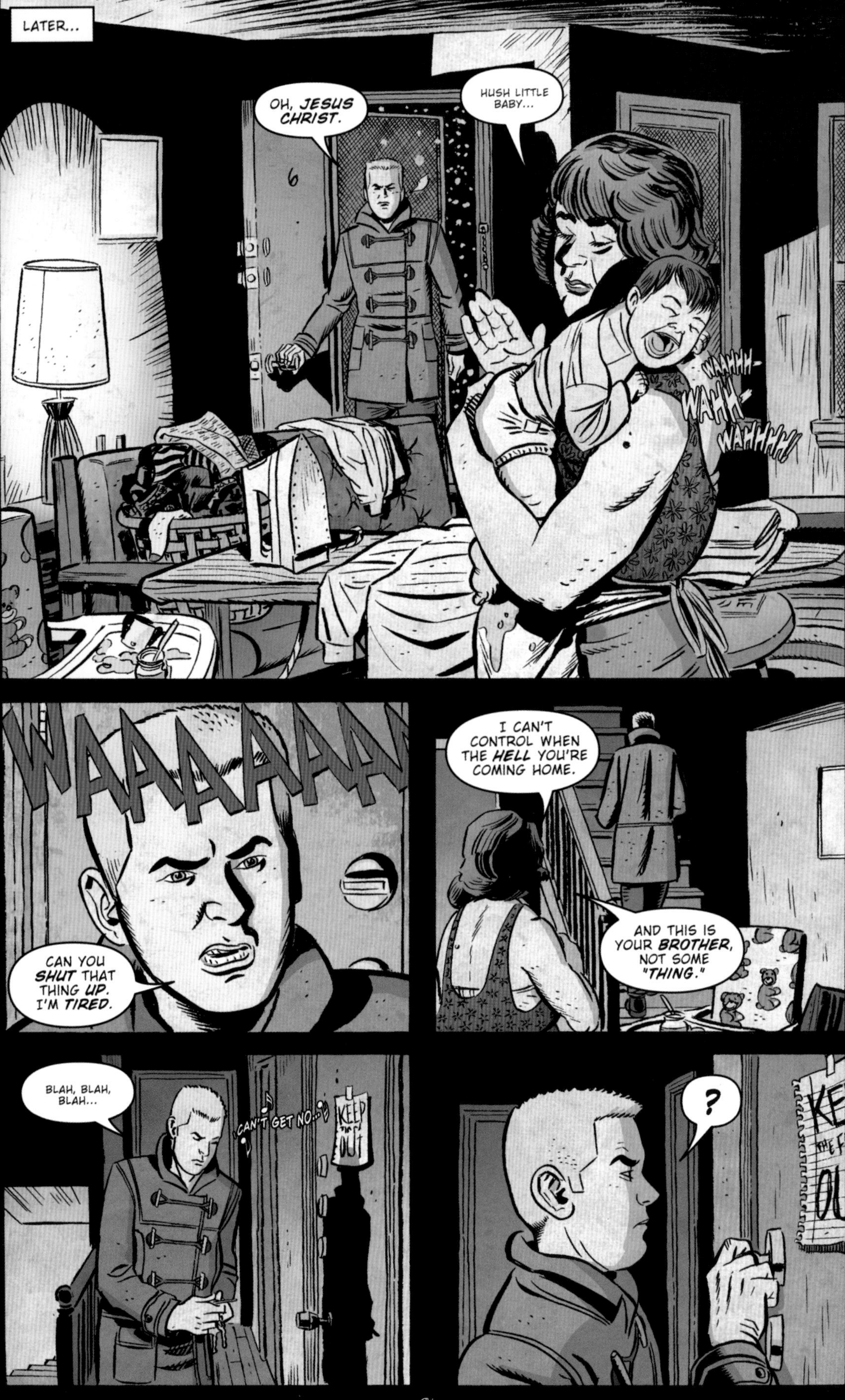
LATER...
OH, JESUS CHRIST.
HUSH LITTLE BABY...
WAHHHH-
WAHH-
WAHHHH!
WAAAAAAA
CAN YOU SHUT THAT THING UP. I'M TIRED.
I CAN'T CONTROL WHEN THE HELL YOU'RE COMING HOME.
AND THIS IS YOUR BROTHER, NOT SOME "THING."
BLAH, BLAH, BLAH...
CAN'T GET NO...
KEEP OUT
?

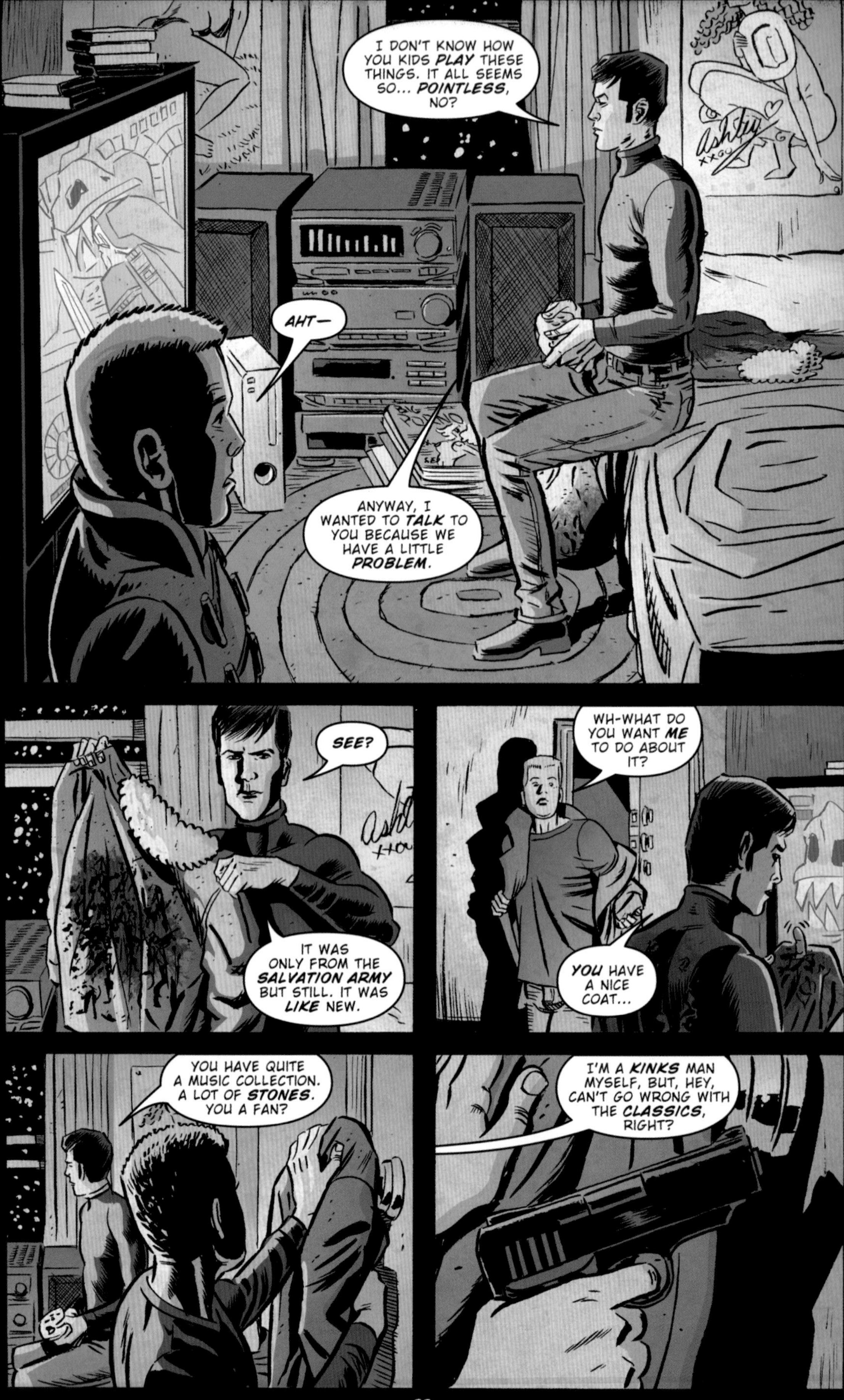
I DON'T KNOW HOW YOU KIDS PLAY THESE THINGS. IT ALL SEEMS SO... POINTLESS, NO?
AHT—
ANYWAY, I WANTED TO TALK TO YOU BECAUSE WE HAVE A LITTLE PROBLEM.
SEE?
IT WAS ONLY FROM THE SALVATION ARMY BUT STILL. IT WAS LIKE NEW.
WH-WHAT DO YOU WANT ME TO DO ABOUT IT?
YOU HAVE A NICE COAT...
YOU HAVE QUITE A MUSIC COLLECTION. A LOT OF STONES. YOU A FAN?
I'M A KINKS MAN MYSELF, BUT, HEY, CAN'T GO WRONG WITH THE CLASSICS, RIGHT?

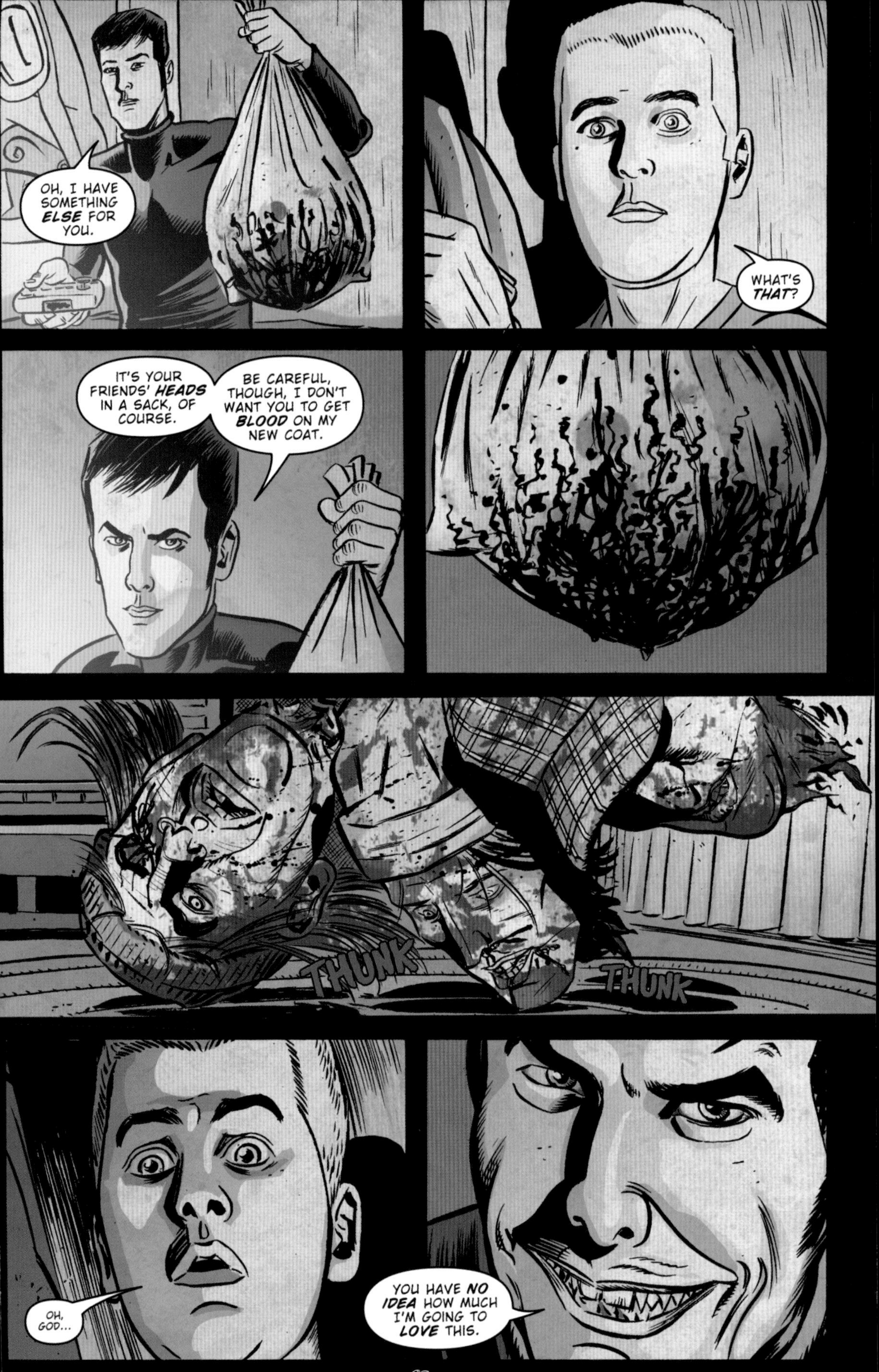
OH, I HAVE SOMETHING ELSE FOR YOU.
WHAT'S THAT?
IT'S YOUR FRIENDS' HEADS IN A SACK, OF COURSE.
BE CAREFUL, THOUGH, I DON'T WANT YOU TO GET BLOOD ON MY NEW COAT.
THUNK
THUNK
OH, GOD...
YOU HAVE NO IDEA HOW MUCH I'M GOING TO LOVE THIS.

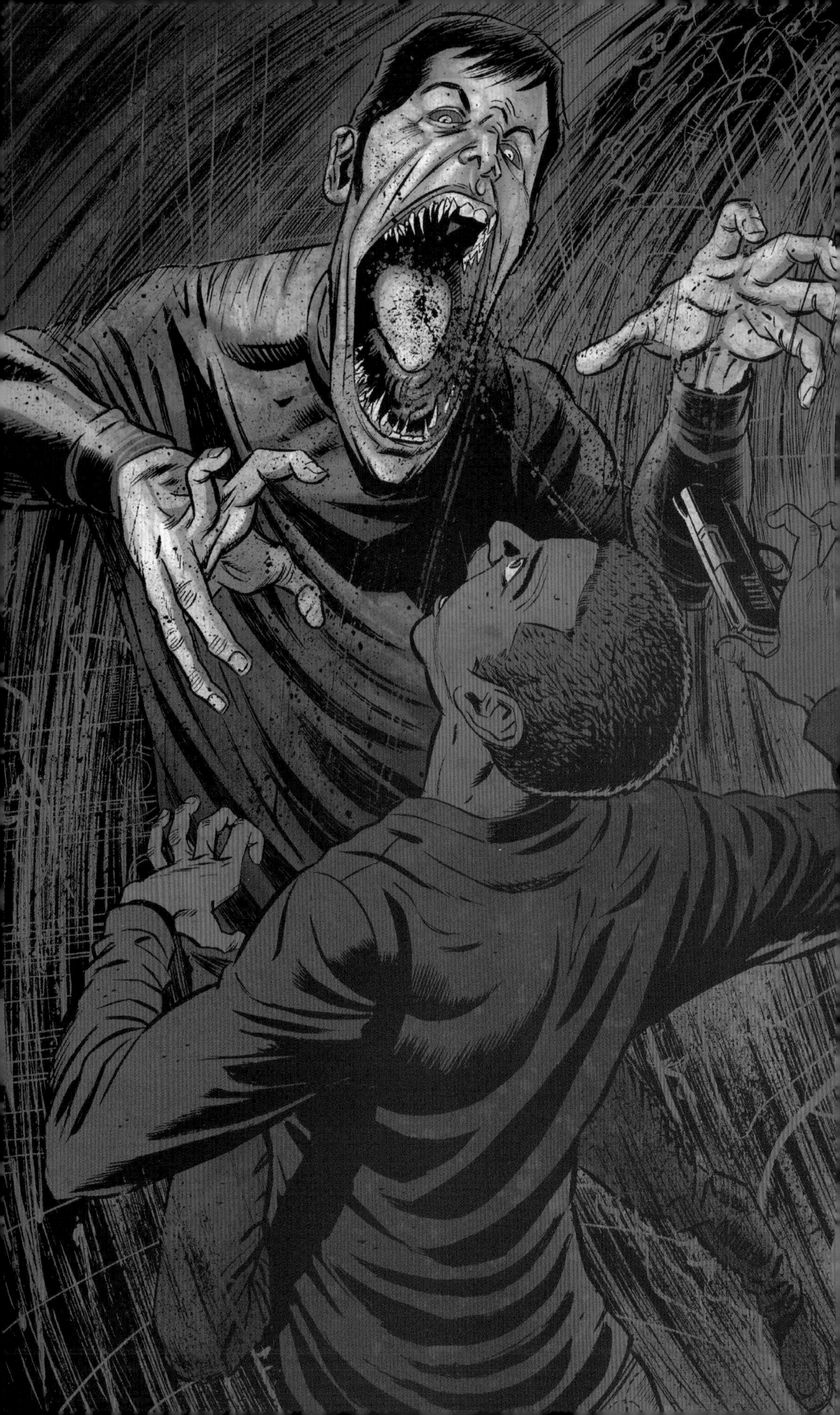

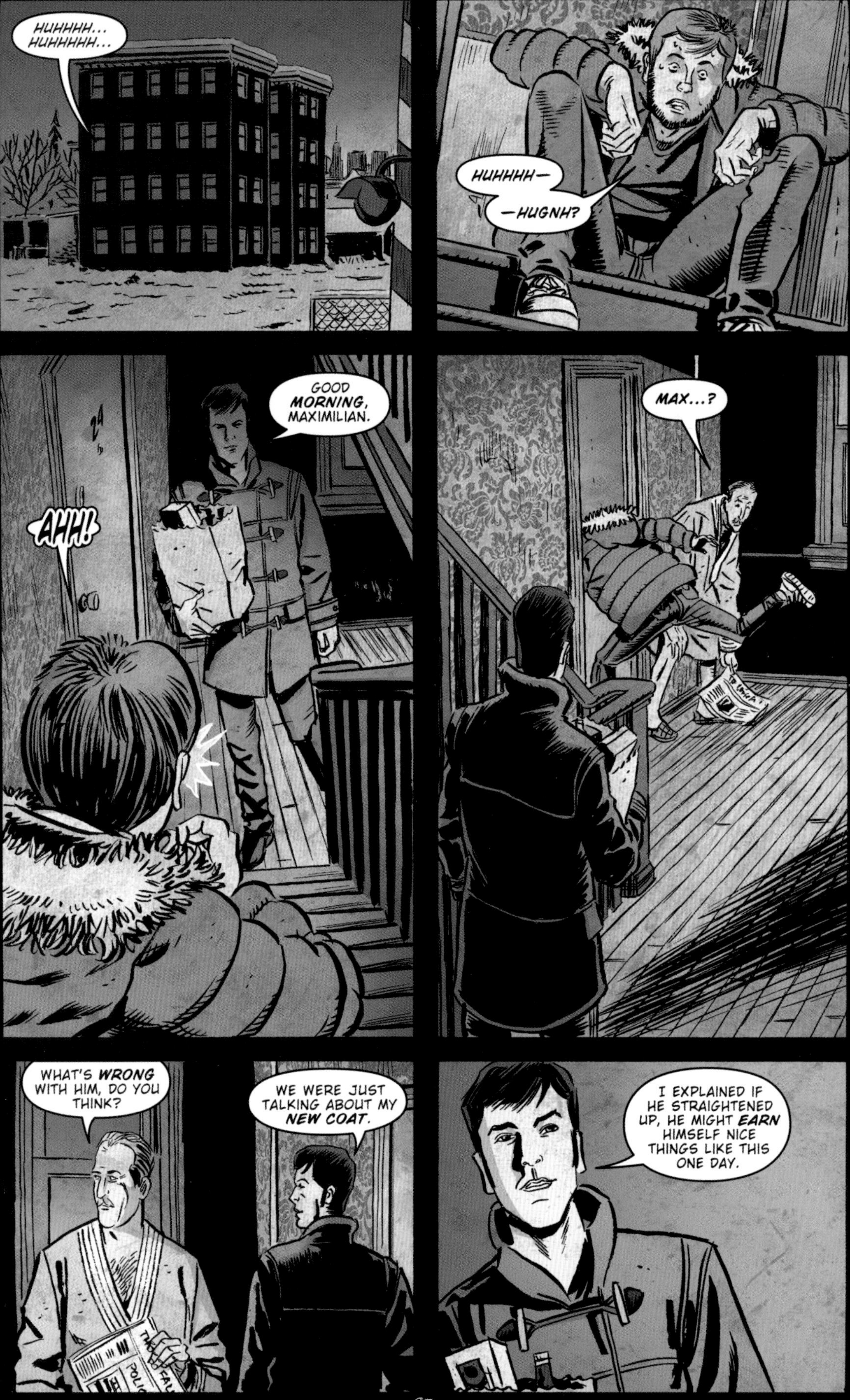
HUHHHH...
HUHHHHH...
HUHHHH—
—HUGNH?
GOOD MORNING, MAXIMILIAN.
AHH!
MAX...?
WHAT'S WRONG WITH HIM, DO YOU THINK?
WE WERE JUST TALKING ABOUT MY NEW COAT.
I EXPLAINED IF HE STRAIGHTENED UP, HE MIGHT EARN HIMSELF NICE THINGS LIKE THIS ONE DAY.

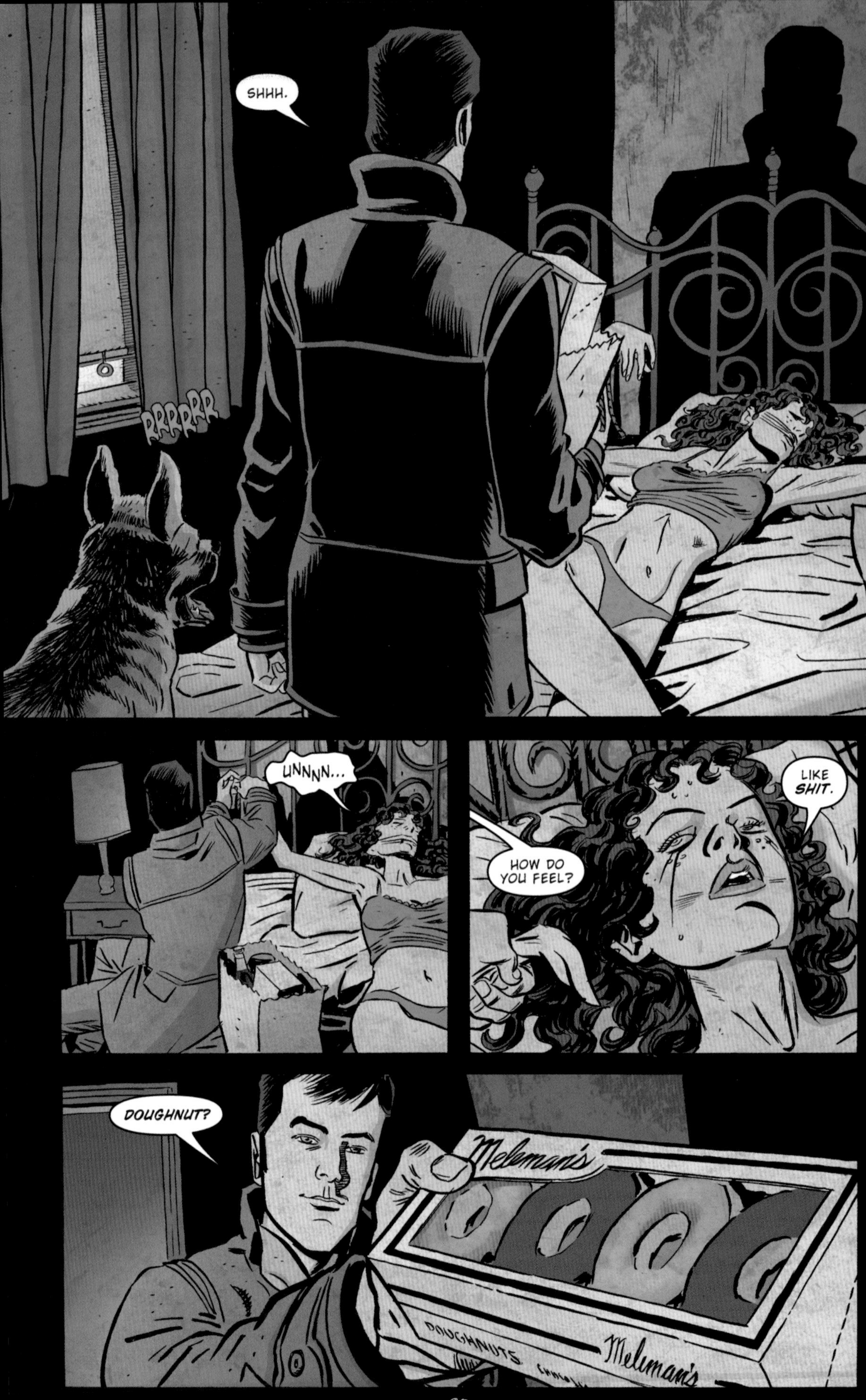
SHHH.
RRRRRR
UNNNN...
HOW DO YOU FEEL?
LIKE SHIT.
DOUGHNUT?
Meleman's
DOUGHNUTS
Meleman's

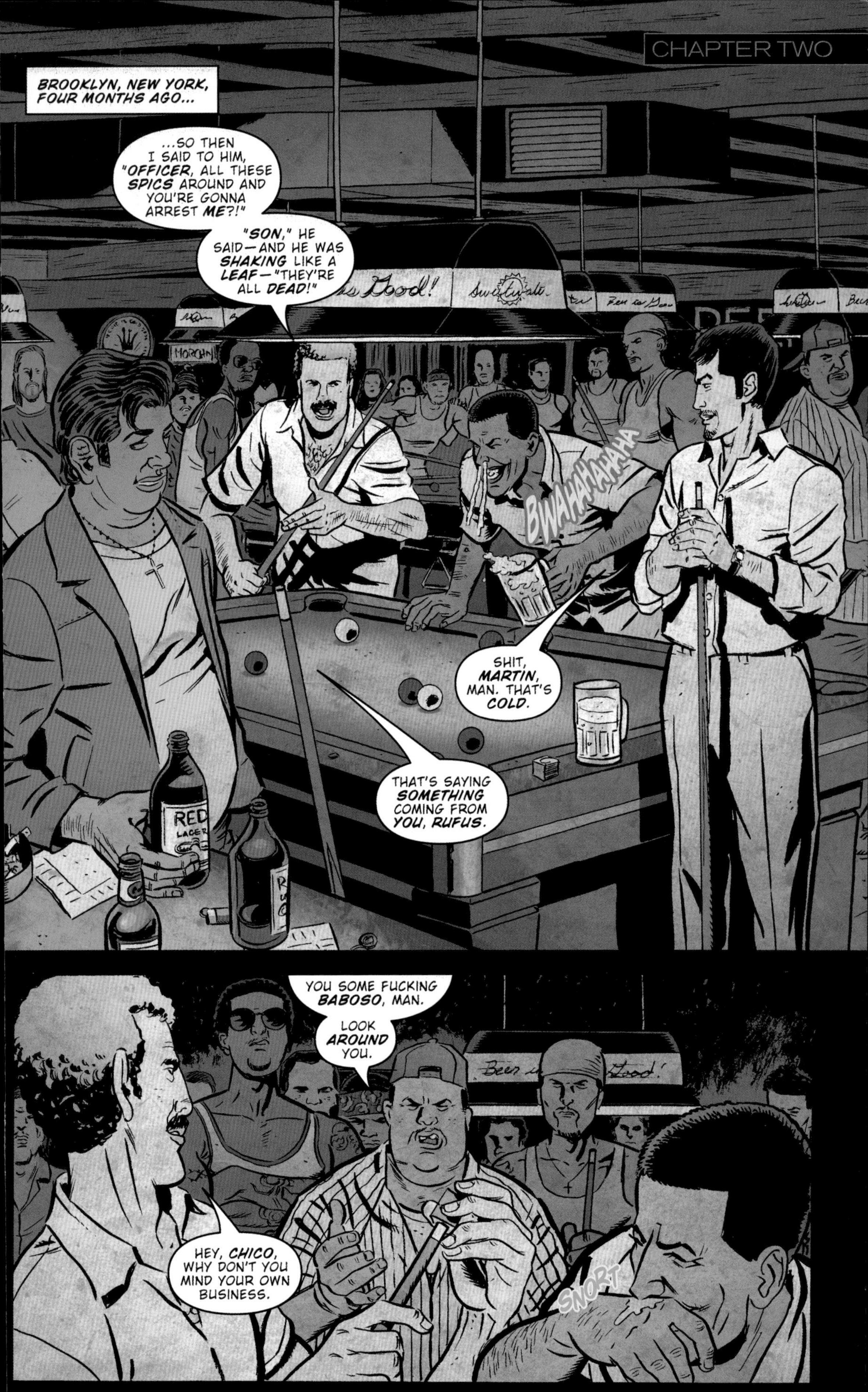
CHAPTER TWO
BROOKLYN, NEW YORK, FOUR MONTHS AGO...
...SO THEN I SAID TO HIM, "OFFICER, ALL THESE SPICS AROUND AND YOU'RE GONNA ARREST ME?!"
"SON," HE SAID—AND HE WAS SHAKING LIKE A LEAF—"THEY'RE ALL DEAD!"
BWAHAHAHAHAHA
SHIT, MARTIN, MAN. THAT'S COLD.
THAT'S SAYING SOMETHING COMING FROM YOU, RUFUS.
YOU SOME FUCKING BABOSO, MAN.
LOOK AROUND YOU.
HEY, CHICO, WHY DON'T YOU MIND YOUR OWN BUSINESS.
SNORT

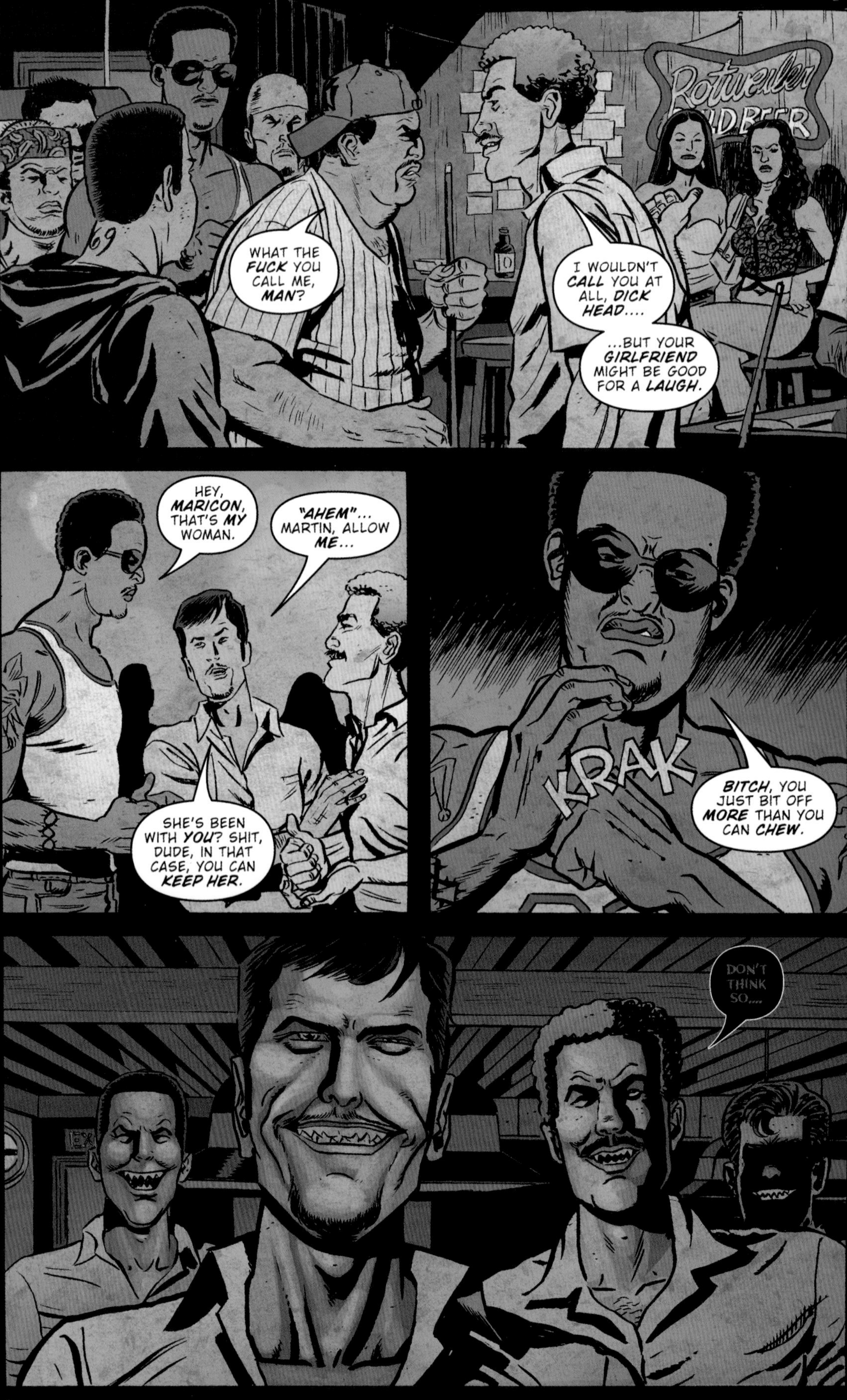
WHAT THE FUCK YOU CALL ME, MAN?
I WOULDN'T CALL YOU AT ALL, DICK HEAD....
...BUT YOUR GIRLFRIEND MIGHT BE GOOD FOR A LAUGH.
HEY, MARICON, THAT'S MY WOMAN.
"AHEM"... MARTIN, ALLOW ME...
SHE'S BEEN WITH YOU? SHIT, DUDE, IN THAT CASE, YOU CAN KEEP HER.
KRAK
BITCH, YOU JUST BIT OFF MORE THAN YOU CAN CHEW.
DON'T THINK SO....

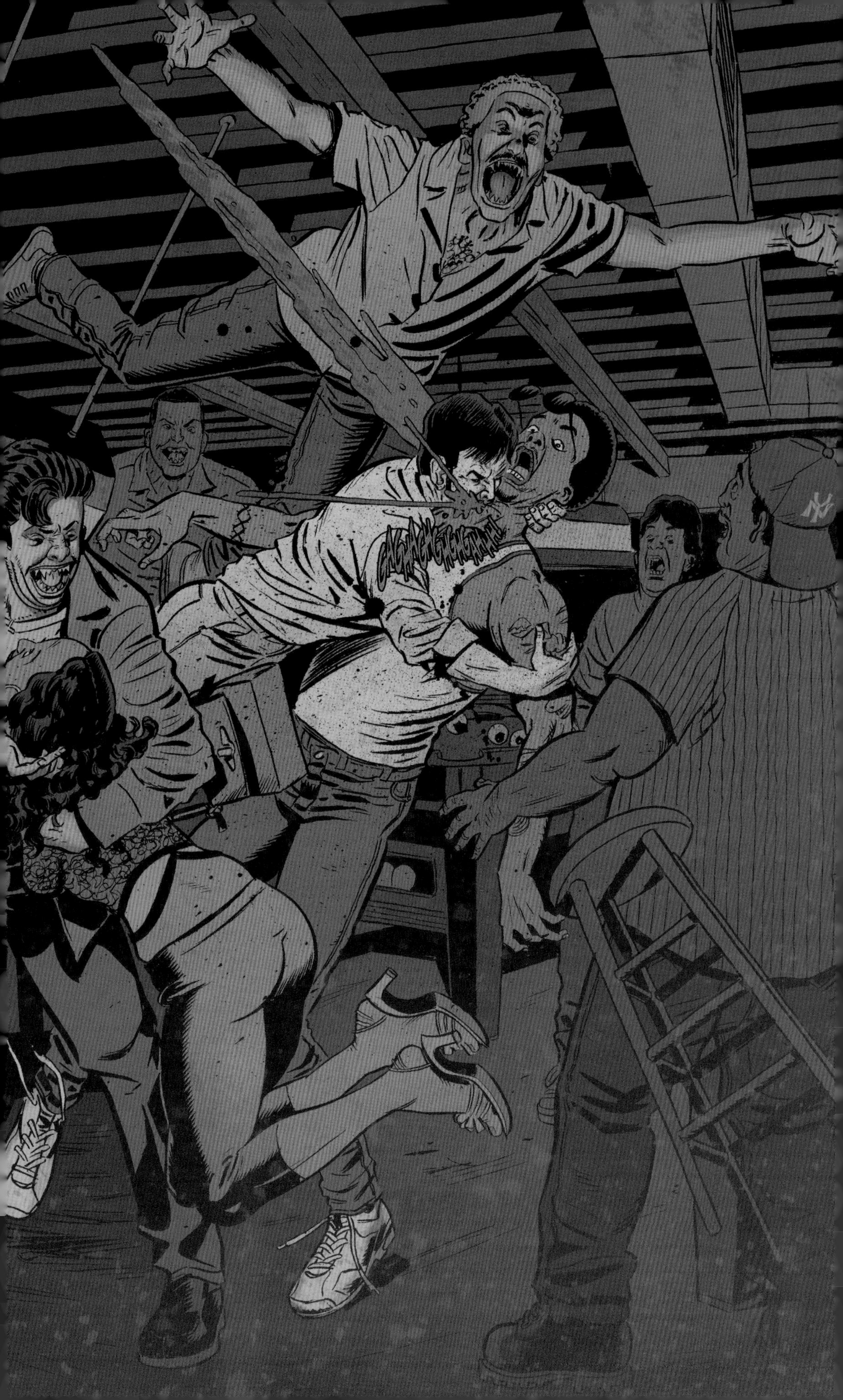

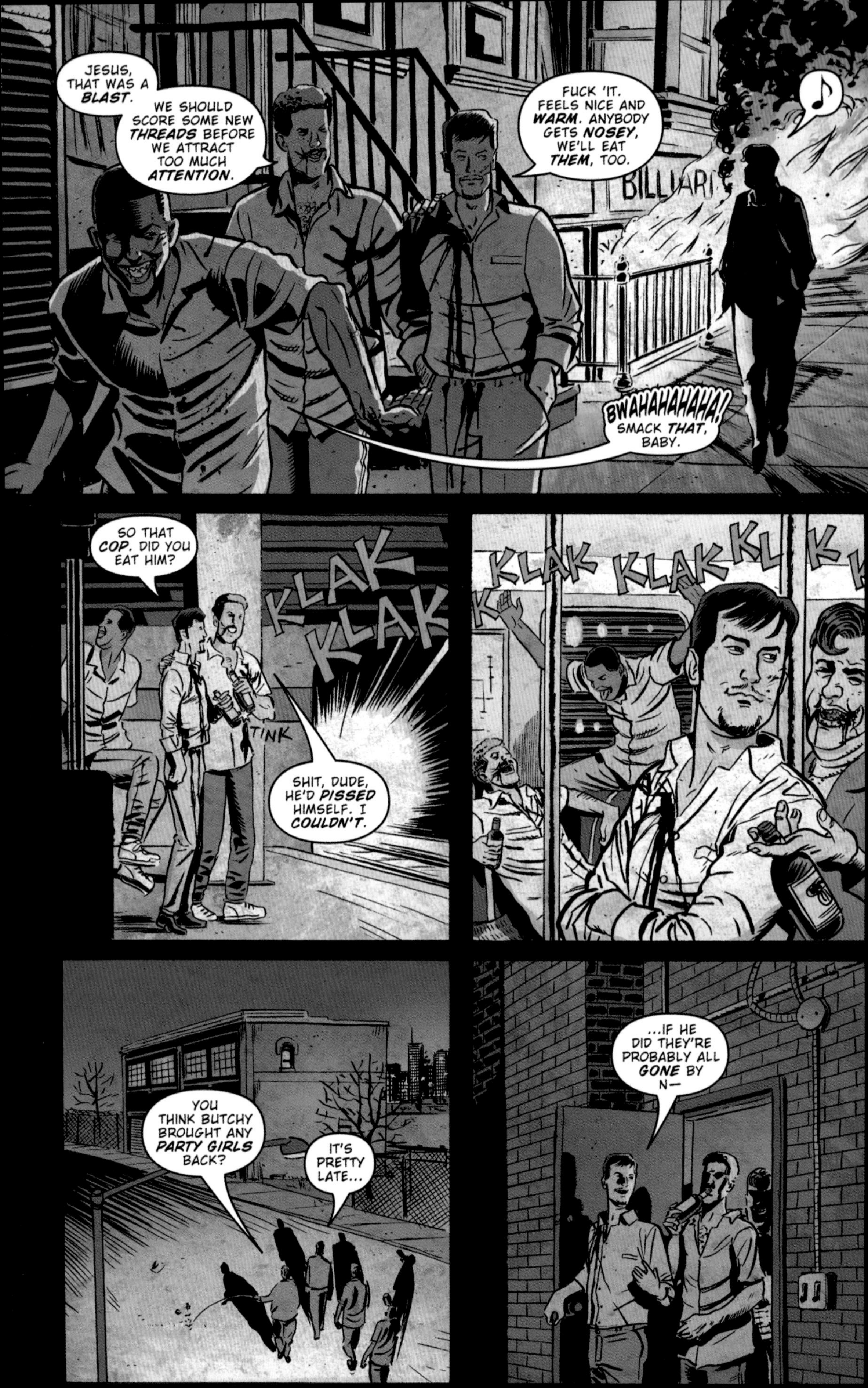

JESUS, THAT WAS A BLAST.
WE SHOULD SCORE SOME NEW THREADS BEFORE WE ATTRACT TOO MUCH ATTENTION.
FUCK 'IT. FEELS NICE AND WARM. ANYBODY GETS NOSEY, WE'LL EAT THEM, TOO.
♪
BILLIARI
BWAHAHAHAHA! SMACK THAT, BABY.
SO THAT COP. DID YOU EAT HIM?
KLAK KLAK
TINK
SHIT, DUDE, HE'D PISSED HIMSELF. I COULDN'T.
KLAK KLAK KLAK KL K
YOU THINK BUTCHY BROUGHT ANY PARTY GIRLS BACK?
IT'S PRETTY LATE...
...IF HE DID THEY'RE PROBABLY ALL GONE BY N—

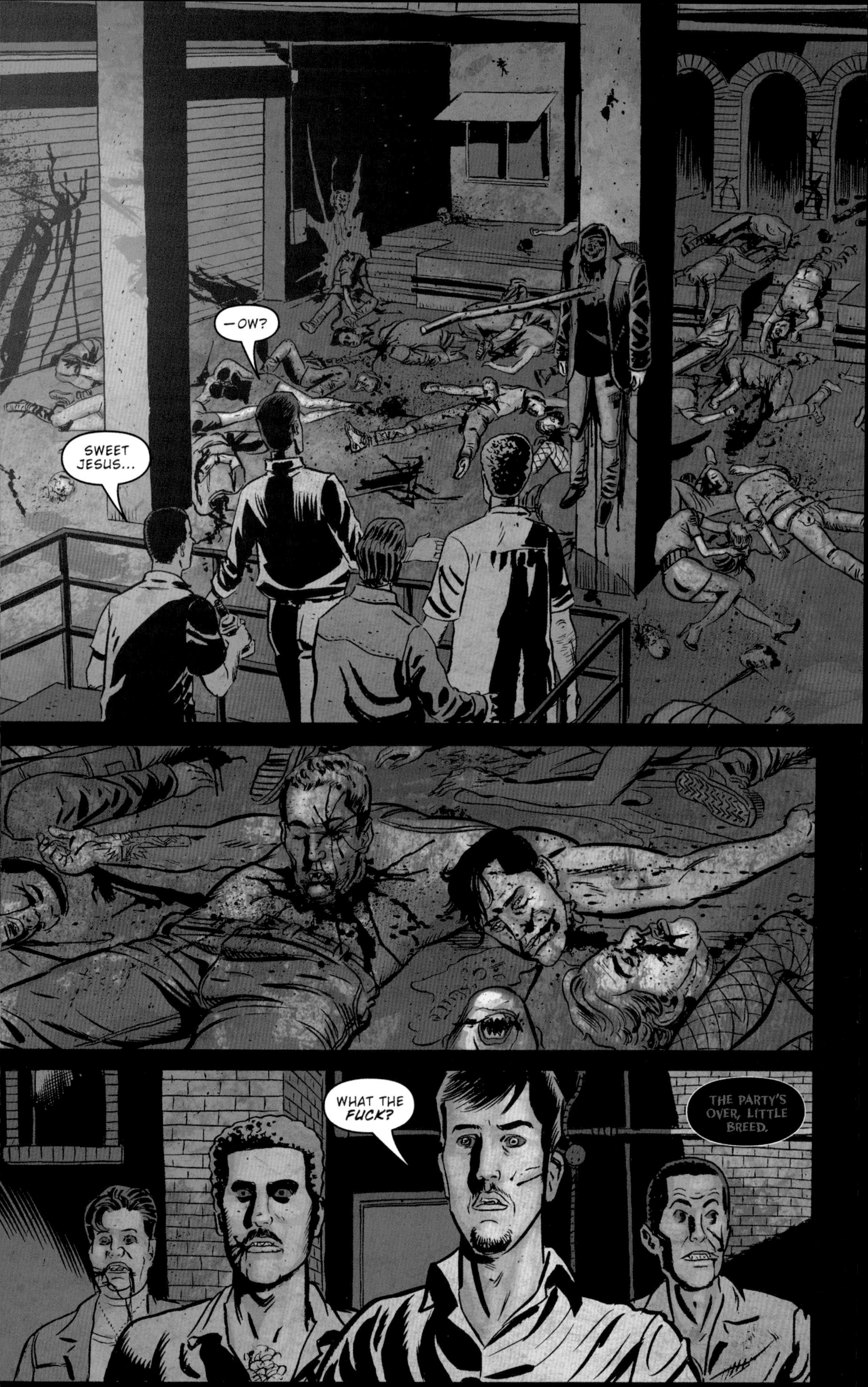
—OW?
SWEET JESUS...
WHAT THE FUCK?
THE PARTY'S OVER, LITTLE BREED.

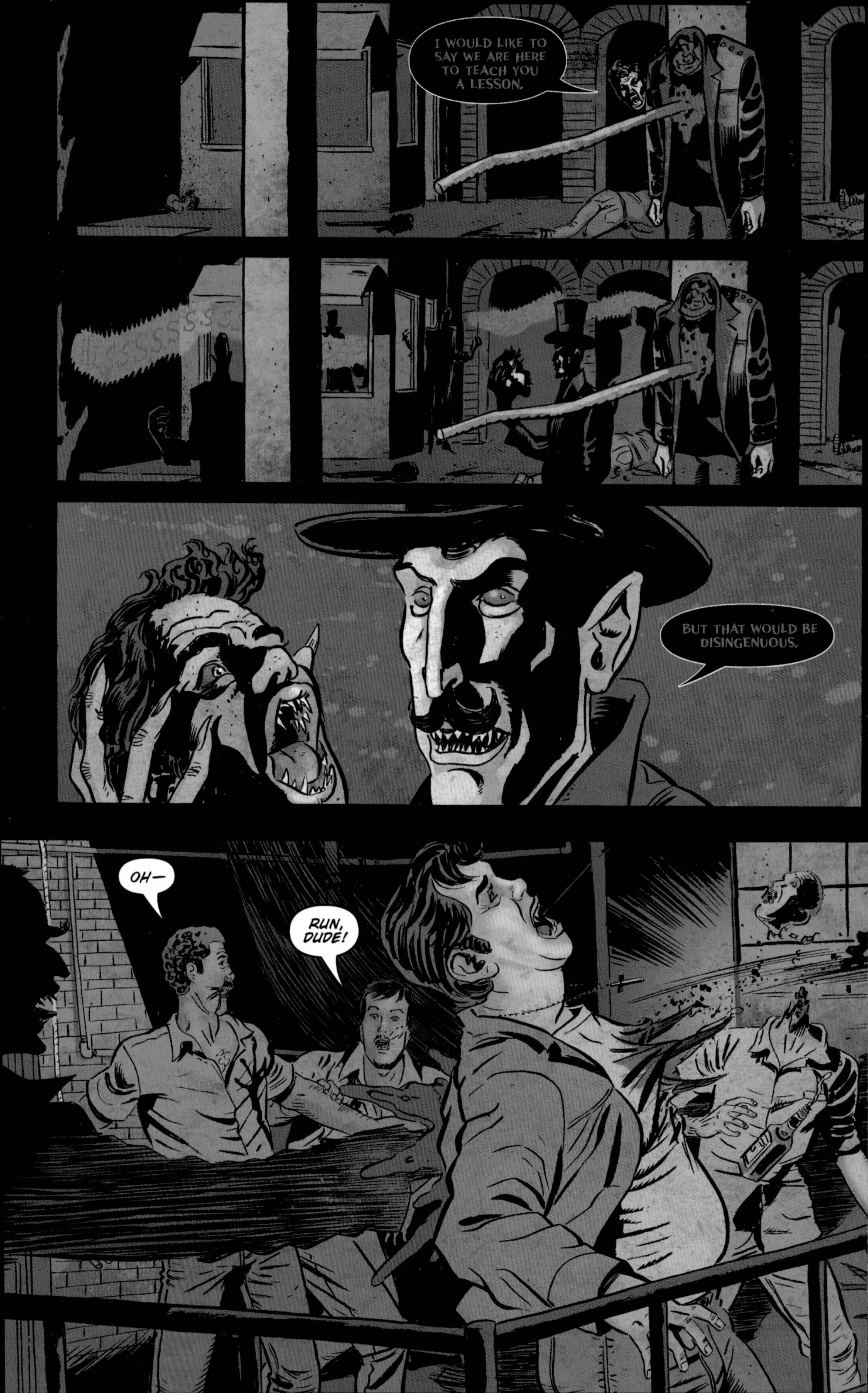
I WOULD LIKE TO SAY WE ARE HERE TO TEACH YOU A LESSON.
HISSSSSSS
BUT THAT WOULD BE DISINGENUOUS.
OH—
RUN, DUDE!

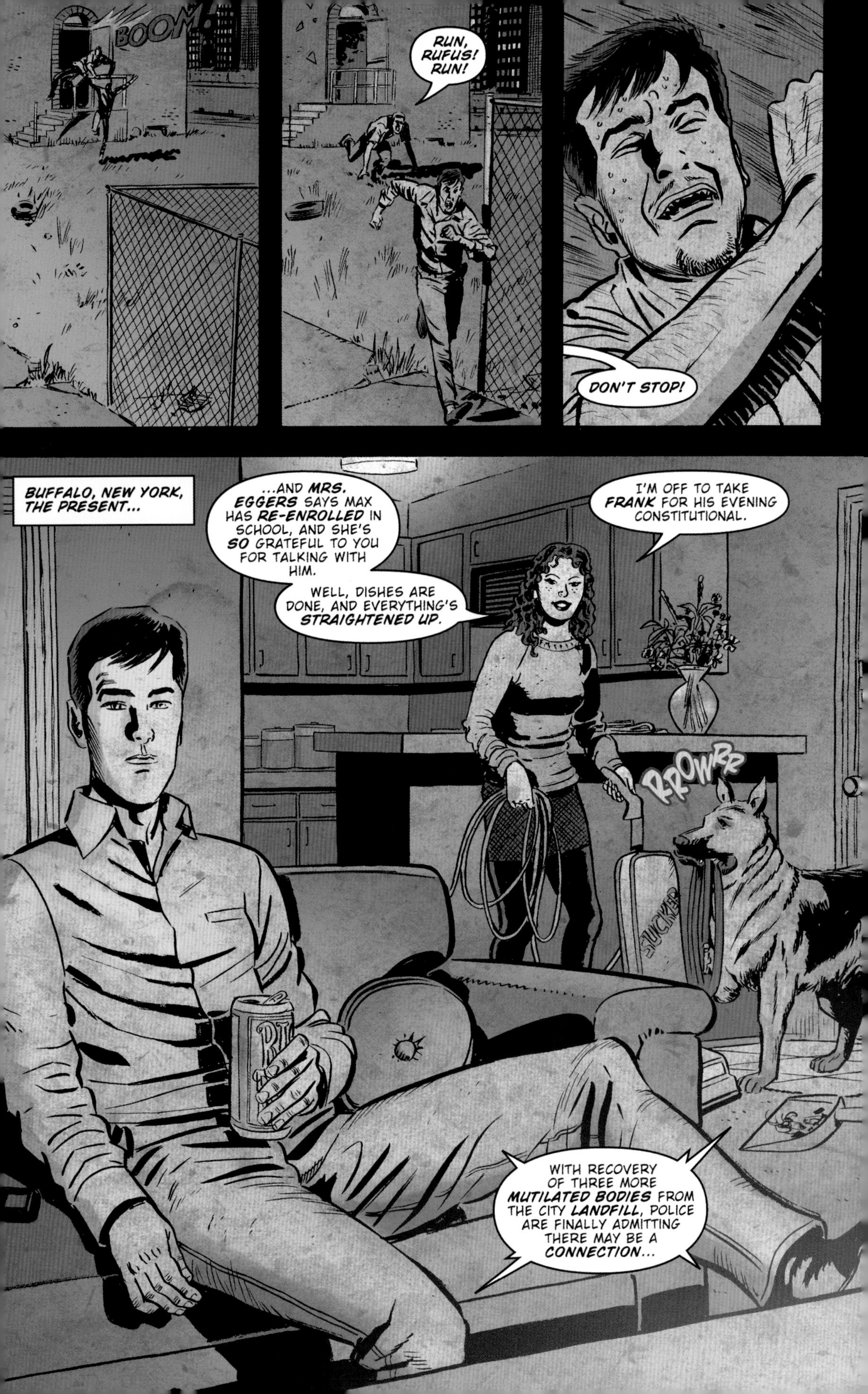

BOOM!
RUN, RUFUS! RUN!
DON'T STOP!
BUFFALO, NEW YORK, THE PRESENT...
...AND MRS. EGGERS SAYS MAX HAS RE-ENROLLED IN SCHOOL, AND SHE'S SO GRATEFUL TO YOU FOR TALKING WITH HIM.
WELL, DISHES ARE DONE, AND EVERYTHING'S STRAIGHTENED UP.
I'M OFF TO TAKE FRANK FOR HIS EVENING CONSTITUTIONAL.
RROWRR
SUCKER
WITH RECOVERY OF THREE MORE MUTILATED BODIES FROM THE CITY LANDFILL, POLICE ARE FINALLY ADMITTING THERE MAY BE A CONNECTION...

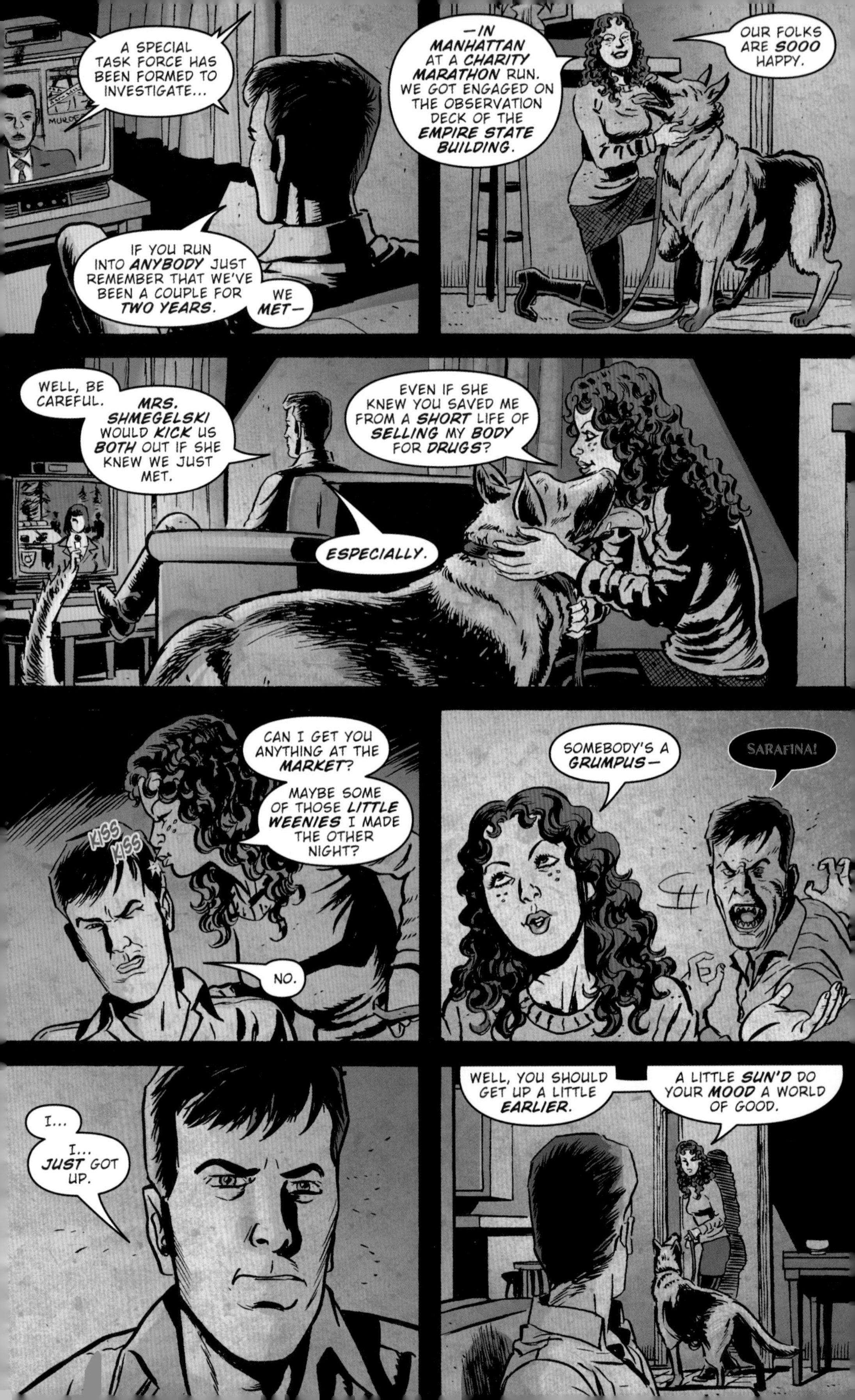
A SPECIAL TASK FORCE HAS BEEN FORMED TO INVESTIGATE...
IF YOU RUN INTO ANYBODY JUST REMEMBER THAT WE'VE BEEN A COUPLE FOR TWO YEARS.
WE MET—
—IN MANHATTAN AT A CHARITY MARATHON RUN. WE GOT ENGAGED ON THE OBSERVATION DECK OF THE EMPIRE STATE BUILDING.
OUR FOLKS ARE SOOO HAPPY.
WELL, BE CAREFUL.
MRS. SHMEGELSKI WOULD KICK US BOTH OUT IF SHE KNEW WE JUST MET.
EVEN IF SHE KNEW YOU SAVED ME FROM A SHORT LIFE OF SELLING MY BODY FOR DRUGS?
ESPECIALLY.
KISS KISS
CAN I GET YOU ANYTHING AT THE MARKET?
MAYBE SOME OF THOSE LITTLE WEENIES I MADE THE OTHER NIGHT?
NO.
SOMEBODY'S A GRUMPUS—
SARAFINA!
I...
I... JUST GOT UP.
WELL, YOU SHOULD GET UP A LITTLE EARLIER.
A LITTLE SUN'D DO YOUR MOOD A WORLD OF GOOD.

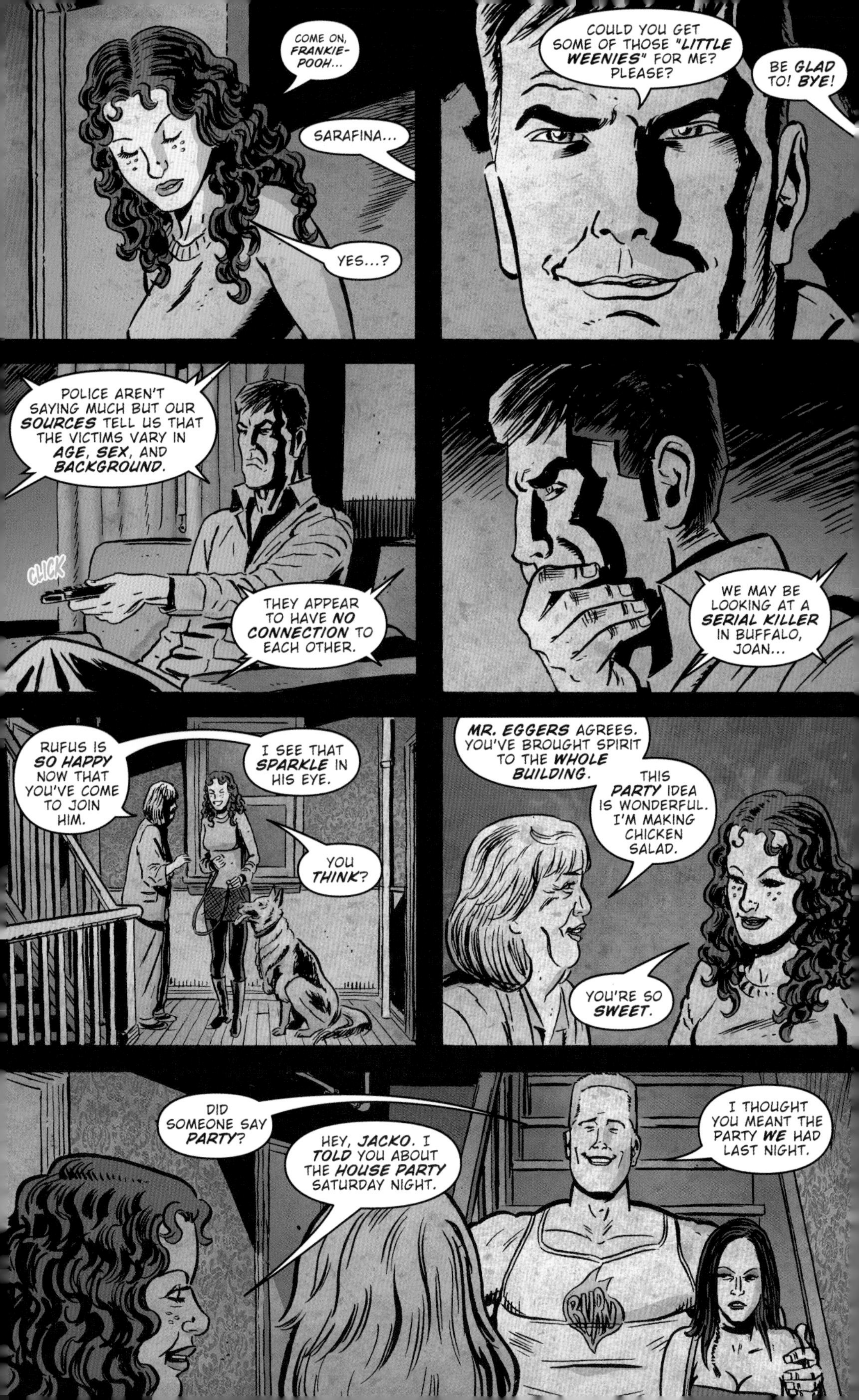
COME ON, FRANKIE-POOH...
SARAFINA...
YES...?
COULD YOU GET SOME OF THOSE "LITTLE WEENIES" FOR ME? PLEASE?
BE GLAD TO! BYE!
POLICE AREN'T SAYING MUCH BUT OUR SOURCES TELL US THAT THE VICTIMS VARY IN AGE, SEX, AND BACKGROUND.
CLICK
THEY APPEAR TO HAVE NO CONNECTION TO EACH OTHER.
WE MAY BE LOOKING AT A SERIAL KILLER IN BUFFALO, JOAN...
RUFUS IS SO HAPPY NOW THAT YOU'VE COME TO JOIN HIM.
I SEE THAT SPARKLE IN HIS EYE.
YOU THINK?
MR. EGGERS AGREES. YOU'VE BROUGHT SPIRIT TO THE WHOLE BUILDING.
THIS PARTY IDEA IS WONDERFUL. I'M MAKING CHICKEN SALAD.
YOU'RE SO SWEET.
DID SOMEONE SAY PARTY?
HEY, JACKO. I TOLD YOU ABOUT THE HOUSE PARTY SATURDAY NIGHT.
I THOUGHT YOU MEANT THE PARTY WE HAD LAST NIGHT.

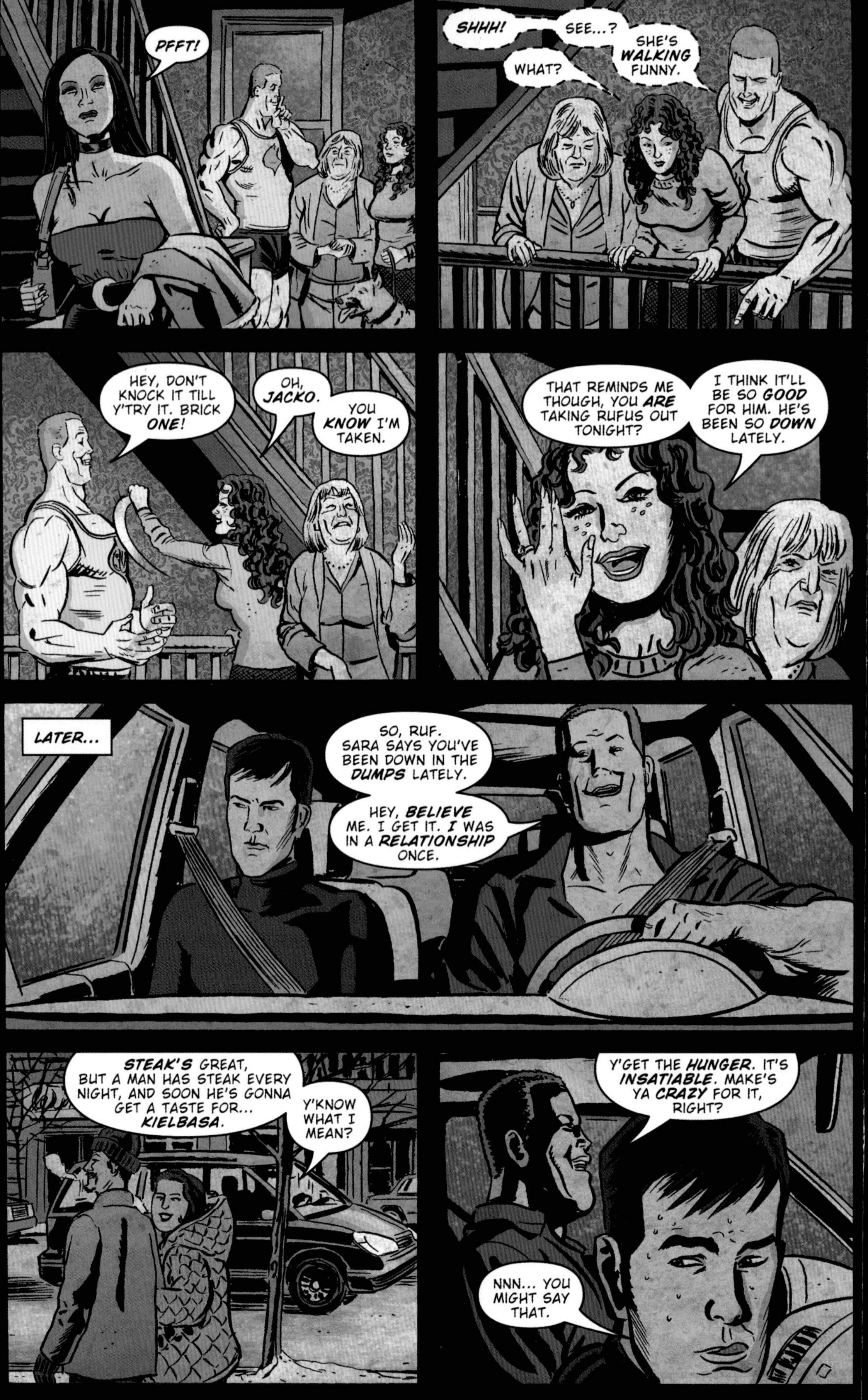
PFFT!
SHHH!
SEE...?
WHAT?
SHE'S WALKING FUNNY.
HEY, DON'T KNOCK IT TILL Y'TRY IT. BRICK ONE!
OH, JACKO.
YOU KNOW I'M TAKEN.
THAT REMINDS ME THOUGH, YOU ARE TAKING RUFUS OUT TONIGHT?
I THINK IT'LL BE SO GOOD FOR HIM. HE'S BEEN SO DOWN LATELY.
LATER...
SO, RUF. SARA SAYS YOU'VE BEEN DOWN IN THE DUMPS LATELY.
HEY, BELIEVE ME. I GET IT. I WAS IN A RELATIONSHIP ONCE.
STEAK'S GREAT, BUT A MAN HAS STEAK EVERY NIGHT, AND SOON HE'S GONNA GET A TASTE FOR... KIELBASA.
Y'KNOW WHAT I MEAN?
Y'GET THE HUNGER. IT'S INSATIABLE. MAKE'S YA CRAZY FOR IT, RIGHT?
NNN... YOU MIGHT SAY THAT.

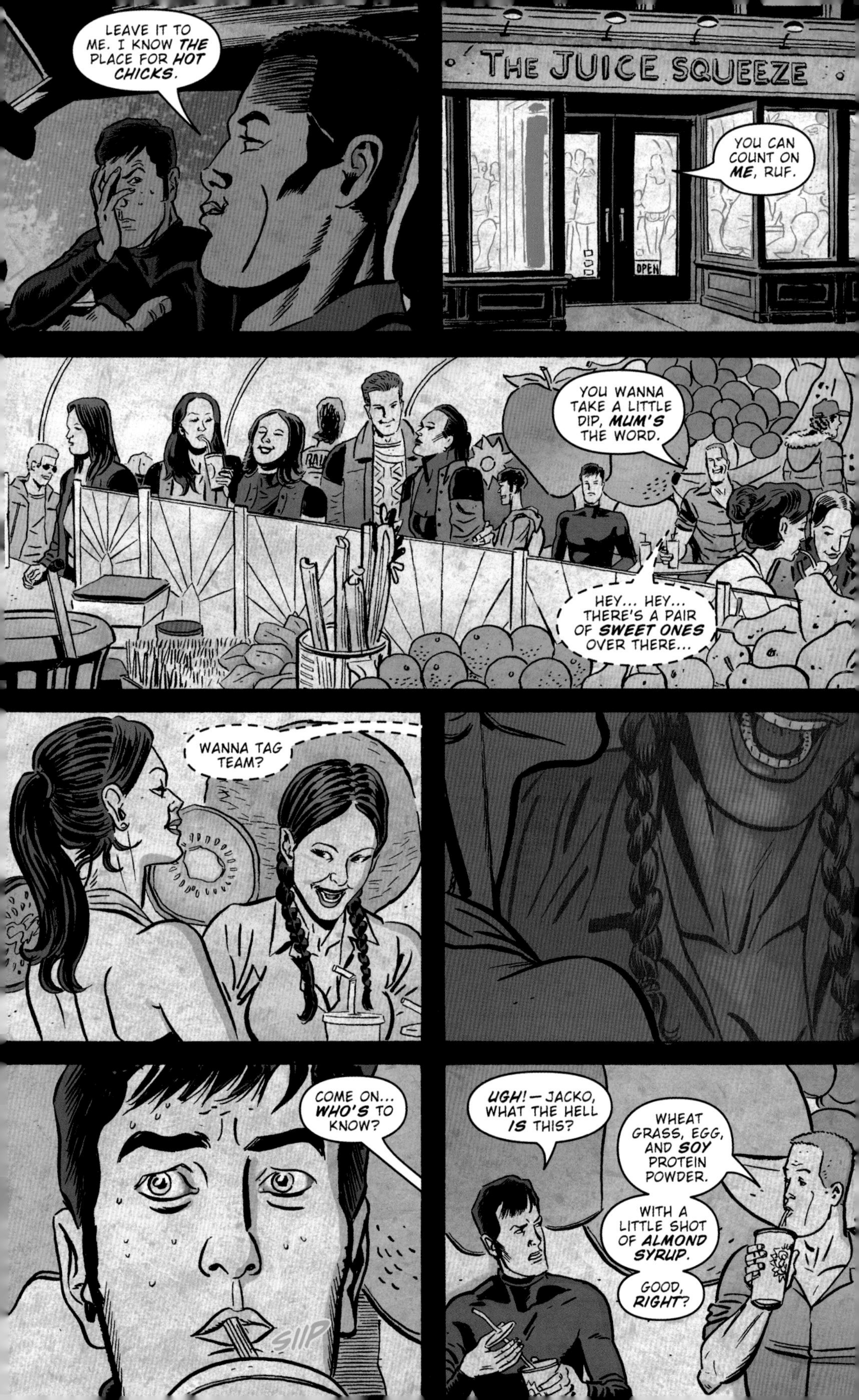
LEAVE IT TO ME. I KNOW THE PLACE FOR HOT CHICKS.
THE JUICE SQUEEZE
OPEN
YOU CAN COUNT ON ME, RUF.
YOU WANNA TAKE A LITTLE DIP, MUM'S THE WORD.
HEY... HEY... THERE'S A PAIR OF SWEET ONES OVER THERE...
WANNA TAG TEAM?
COME ON... WHO'S TO KNOW?
SIIP
UGH!—JACKO, WHAT THE HELL IS THIS?
WHEAT GRASS, EGG, AND SOY PROTEIN POWDER.
WITH A LITTLE SHOT OF ALMOND SYRUP.
GOOD, RIGHT?

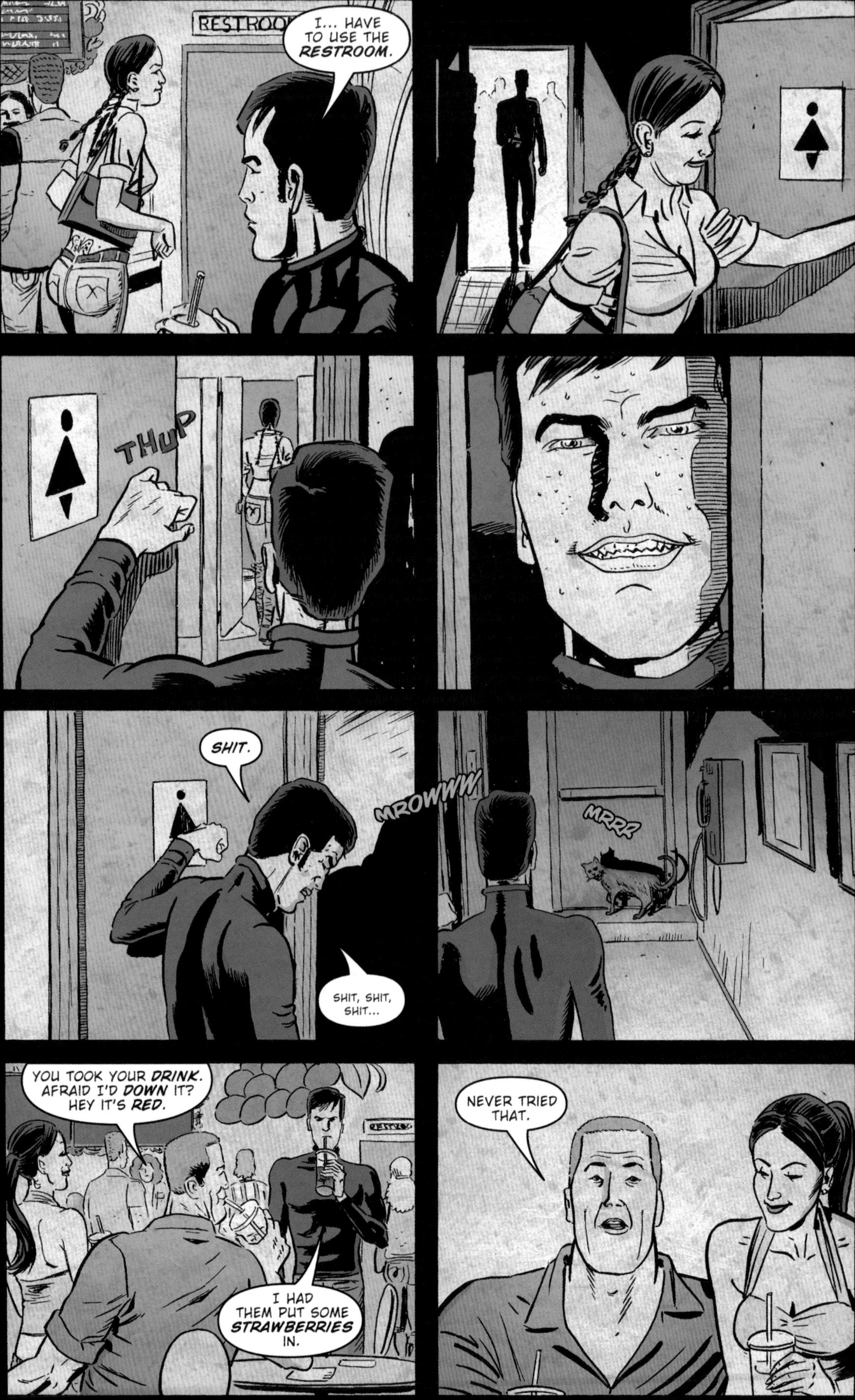

RESTROOM
I... HAVE TO USE THE RESTROOM.
THUP
SHIT.
SHIT, SHIT, SHIT...
MROWWW
MRRR
YOU TOOK YOUR DRINK. AFRAID I'D DOWN IT? HEY IT'S RED.
I HAD THEM PUT SOME STRAWBERRIES IN.
NEVER TRIED THAT.

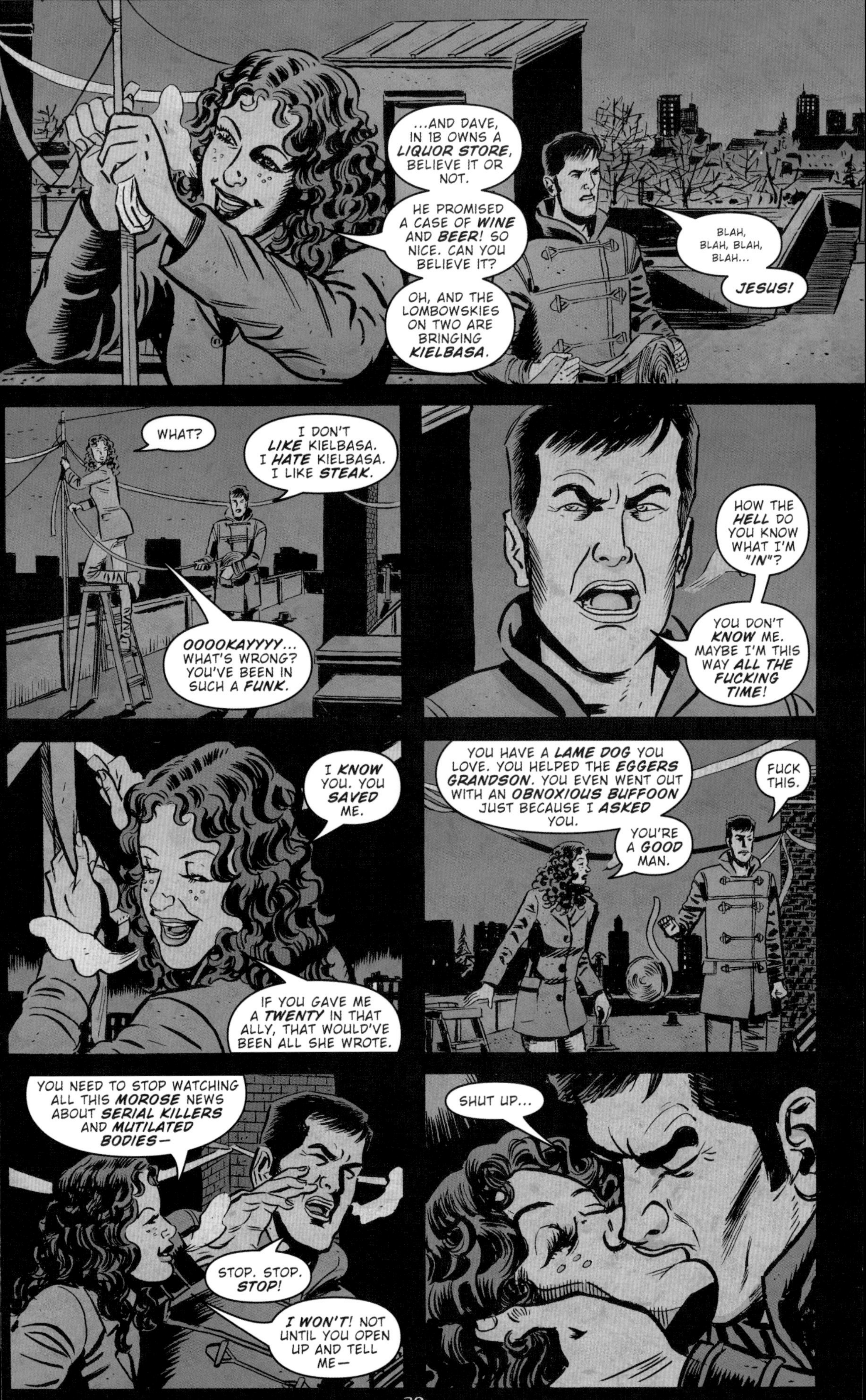
...AND DAVE, IN 1B OWNS A LIQUOR STORE, BELIEVE IT OR NOT.
HE PROMISED A CASE OF WINE AND BEER! SO NICE. CAN YOU BELIEVE IT?
OH, AND THE LOMBOWSKIES ON TWO ARE BRINGING KIELBASA.
BLAH, BLAH, BLAH, BLAH...
JESUS!
WHAT?
I DON'T LIKE KIELBASA. I HATE KIELBASA. I LIKE STEAK.
OOOOKAYYYY... WHAT'S WRONG? YOU'VE BEEN IN SUCH A FUNK.
HOW THE HELL DO YOU KNOW WHAT I'M "IN"?
YOU DON'T KNOW ME. MAYBE I'M THIS WAY ALL THE FUCKING TIME!
I KNOW YOU. YOU SAVED ME.
IF YOU GAVE ME A TWENTY IN THAT ALLY, THAT WOULD'VE BEEN ALL SHE WROTE.
YOU HAVE A LAME DOG YOU LOVE. YOU HELPED THE EGGERS GRANDSON. YOU EVEN WENT OUT WITH AN OBNOXIOUS BUFFOON JUST BECAUSE I ASKED YOU.
YOU'RE A GOOD MAN.
FUCK THIS.
YOU NEED TO STOP WATCHING ALL THIS MOROSE NEWS ABOUT SERIAL KILLERS AND MUTILATED BODIES—
STOP. STOP. STOP!
I WON'T! NOT UNTIL YOU OPEN UP AND TELL ME—
SHUT UP...

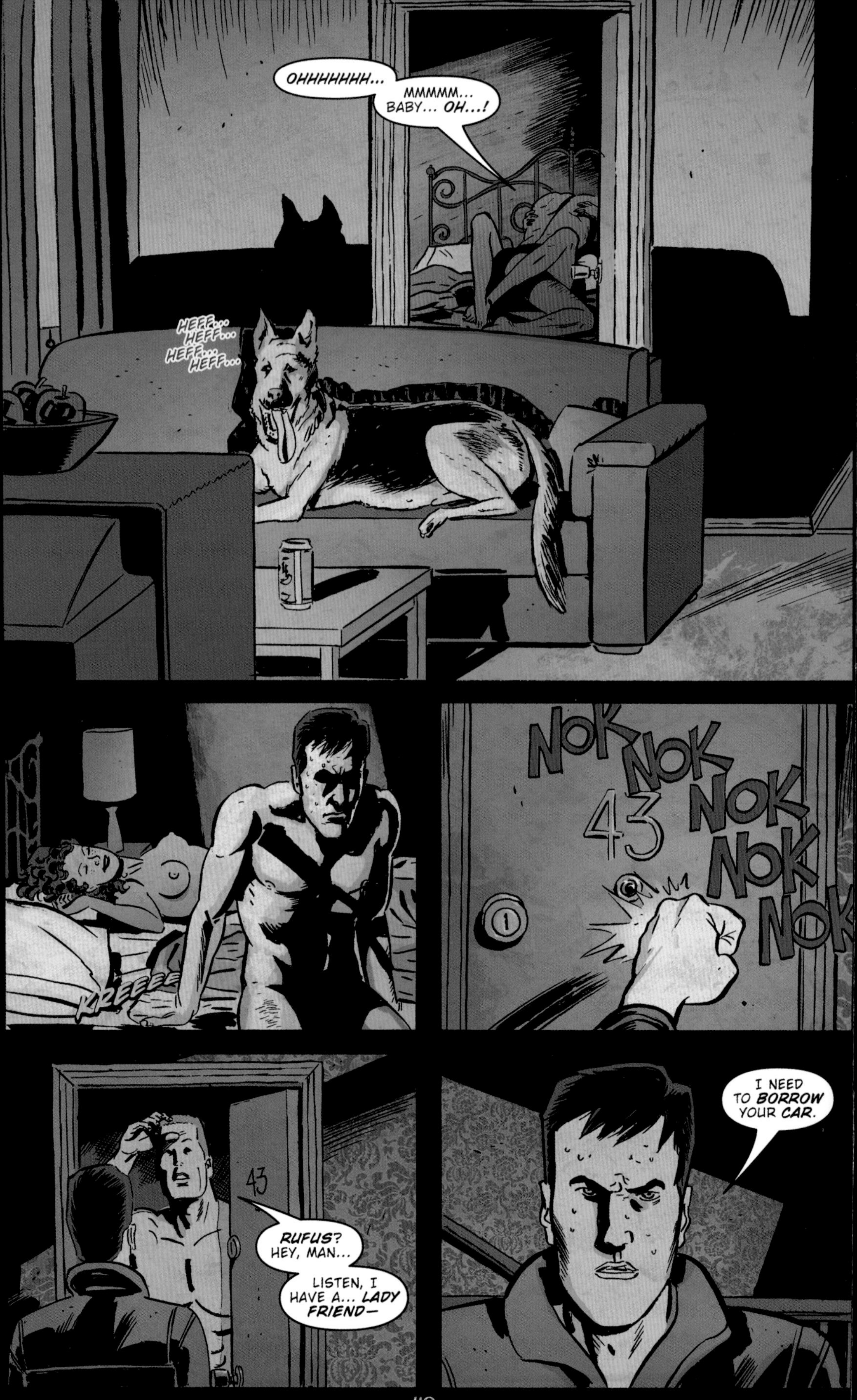

OHHHHHHHH...
MMMMM... BABY... OH...!
HEFF... HEFF... HEFF... HEFF...
KREEEEE
NOK NOK NOK NOK NOK
43
43
RUFUS? HEY, MAN...
LISTEN, I HAVE A... LADY FRIEND—
I NEED TO BORROW YOUR CAR.

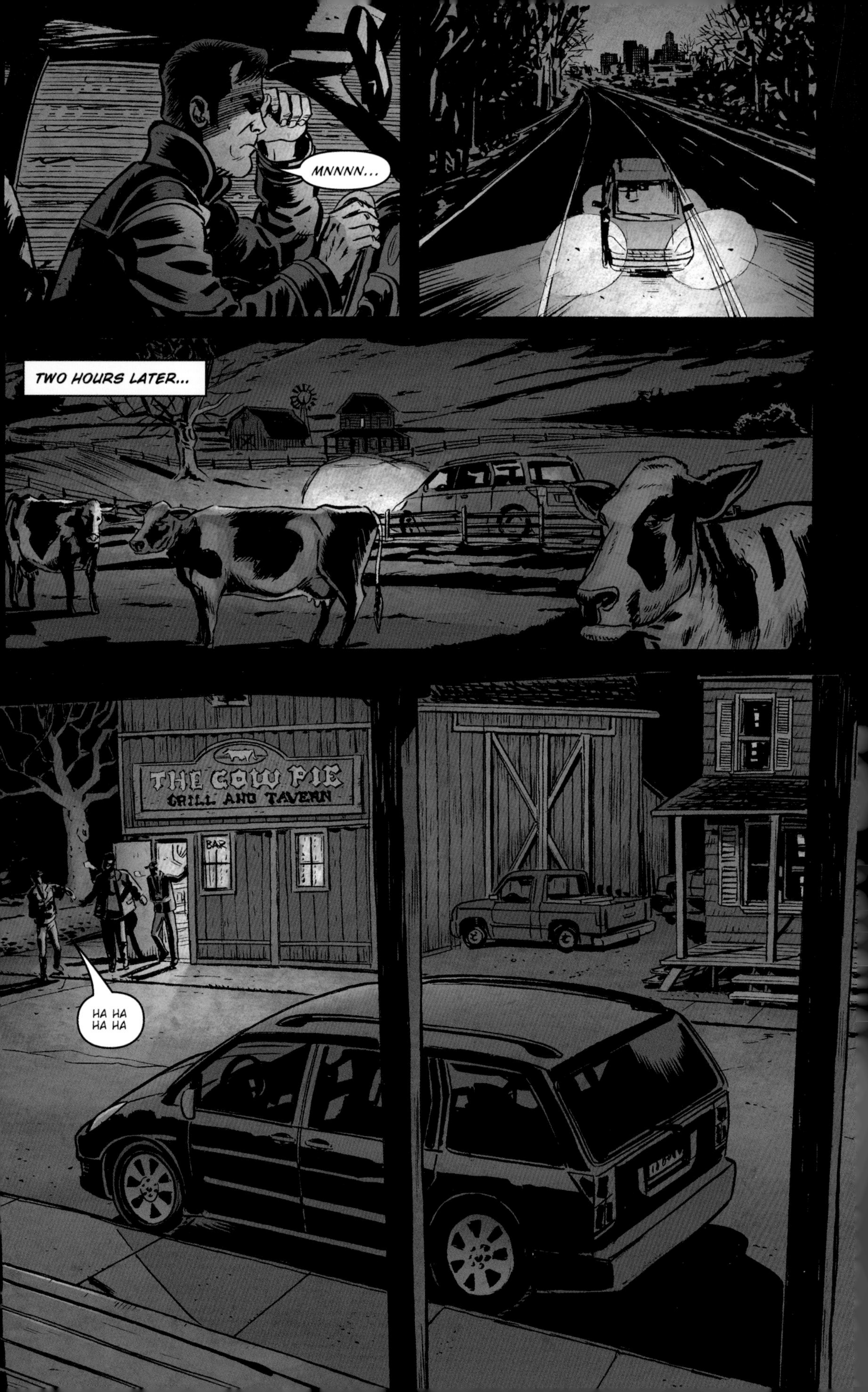
MNNNN...
TWO HOURS LATER...
THE COW PIE
GRILL AND TAVERN
BAR
HA HA
HA HA

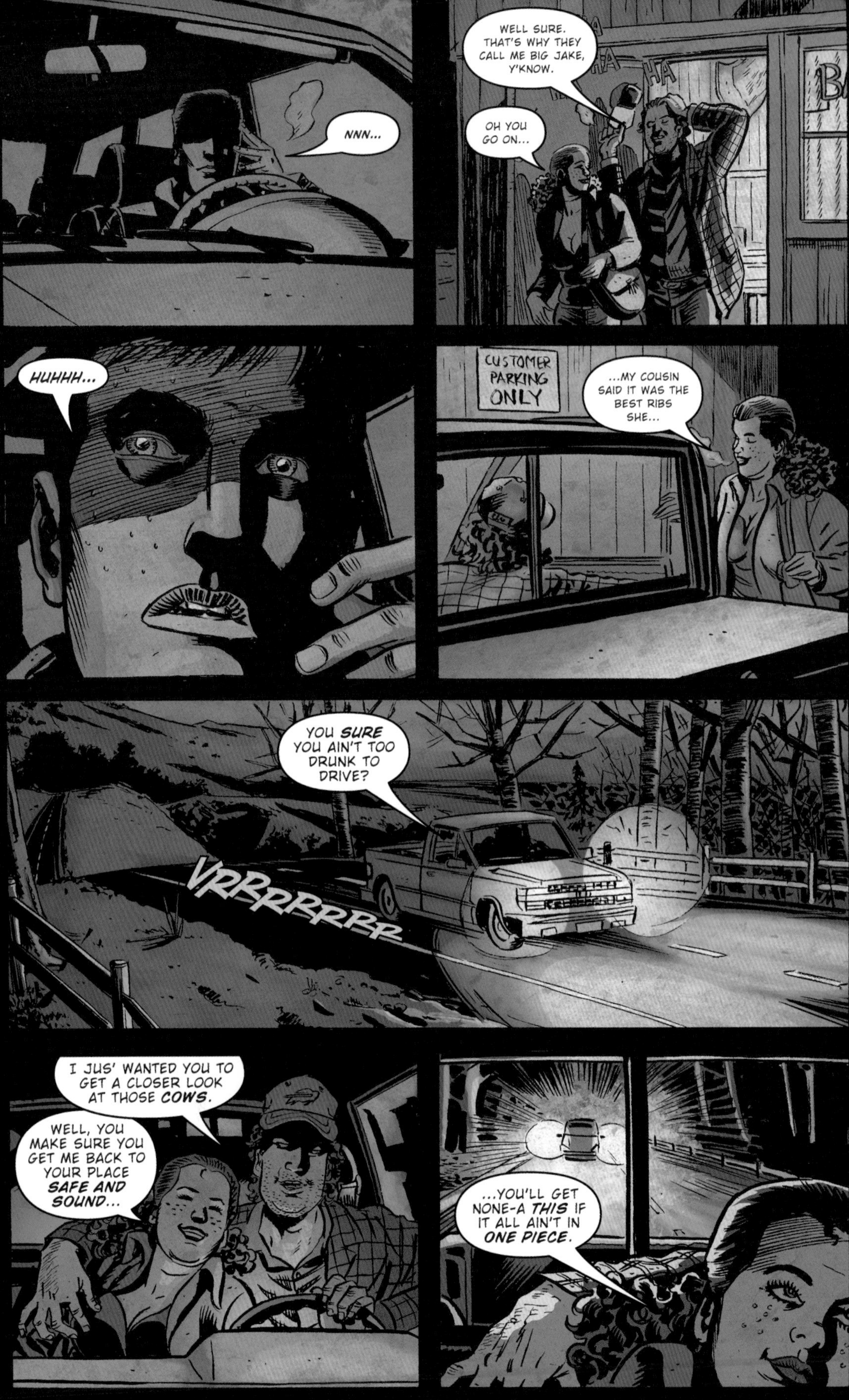
NNN...
WELL SURE. THAT'S WHY THEY CALL ME BIG JAKE, Y'KNOW.
OH YOU GO ON...
HUHHH...
CUSTOMER PARKING ONLY
...MY COUSIN SAID IT WAS THE BEST RIBS SHE...
YOU *SURE* YOU AIN'T TOO DRUNK TO DRIVE?
VRRRRRRRR
I JUS' WANTED YOU TO GET A CLOSER LOOK AT THOSE *COWS*.
WELL, YOU MAKE SURE YOU GET ME BACK TO YOUR PLACE *SAFE AND SOUND*...
...YOU'LL GET NONE-A *THIS* IF IT ALL AIN'T IN *ONE PIECE*.

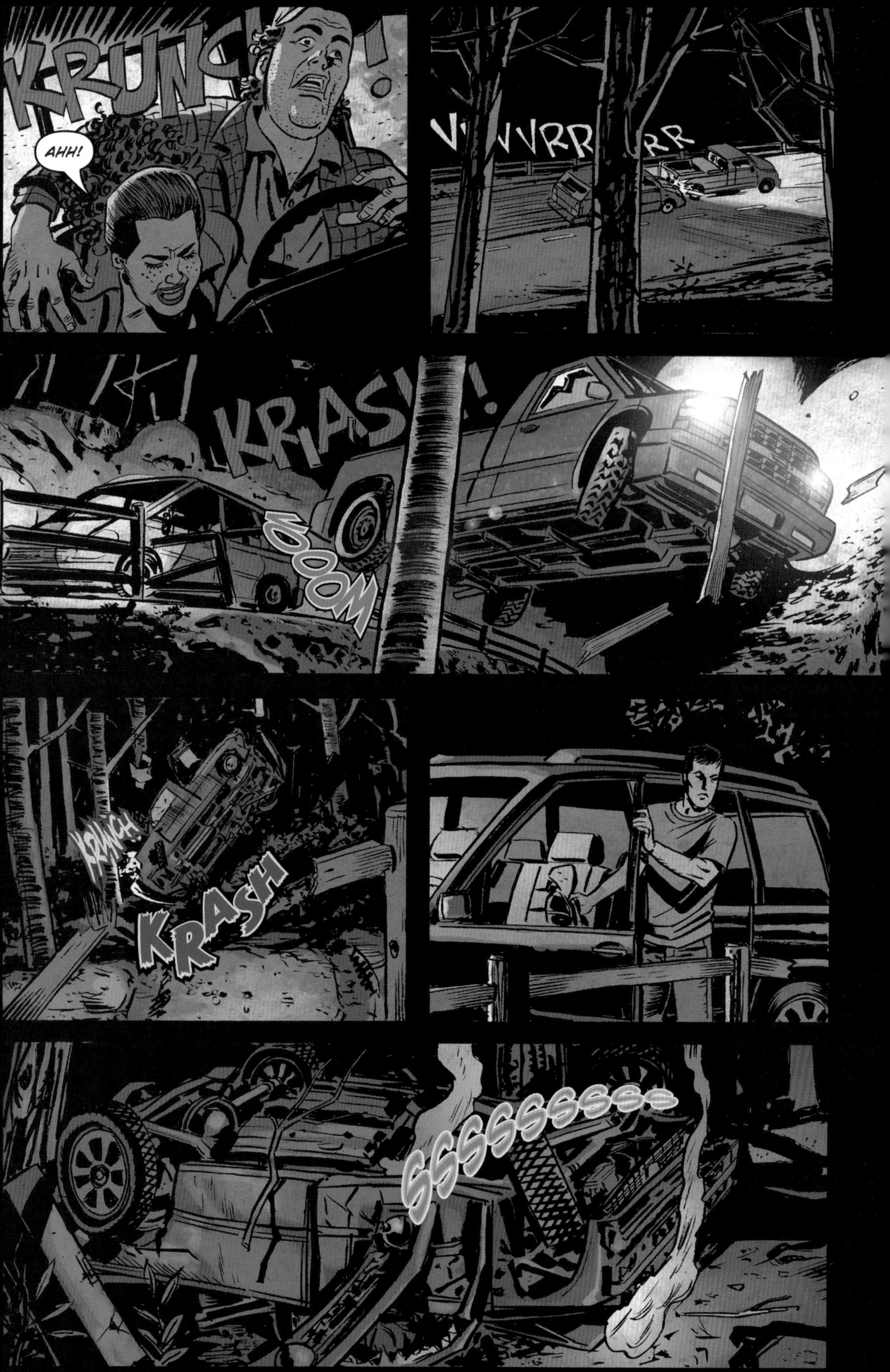
KRUNCH!
AHH!
VVVVVRRRRRR
KRASH!
VOOOM
KRUNCH
KRASH
SSSSSSSSSS

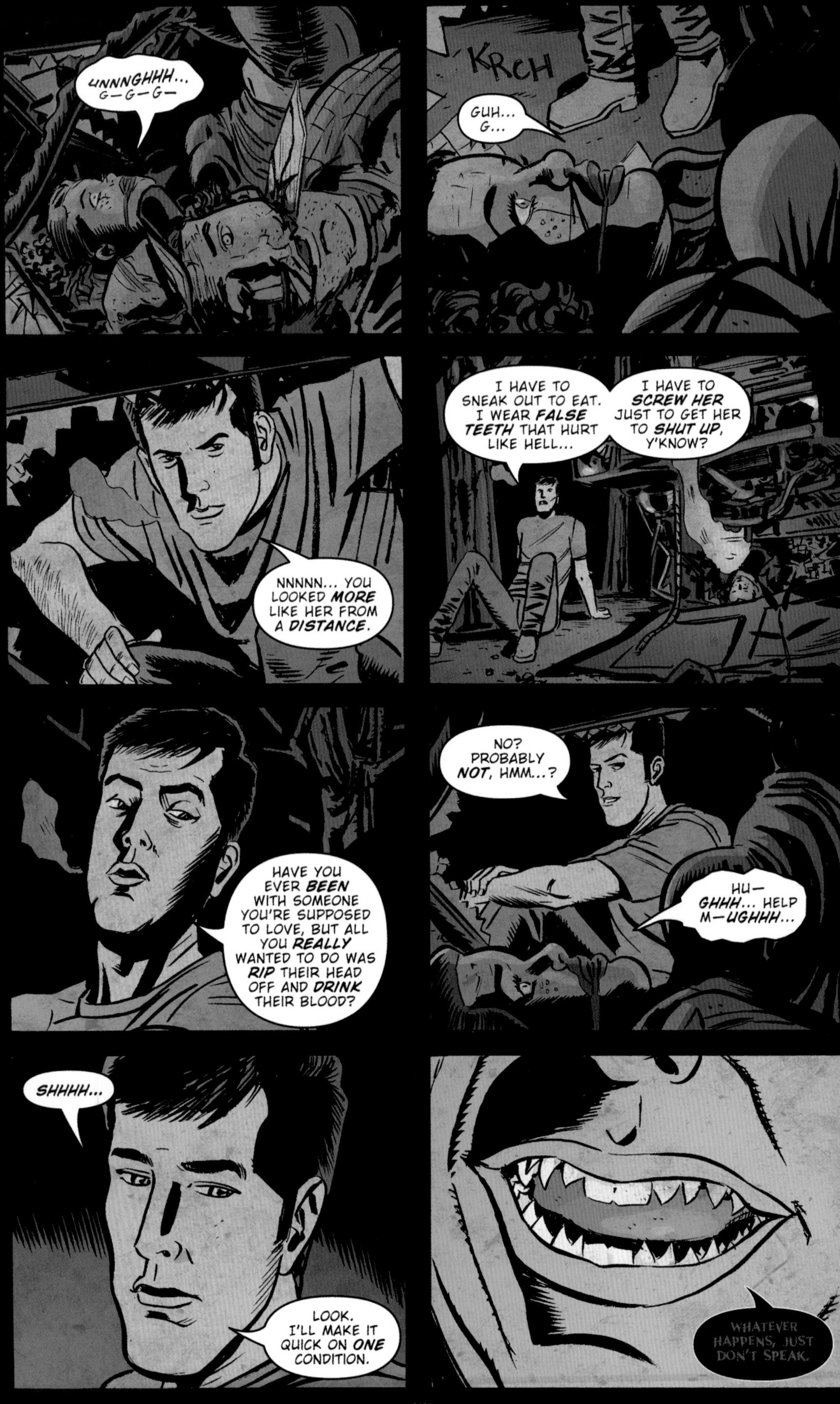
UNNNGHHH... G—G—G—
KRCH
GUH... G...
NNNNN... YOU LOOKED MORE LIKE HER FROM A DISTANCE.
I HAVE TO SNEAK OUT TO EAT. I WEAR FALSE TEETH THAT HURT LIKE HELL...
I HAVE TO SCREW HER JUST TO GET HER TO SHUT UP, Y'KNOW?
HAVE YOU EVER BEEN WITH SOMEONE YOU'RE SUPPOSED TO LOVE, BUT ALL YOU REALLY WANTED TO DO WAS RIP THEIR HEAD OFF AND DRINK THEIR BLOOD?
NO? PROBABLY NOT, HMM...?
HU— GHHH... HELP M—UGHHH...
SHHHH...
LOOK. I'LL MAKE IT QUICK ON ONE CONDITION.
WHATEVER HAPPENS, JUST DON'T SPEAK.

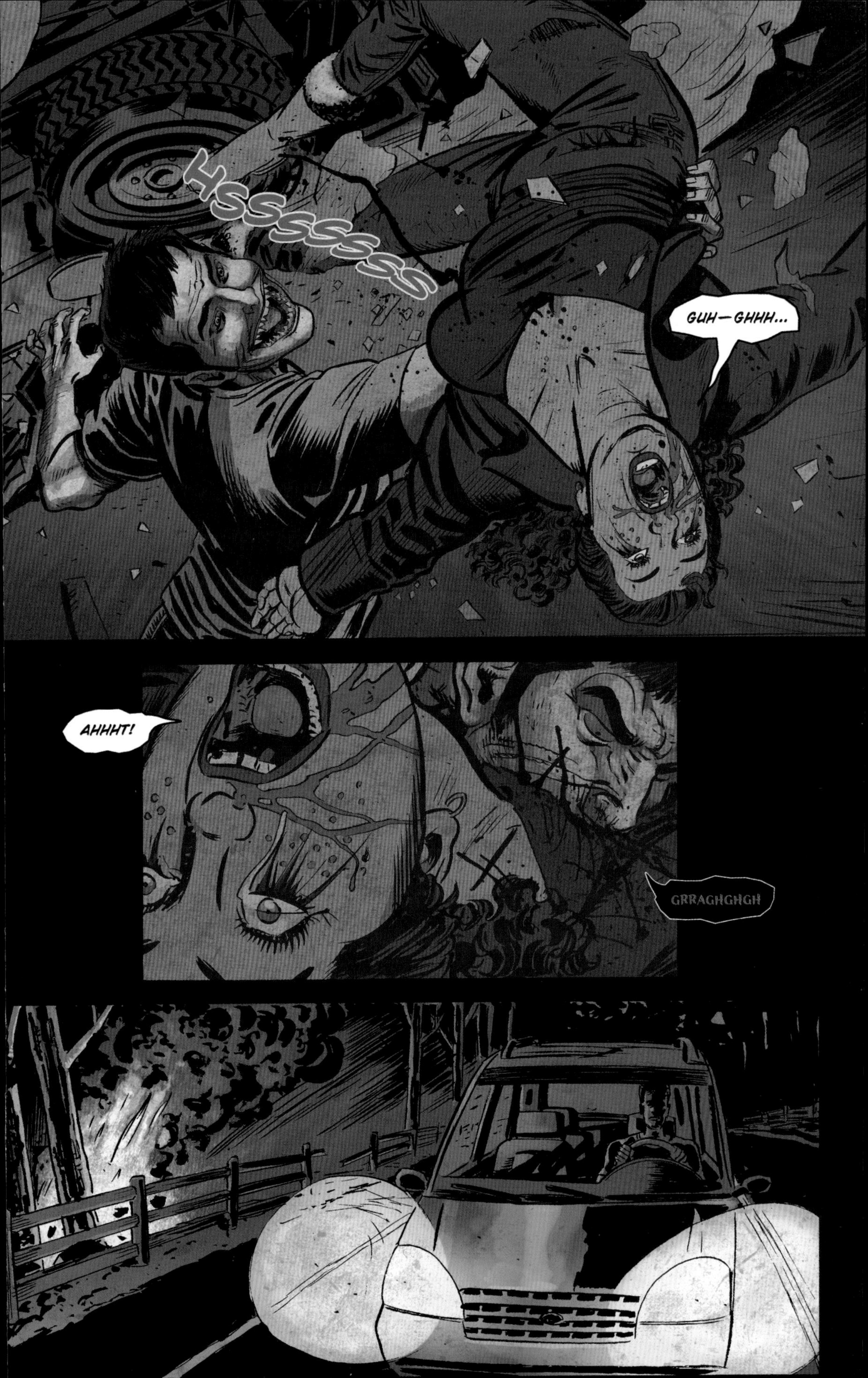
HSSSSSSS
GUH—GHHH...
AHHHT!
GRRAGHGHGH

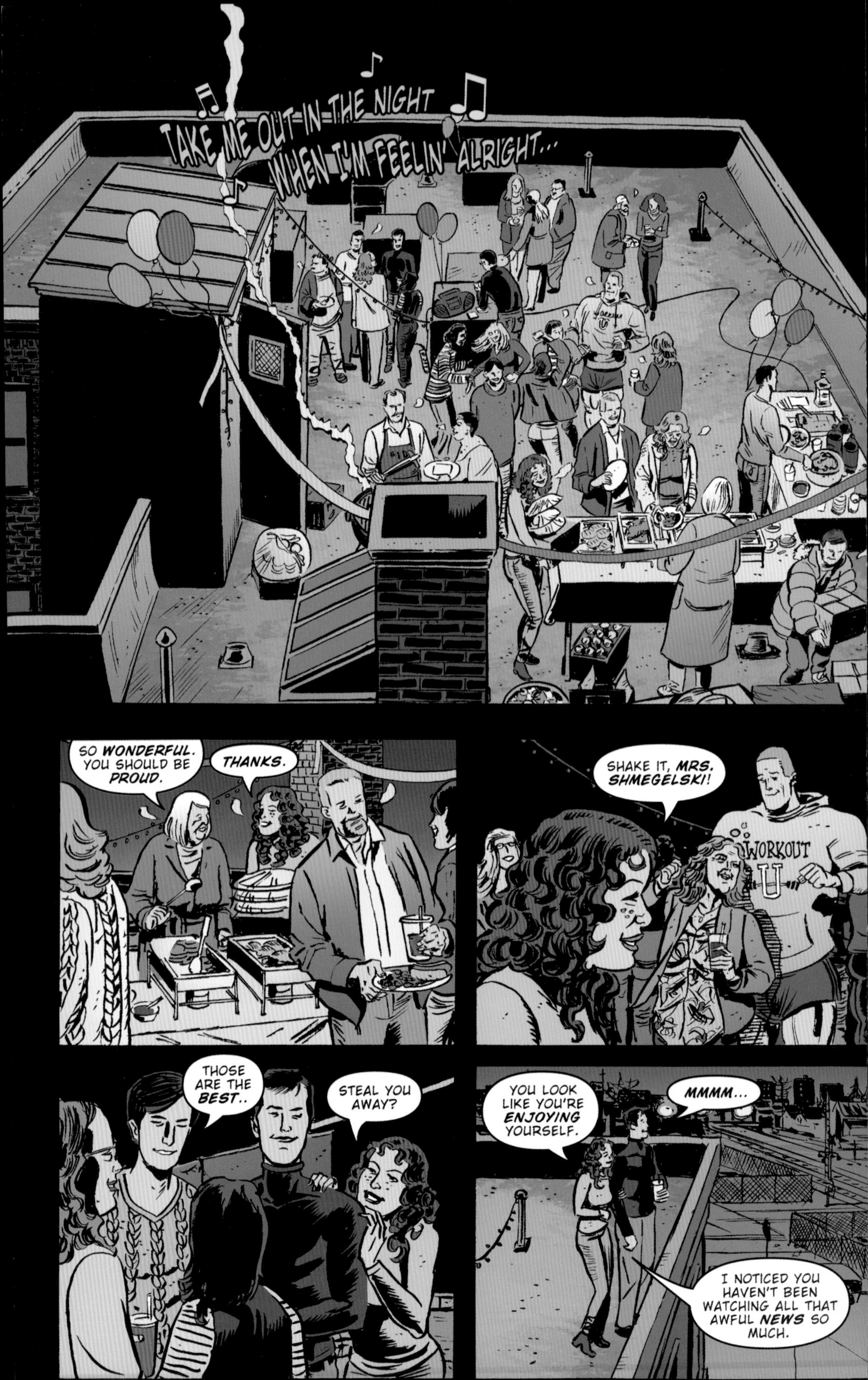
TAKE ME OUT IN THE NIGHT
WHEN I'M FEELIN' ALRIGHT...
SO WONDERFUL. YOU SHOULD BE PROUD.
THANKS.
SHAKE IT, MRS. SHMEGELSKI!
WORKOUT U
THOSE ARE THE BEST..
STEAL YOU AWAY?
YOU LOOK LIKE YOU'RE ENJOYING YOURSELF.
MMMM...
I NOTICED YOU HAVEN'T BEEN WATCHING ALL THAT AWFUL NEWS SO MUCH.

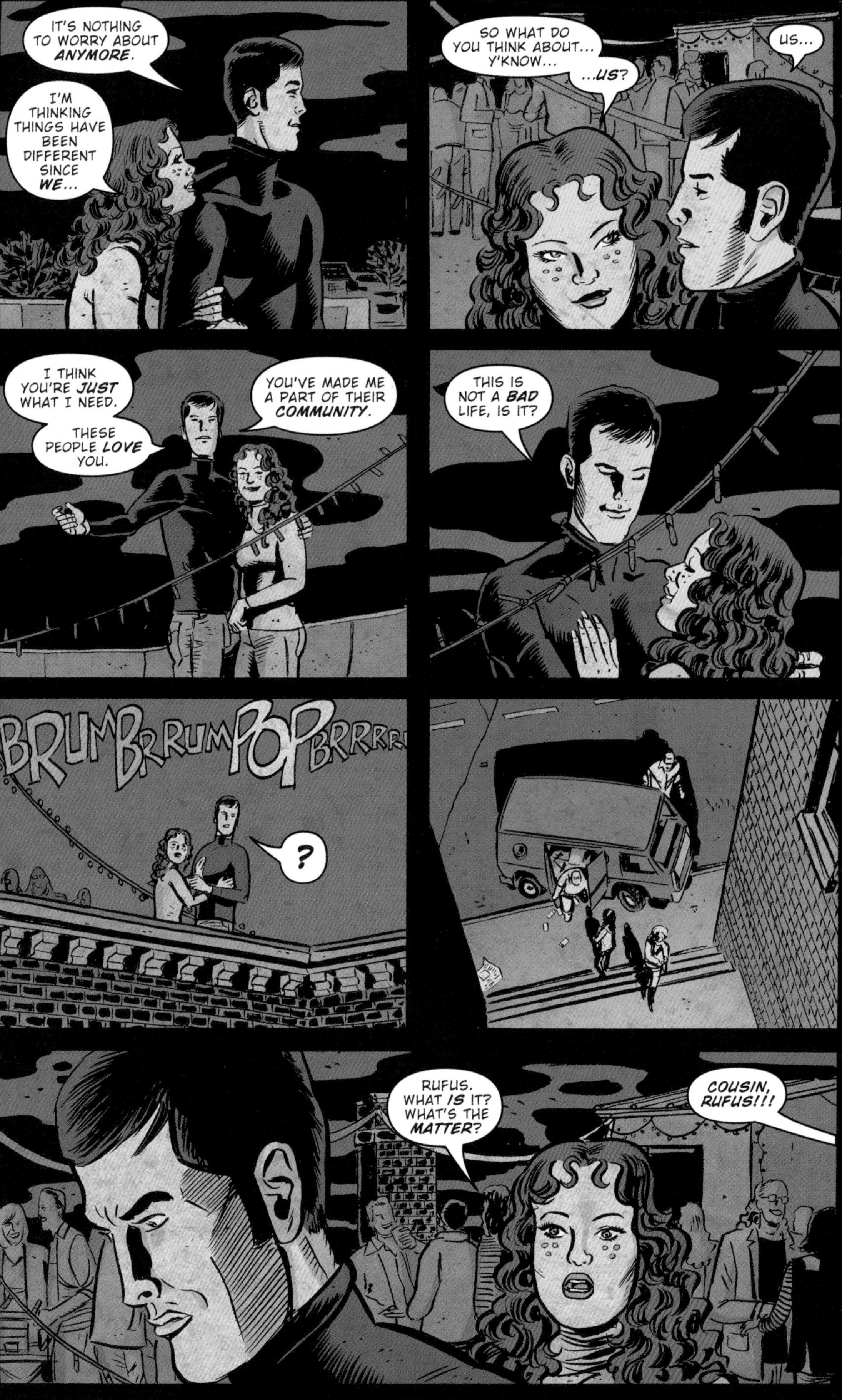

IT'S NOTHING TO WORRY ABOUT ANYMORE.
I'M THINKING THINGS HAVE BEEN DIFFERENT SINCE WE...
SO WHAT DO YOU THINK ABOUT... Y'KNOW...
...US?
US...
I THINK YOU'RE JUST WHAT I NEED.
THESE PEOPLE LOVE YOU.
YOU'VE MADE ME A PART OF THEIR COMMUNITY.
THIS IS NOT A BAD LIFE, IS IT?
BRUMBRRUMPOPBRRRR
?
RUFUS. WHAT IS IT? WHAT'S THE MATTER?
COUSIN, RUFUS!!!

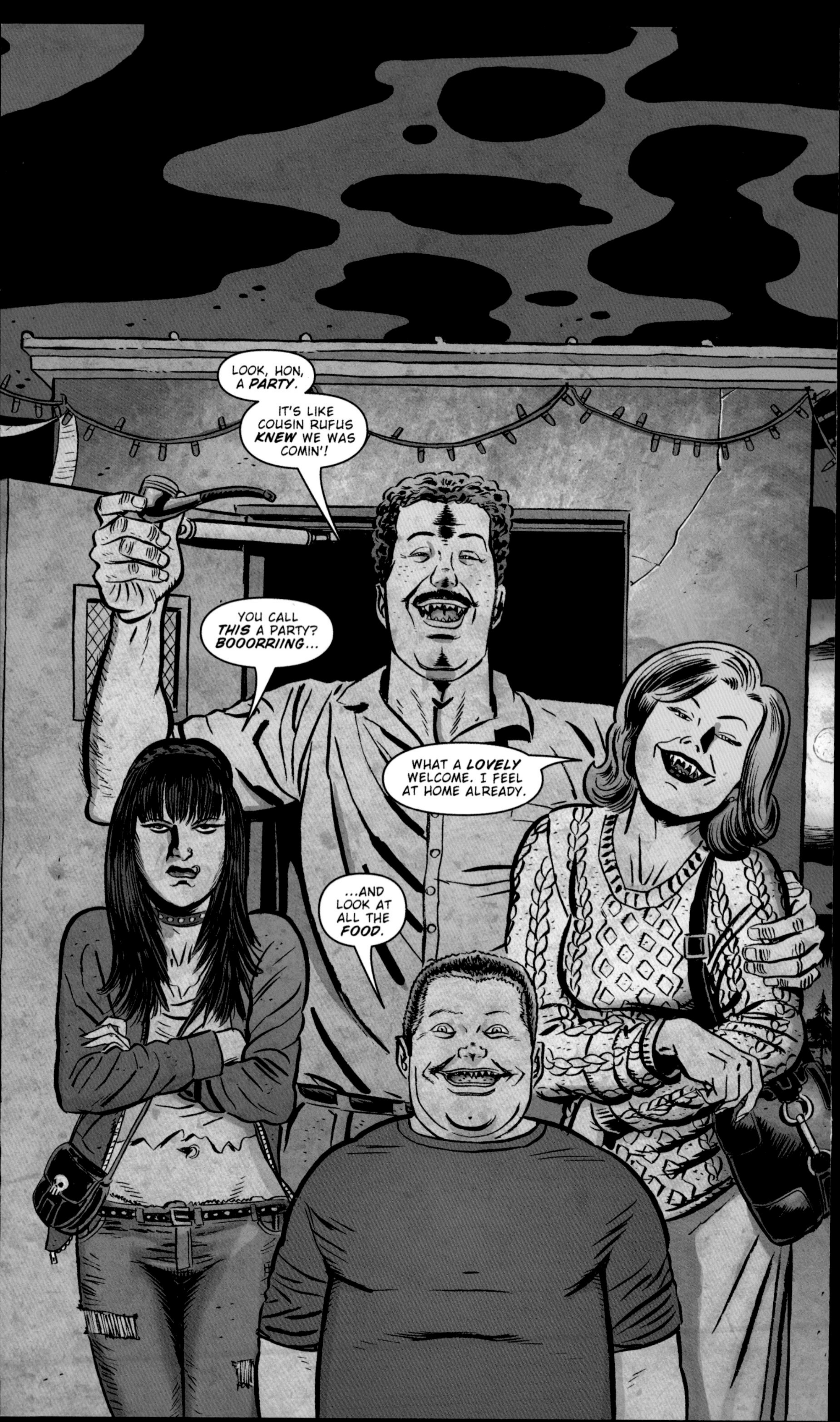
LOOK, HON, A PARTY.
IT'S LIKE COUSIN RUFUS KNEW WE WAS COMIN'!
YOU CALL THIS A PARTY? BOOORRIING...
WHAT A LOVELY WELCOME. I FEEL AT HOME ALREADY.
...AND LOOK AT ALL THE FOOD.

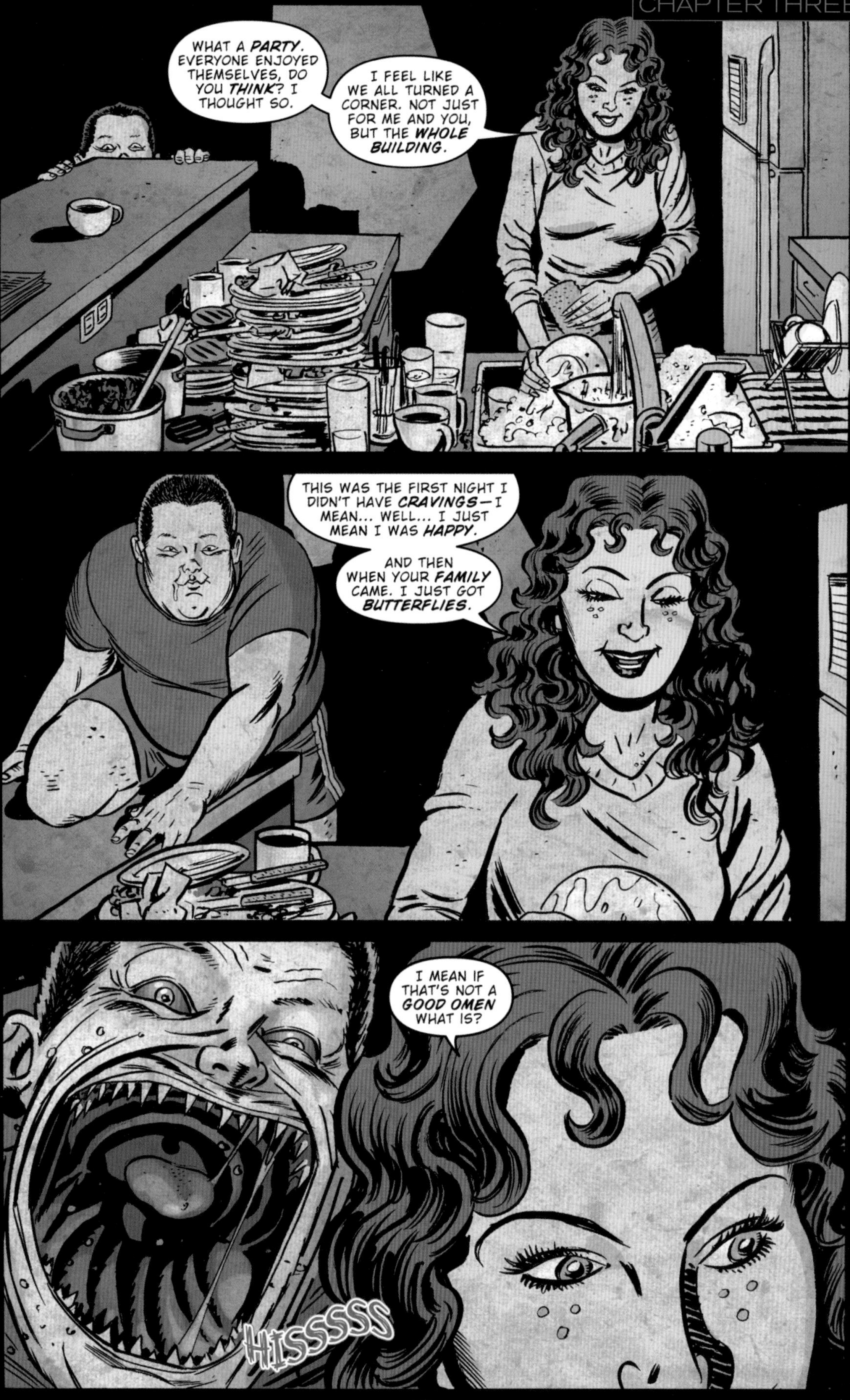
WHAT A PARTY. EVERYONE ENJOYED THEMSELVES, DO YOU THINK? I THOUGHT SO.
I FEEL LIKE WE ALL TURNED A CORNER. NOT JUST FOR ME AND YOU, BUT THE WHOLE BUILDING.
THIS WAS THE FIRST NIGHT I DIDN'T HAVE CRAVINGS—I MEAN... WELL... I JUST MEAN I WAS HAPPY.
AND THEN WHEN YOUR FAMILY CAME. I JUST GOT BUTTERFLIES.
I MEAN IF THAT'S NOT A GOOD OMEN WHAT IS?
HISSSSSS

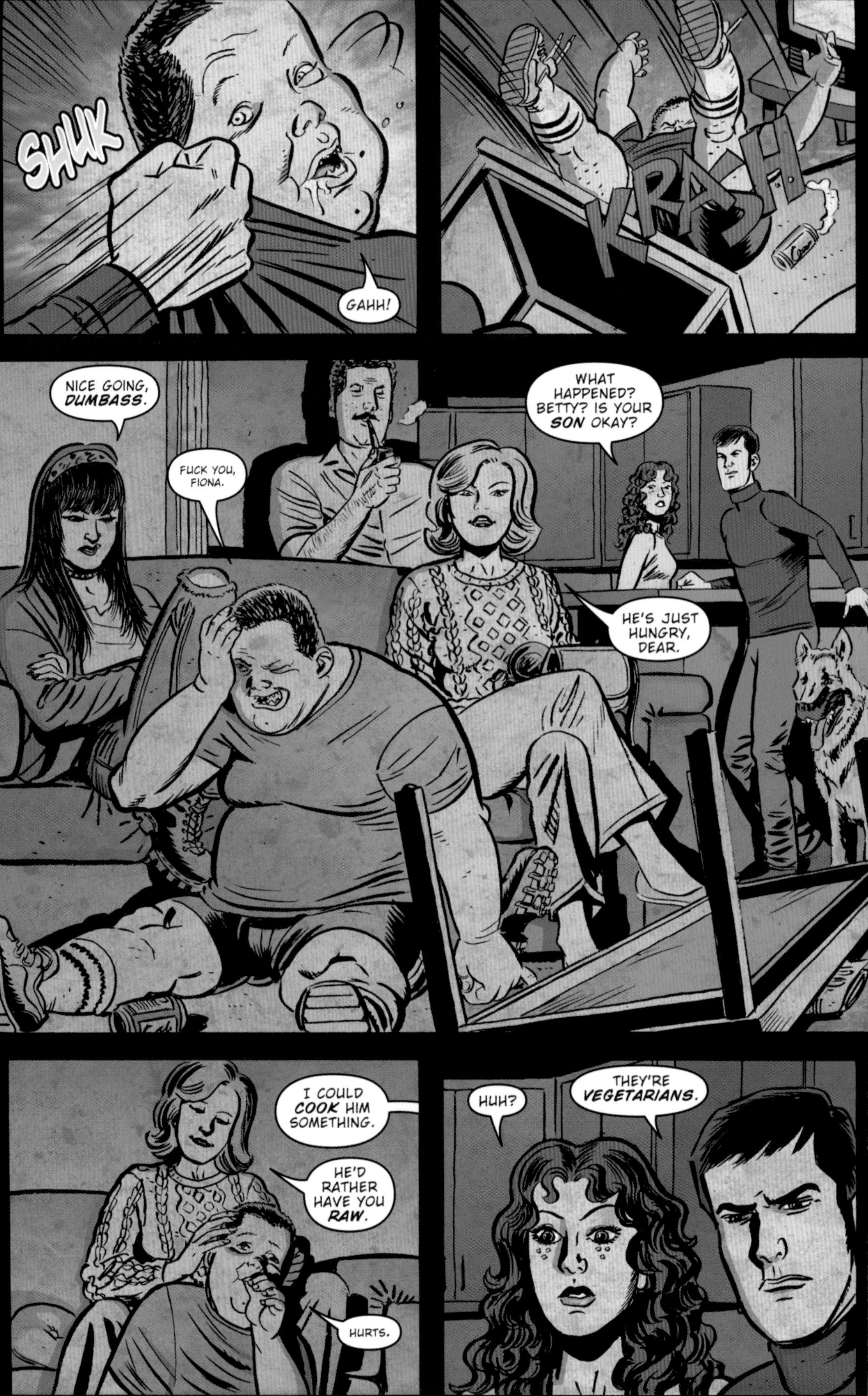
SHUK
GAHH!
KRASH
NICE GOING, DUMBASS.
FUCK YOU, FIONA.
WHAT HAPPENED? BETTY? IS YOUR SON OKAY?
HE'S JUST HUNGRY, DEAR.
I COULD COOK HIM SOMETHING.
HE'D RATHER HAVE YOU RAW.
HURTS.
HUH?
THEY'RE VEGETARIANS.

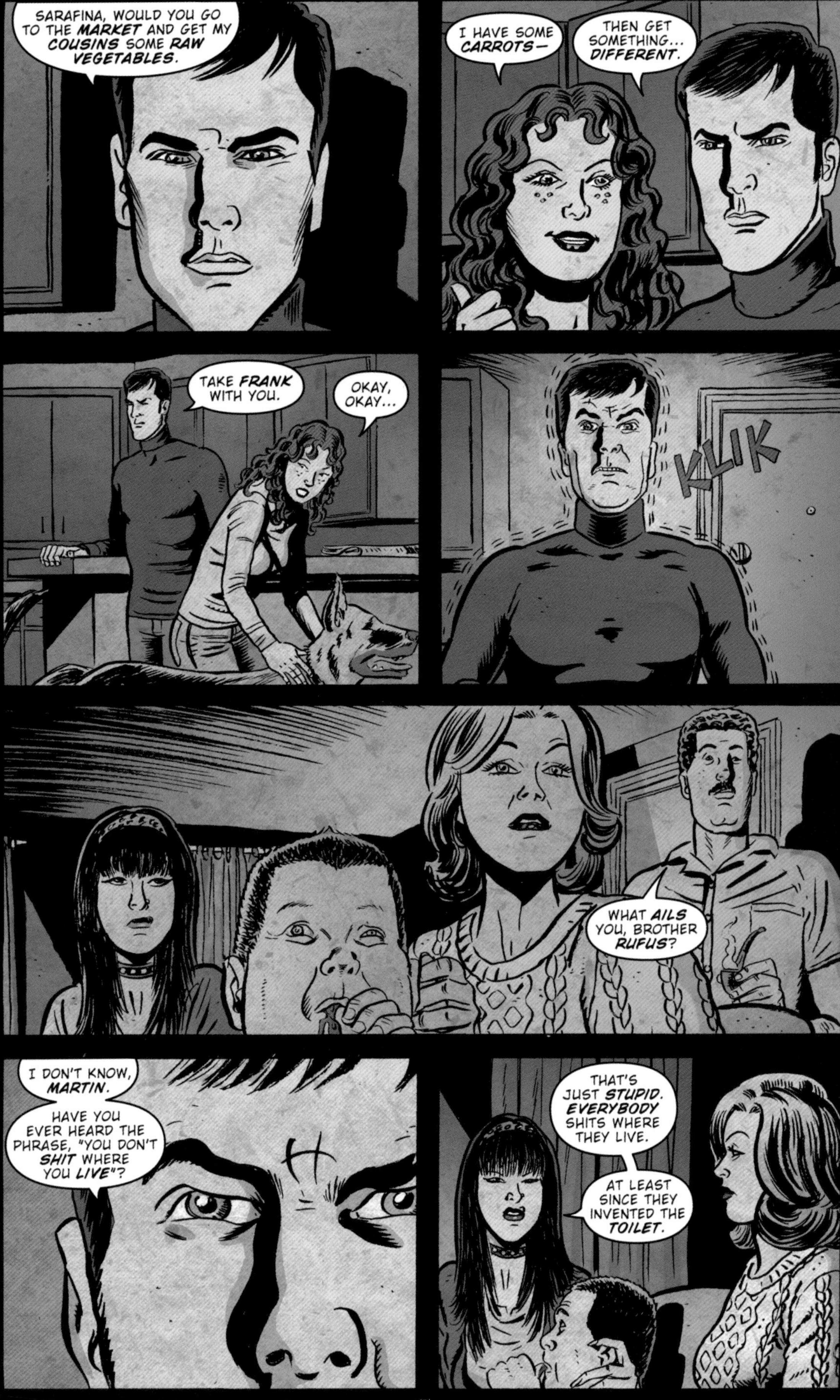

SARAFINA, WOULD YOU GO TO THE MARKET AND GET MY COUSINS SOME RAW VEGETABLES.
I HAVE SOME CARROTS—
THEN GET SOMETHING... DIFFERENT.
TAKE FRANK WITH YOU.
OKAY, OKAY...
KLIK
WHAT AILS YOU, BROTHER RUFUS?
I DON'T KNOW, MARTIN.
HAVE YOU EVER HEARD THE PHRASE, "YOU DON'T SHIT WHERE YOU LIVE"?
THAT'S JUST STUPID. EVERYBODY SHITS WHERE THEY LIVE.
AT LEAST SINCE THEY INVENTED THE TOILET.

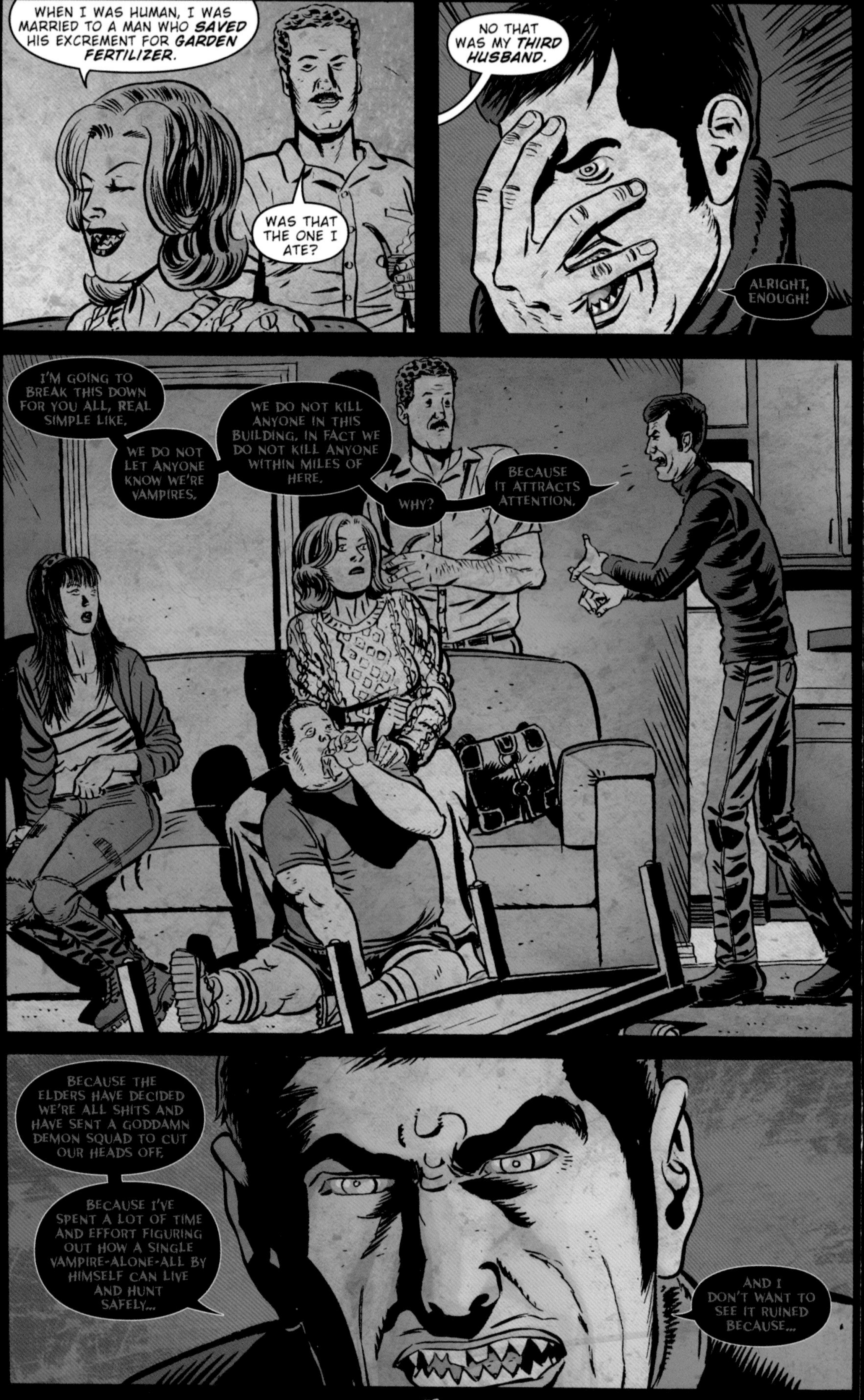
WHEN I WAS HUMAN, I WAS MARRIED TO A MAN WHO SAVED HIS EXCREMENT FOR GARDEN FERTILIZER.
WAS THAT THE ONE I ATE?
NO THAT WAS MY THIRD HUSBAND.
ALRIGHT, ENOUGH!
I'M GOING TO BREAK THIS DOWN FOR YOU ALL, REAL SIMPLE LIKE,
WE DO NOT LET ANYONE KNOW WE'RE VAMPIRES,
WE DO NOT KILL ANYONE IN THIS BUILDING, IN FACT WE DO NOT KILL ANYONE WITHIN MILES OF HERE,
WHY?
BECAUSE IT ATTRACTS ATTENTION,
BECAUSE THE ELDERS HAVE DECIDED WE'RE ALL SHITS AND HAVE SENT A GODDAMN DEMON SQUAD TO CUT OUR HEADS OFF,
BECAUSE I'VE SPENT A LOT OF TIME AND EFFORT FIGURING OUT HOW A SINGLE VAMPIRE-ALONE-ALL BY HIMSELF CAN LIVE AND HUNT SAFELY...
AND I DON'T WANT TO SEE IT RUINED BECAUSE...

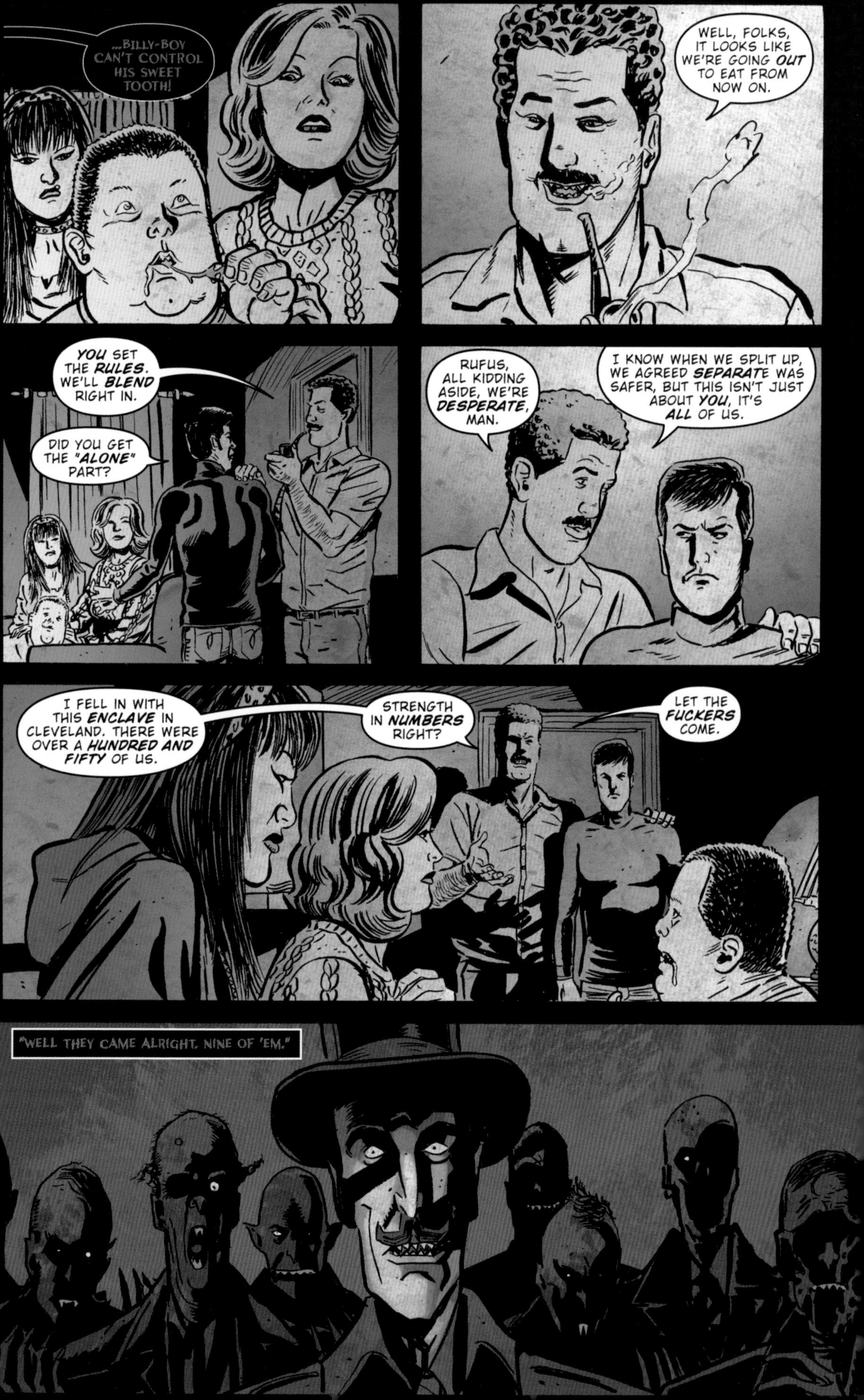
...BILLY-BOY CAN'T CONTROL HIS SWEET TOOTH!
WELL, FOLKS, IT LOOKS LIKE WE'RE GOING OUT TO EAT FROM NOW ON.
YOU SET THE RULES. WE'LL BLEND RIGHT IN.
DID YOU GET THE "ALONE" PART?
RUFUS, ALL KIDDING ASIDE, WE'RE DESPERATE, MAN.
I KNOW WHEN WE SPLIT UP, WE AGREED SEPARATE WAS SAFER, BUT THIS ISN'T JUST ABOUT YOU, IT'S ALL OF US.
I FELL IN WITH THIS ENCLAVE IN CLEVELAND. THERE WERE OVER A HUNDRED AND FIFTY OF US.
STRENGTH IN NUMBERS RIGHT?
LET THE FUCKERS COME.
"WELL THEY CAME ALRIGHT. NINE OF 'EM."

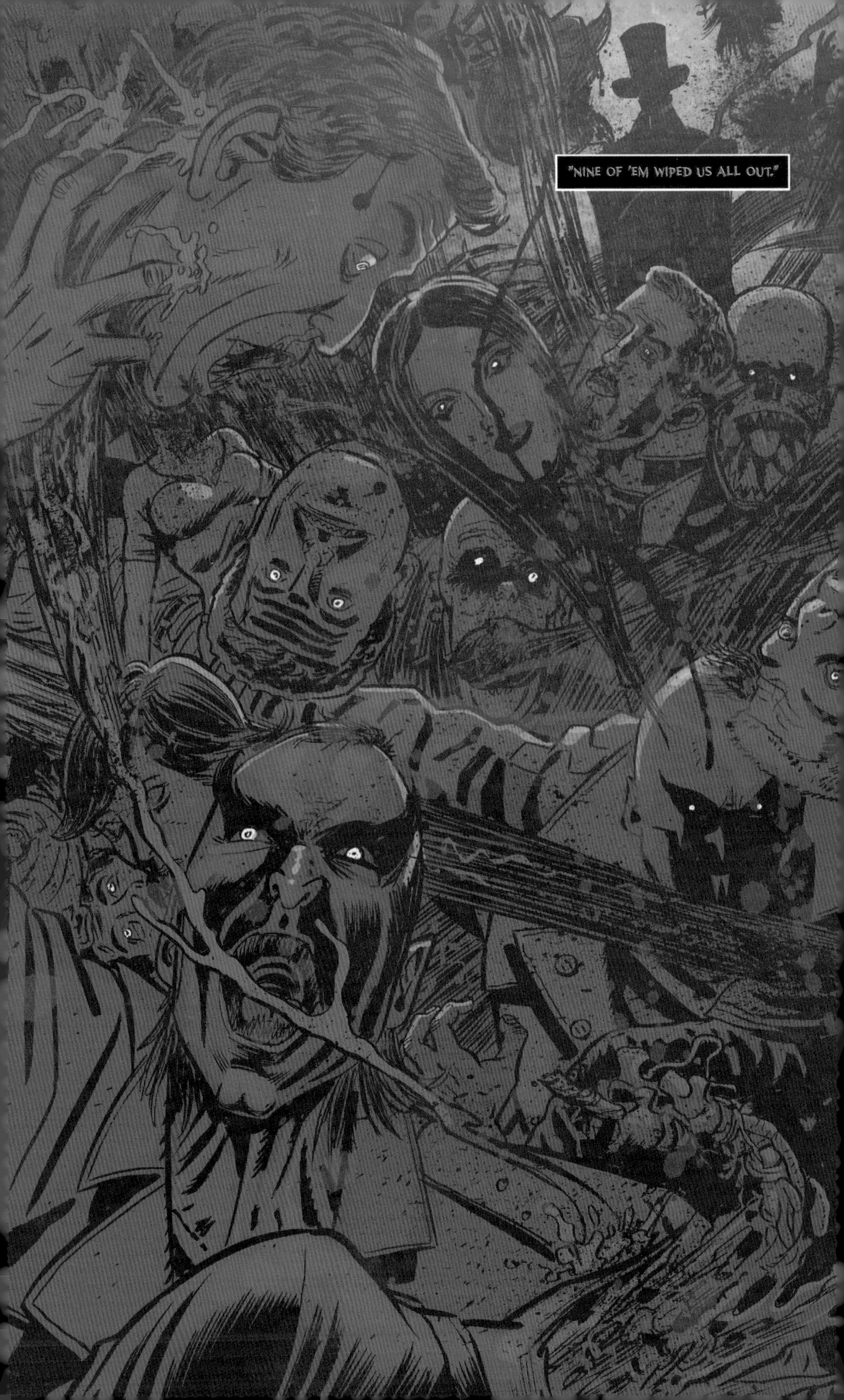
"NINE OF 'EM WIPED US ALL OUT."

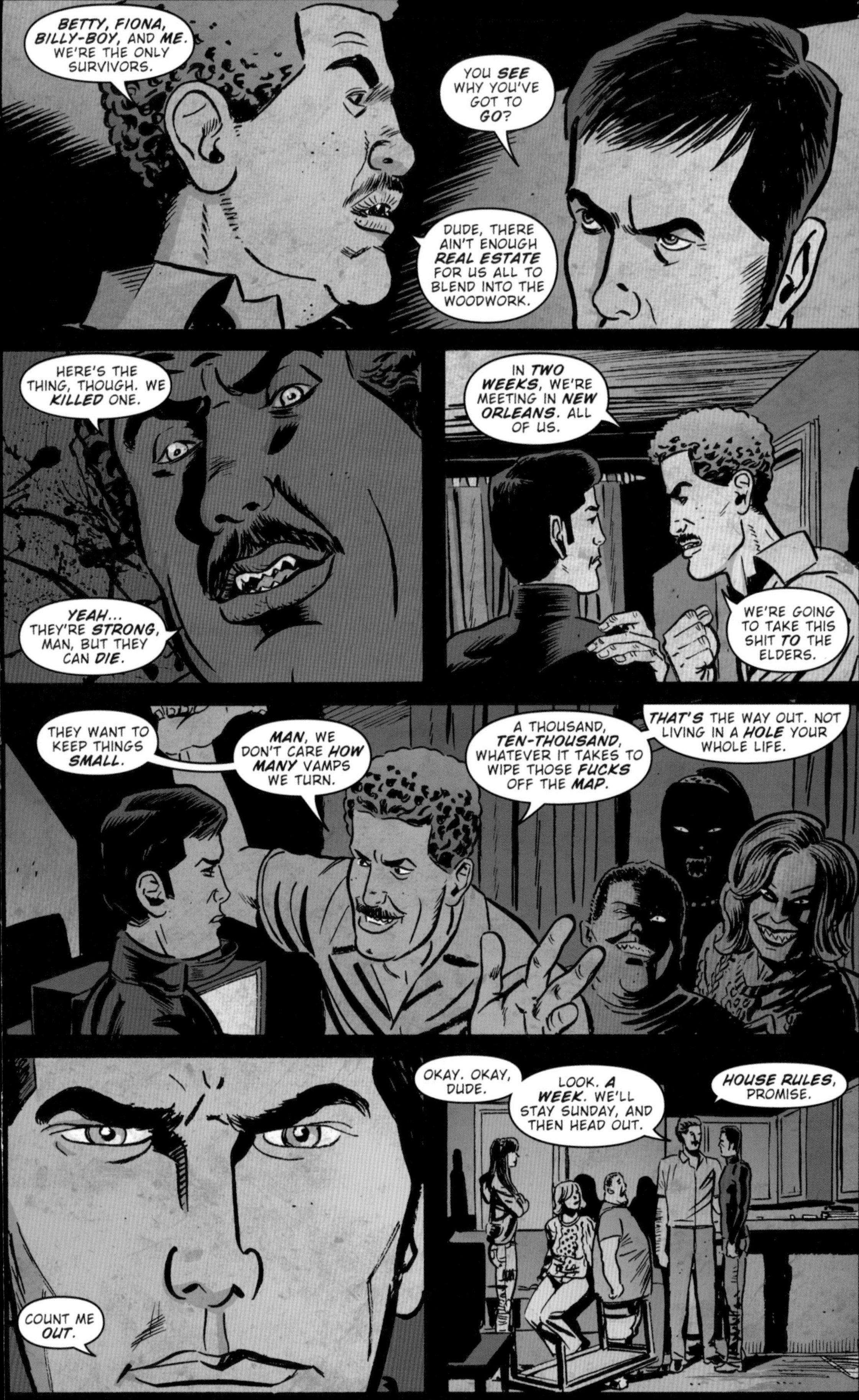

BETTY, FIONA, BILLY-BOY, AND ME. WE'RE THE ONLY SURVIVORS.
YOU SEE WHY YOU'VE GOT TO GO?
DUDE, THERE AIN'T ENOUGH REAL ESTATE FOR US ALL TO BLEND INTO THE WOODWORK.
HERE'S THE THING, THOUGH. WE KILLED ONE.
YEAH... THEY'RE STRONG, MAN, BUT THEY CAN DIE.
IN TWO WEEKS, WE'RE MEETING IN NEW ORLEANS. ALL OF US.
WE'RE GOING TO TAKE THIS SHIT TO THE ELDERS.
THEY WANT TO KEEP THINGS SMALL.
MAN, WE DON'T CARE HOW MANY VAMPS WE TURN.
A THOUSAND, TEN-THOUSAND, WHATEVER IT TAKES TO WIPE THOSE FUCKS OFF THE MAP.
THAT'S THE WAY OUT. NOT LIVING IN A HOLE YOUR WHOLE LIFE.
COUNT ME OUT.
OKAY. OKAY, DUDE.
LOOK. A WEEK. WE'LL STAY SUNDAY, AND THEN HEAD OUT.
HOUSE RULES, PROMISE.

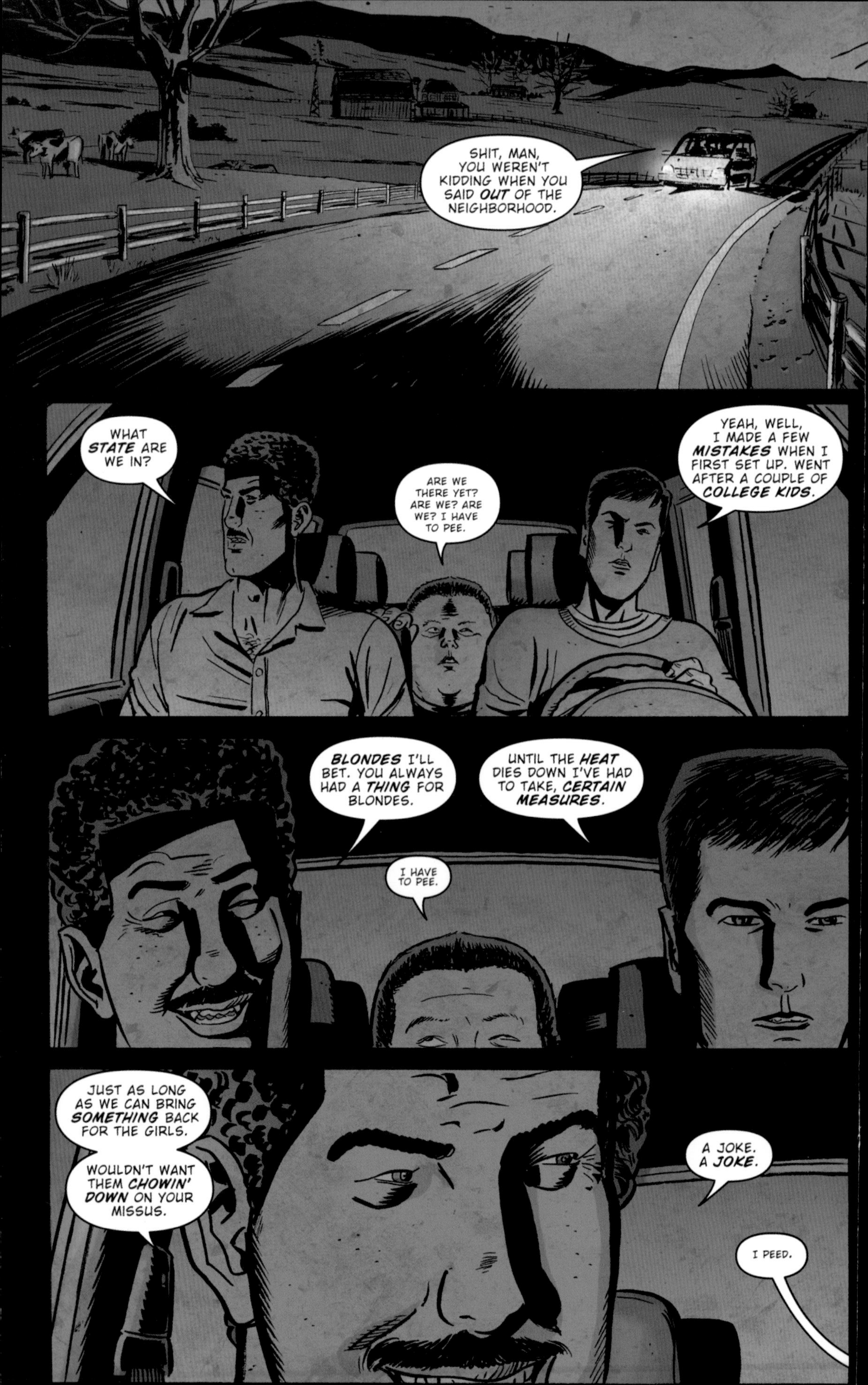
SHIT, MAN, YOU WEREN'T KIDDING WHEN YOU SAID OUT OF THE NEIGHBORHOOD.
WHAT STATE ARE WE IN?
ARE WE THERE YET? ARE WE? ARE WE? I HAVE TO PEE.
YEAH, WELL, I MADE A FEW MISTAKES WHEN I FIRST SET UP. WENT AFTER A COUPLE OF COLLEGE KIDS.
BLONDES I'LL BET. YOU ALWAYS HAD A THING FOR BLONDES.
UNTIL THE HEAT DIES DOWN I'VE HAD TO TAKE, CERTAIN MEASURES.
I HAVE TO PEE.
JUST AS LONG AS WE CAN BRING SOMETHING BACK FOR THE GIRLS.
WOULDN'T WANT THEM CHOWIN' DOWN ON YOUR MISSUS.
A JOKE. A JOKE.
I PEED.

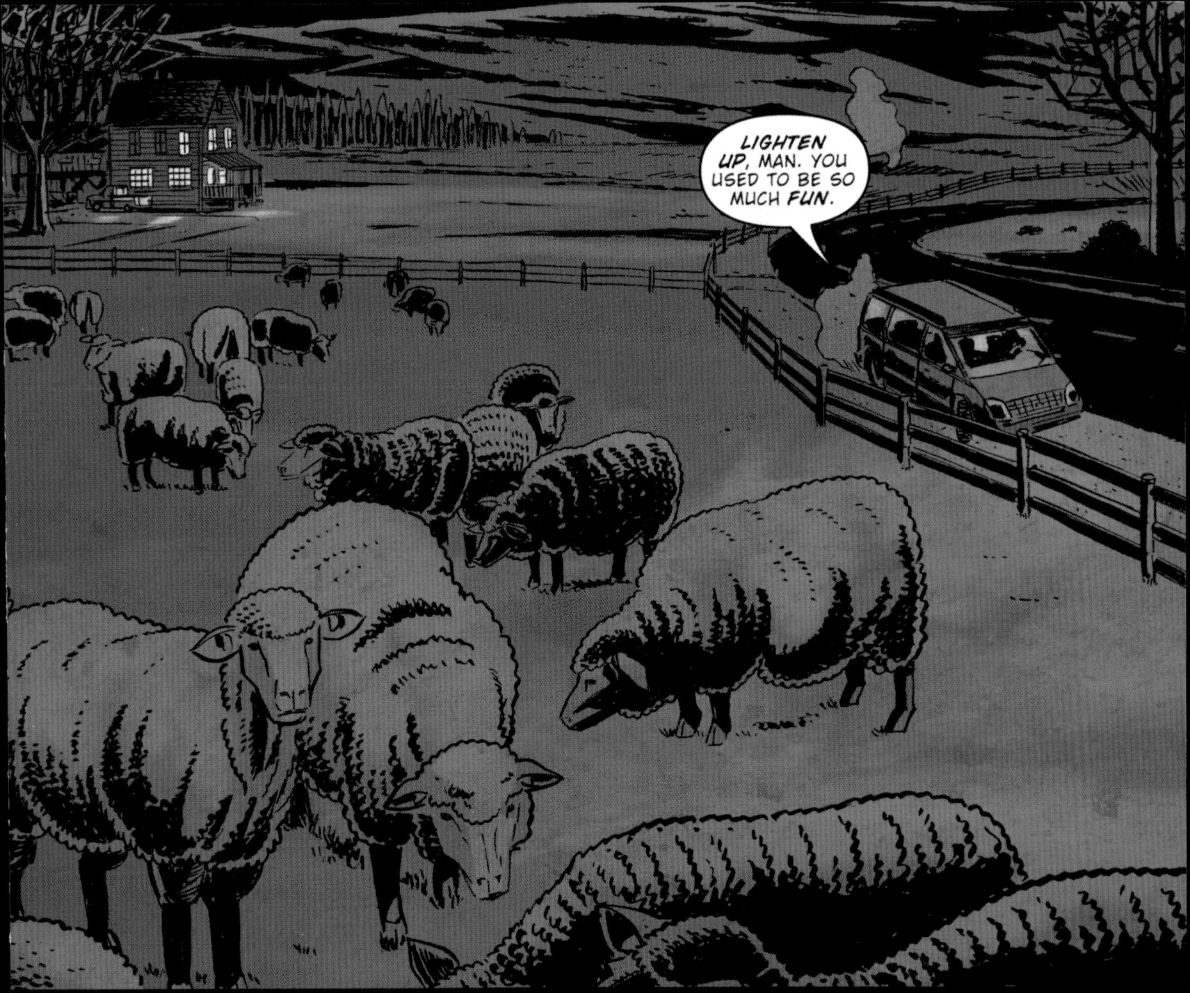
LIGHTEN UP, MAN. YOU USED TO BE SO MUCH FUN.

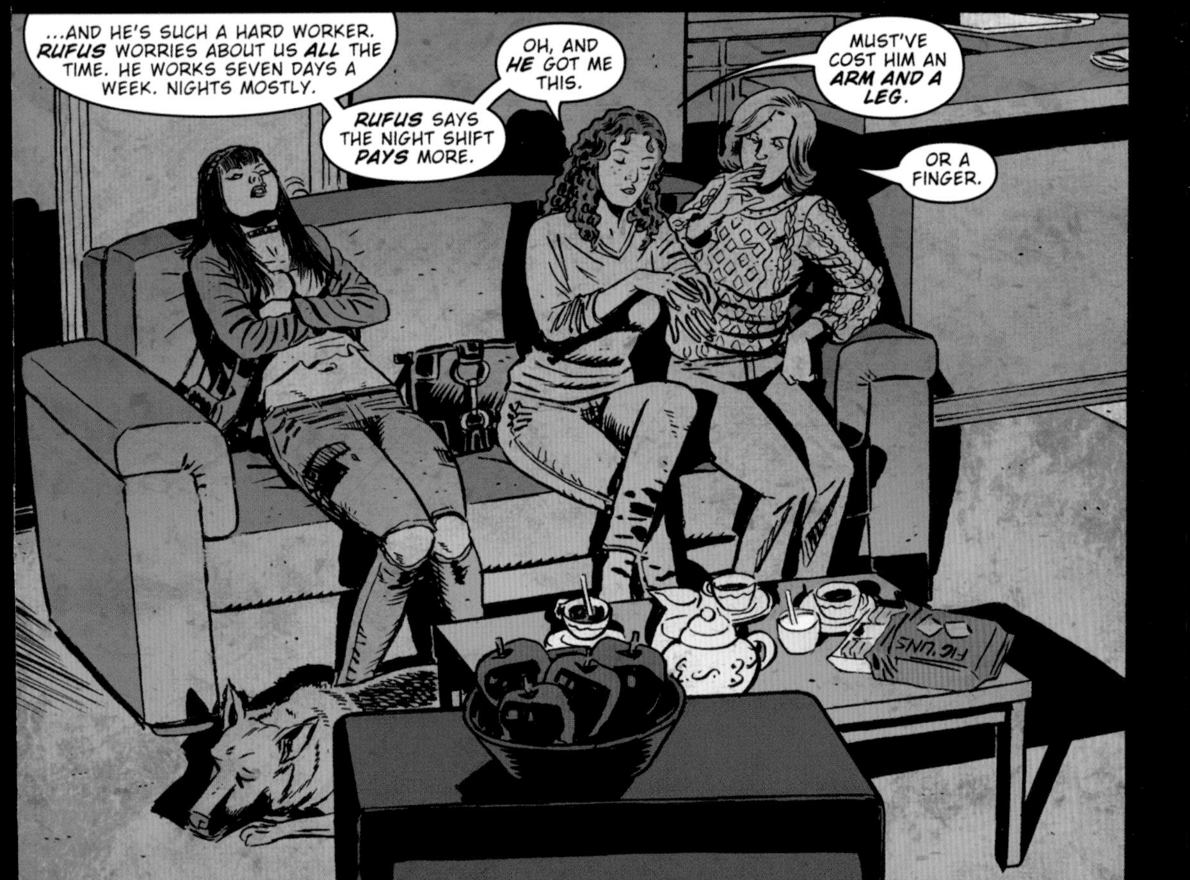
...AND HE'S SUCH A HARD WORKER. RUFUS WORRIES ABOUT US ALL THE TIME. HE WORKS SEVEN DAYS A WEEK. NIGHTS MOSTLY.
RUFUS SAYS THE NIGHT SHIFT PAYS MORE.
OH, AND HE GOT ME THIS.
MUST'VE COST HIM AN ARM AND A LEG.
OR A FINGER.

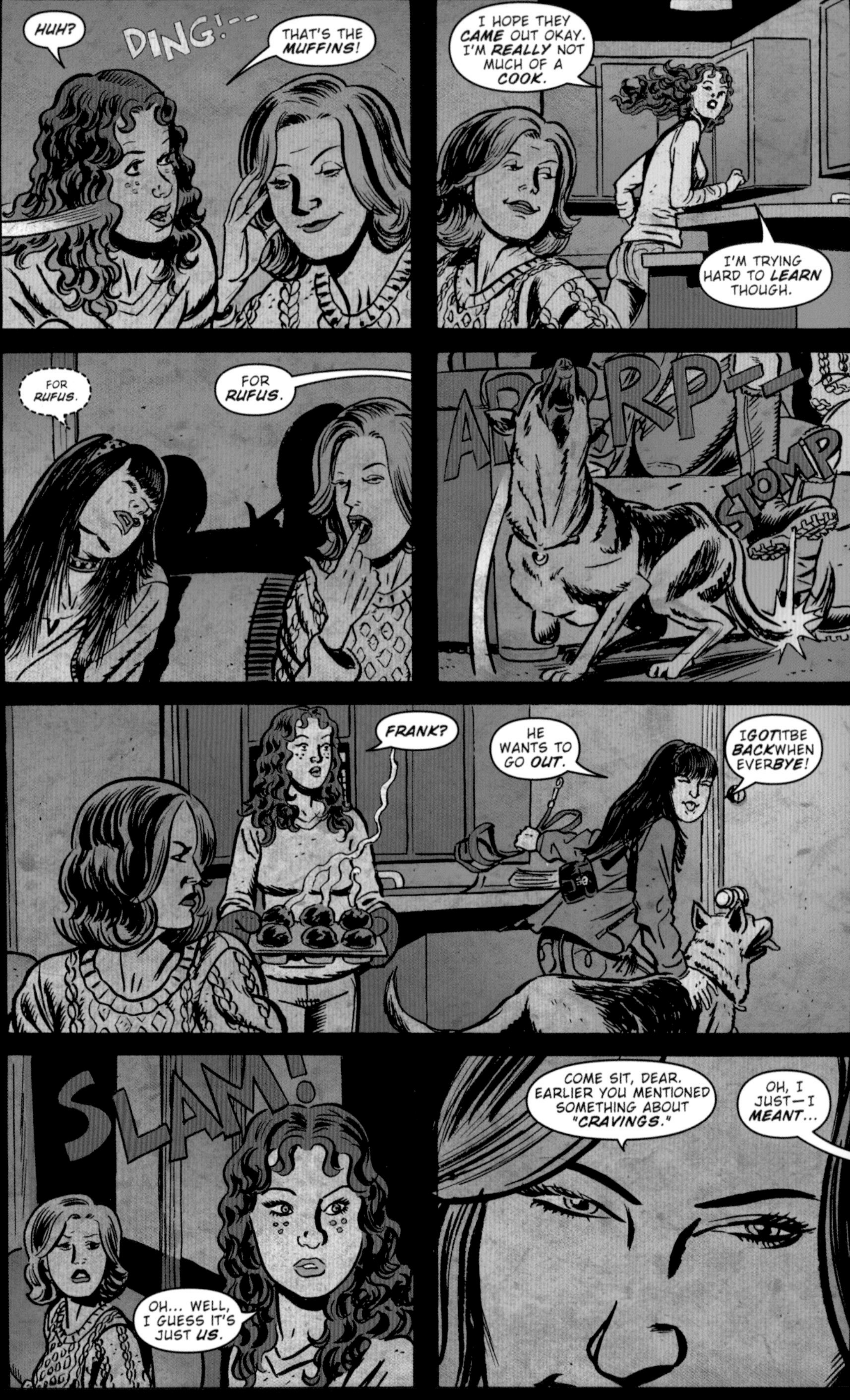
HUH?
DING!--
THAT'S THE MUFFINS!
I HOPE THEY CAME OUT OKAY. I'M REALLY NOT MUCH OF A COOK.
I'M TRYING HARD TO LEARN THOUGH.
FOR RUFUS.
FOR RUFUS.
ARRRP--
STOMP
FRANK?
HE WANTS TO GO OUT.
IGOTTBE BACKWHEN EVERBYE!
SLAM!
OH... WELL, I GUESS IT'S JUST US.
COME SIT, DEAR. EARLIER YOU MENTIONED SOMETHING ABOUT "CRAVINGS."
OH, I JUST—I MEANT...

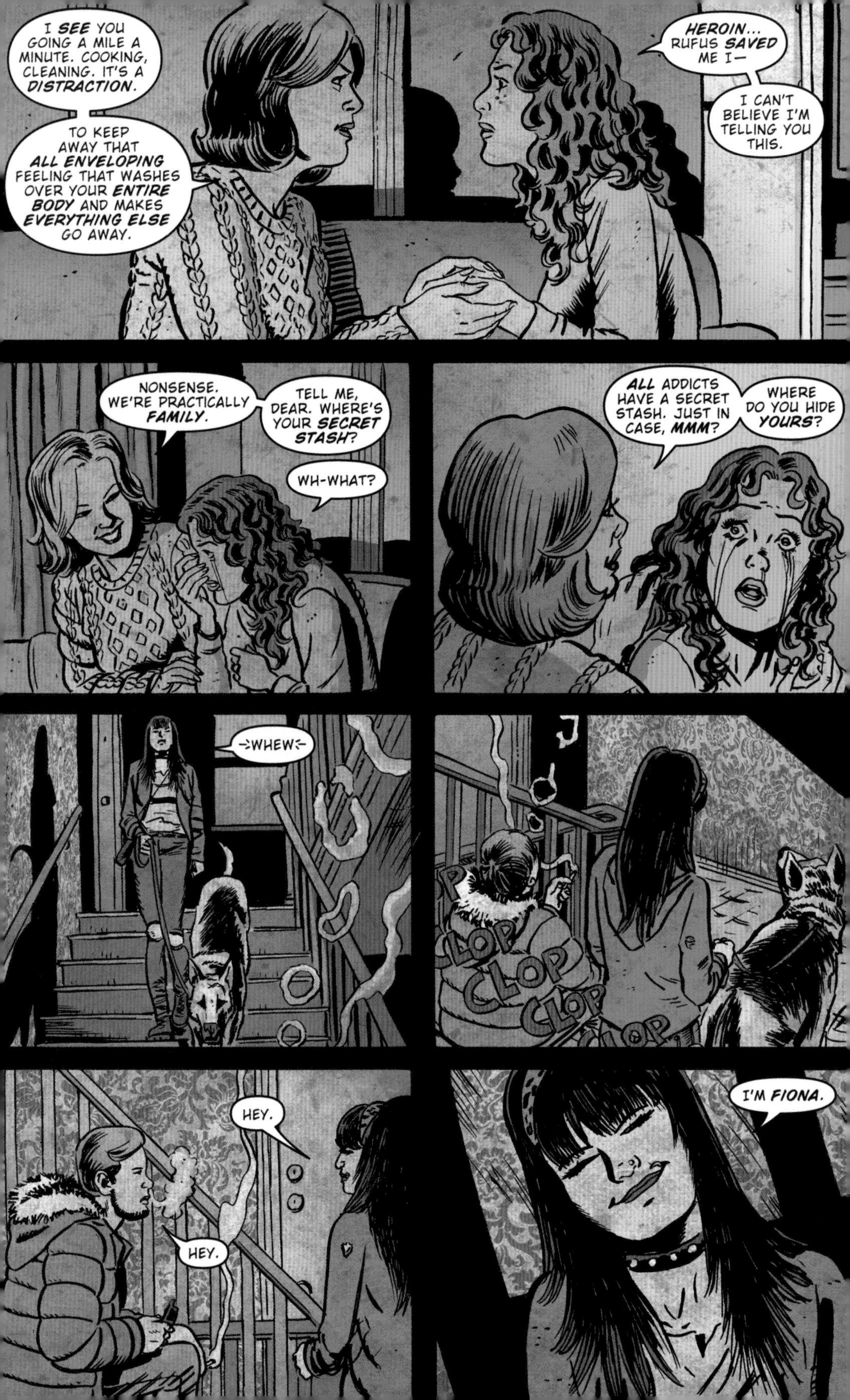
I SEE YOU GOING A MILE A MINUTE. COOKING, CLEANING. IT'S A DISTRACTION.
TO KEEP AWAY THAT ALL ENVELOPING FEELING THAT WASHES OVER YOUR ENTIRE BODY AND MAKES EVERYTHING ELSE GO AWAY.
HEROIN... RUFUS SAVED ME I—
I CAN'T BELIEVE I'M TELLING YOU THIS.
NONSENSE. WE'RE PRACTICALLY FAMILY.
TELL ME, DEAR. WHERE'S YOUR SECRET STASH?
WH-WHAT?
ALL ADDICTS HAVE A SECRET STASH. JUST IN CASE, MMM?
WHERE DO YOU HIDE YOURS?
WHEW
CLOP CLOP CLOP CLOP
HEY.
HEY.
I'M FIONA.

BAAA

BAAA

BAAA

LOOK, GUYS, I'M *SORRY* ABOUT THIS. I KNOW THIS ISN'T IDEAL.

I'M NOT PICKY LIKE *YOU* AND YOUR *COEDS*, RUFUS. JETHRO AND THE *KIDS'LL* DO.

YEAH, YEAH...

UM... WELL... I TOLD YOU. THERE ARE *TOO MANY* OF YOU. WE CAN'T JUST GO *MASSACRING* HOUSES FULL OF PEOPLE.

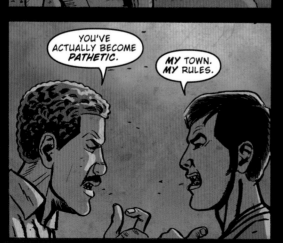

SO, WHAT ARE WE DOING OUT *HERE*—

BAAA

OH, NO. NO, NO, NO.

YOU'RE *JOKING*?

THEY'RE FULL OF *BLOOD*, AND NOT AS TOUGH AS THE *COWS*.

BAAA

YOU'VE ACTUALLY BECOME *PATHETIC*.

MY TOWN. *MY* RULES.

DUDE, I'D RATHER GO *SUNBATHING*.

THEN *LEAVE*—

EEEEEEE!

60

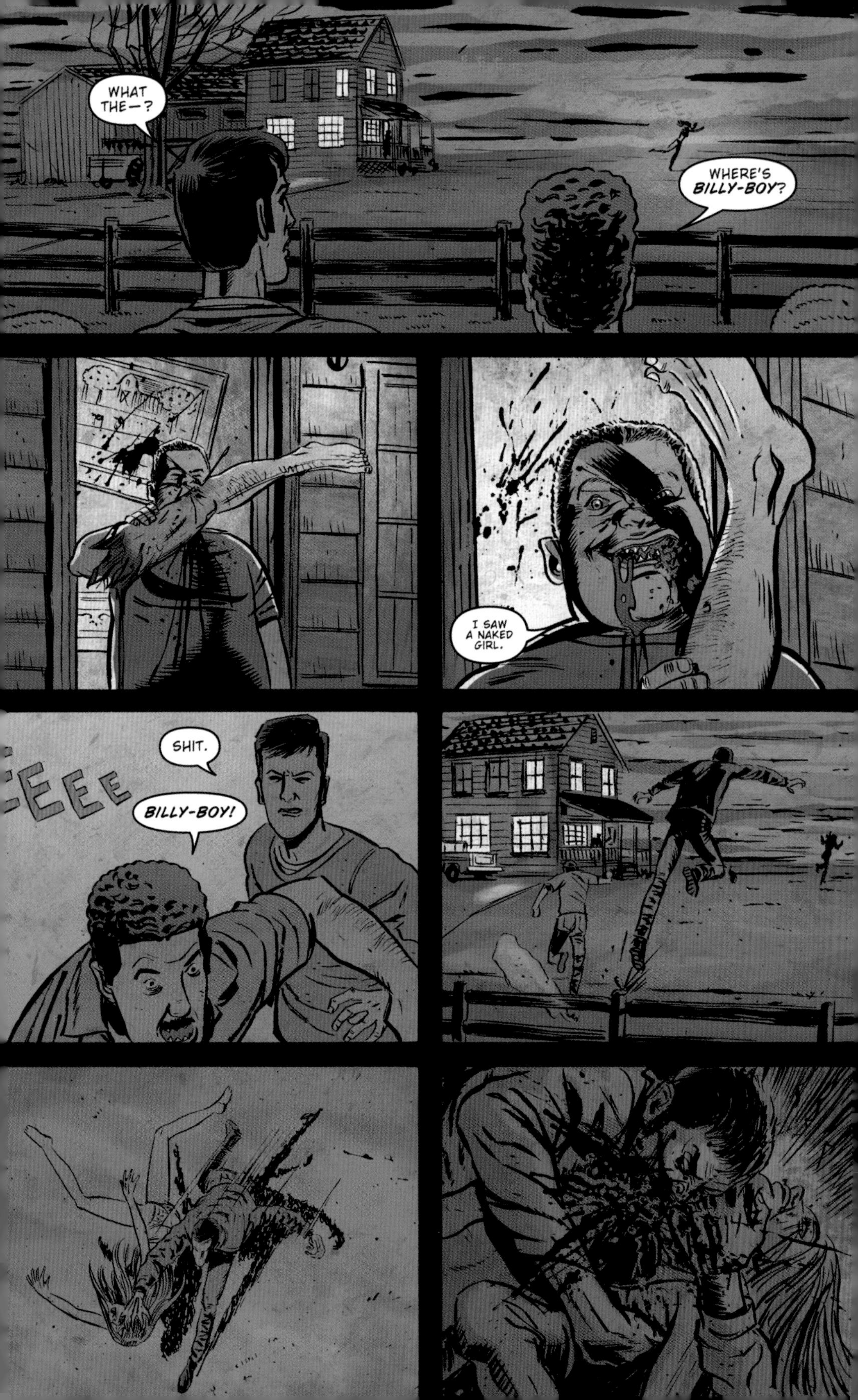
WHAT THE—?
WHERE'S BILLY-BOY?
I SAW A NAKED GIRL.
SHIT.
EEEE
BILLY-BOY!

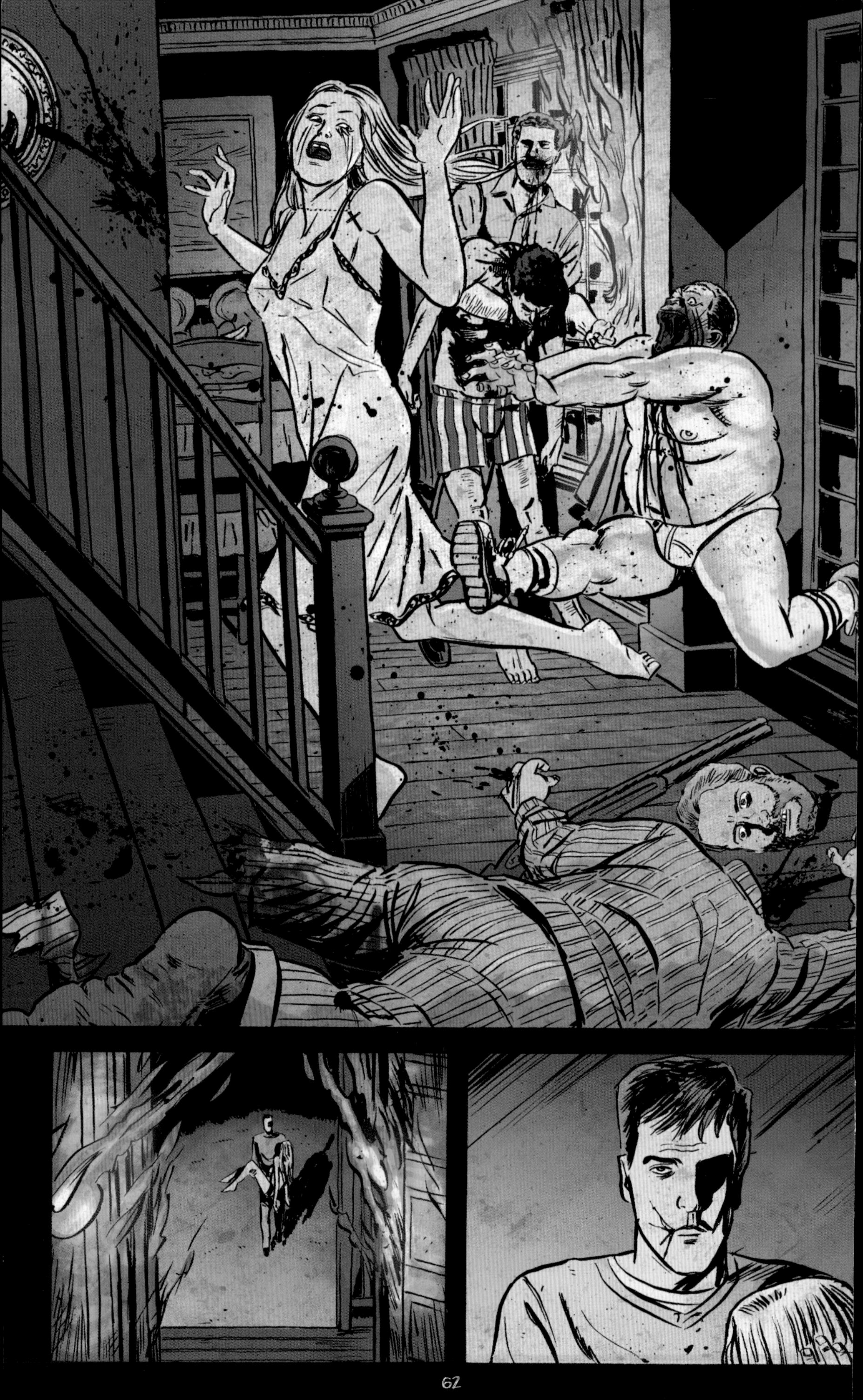

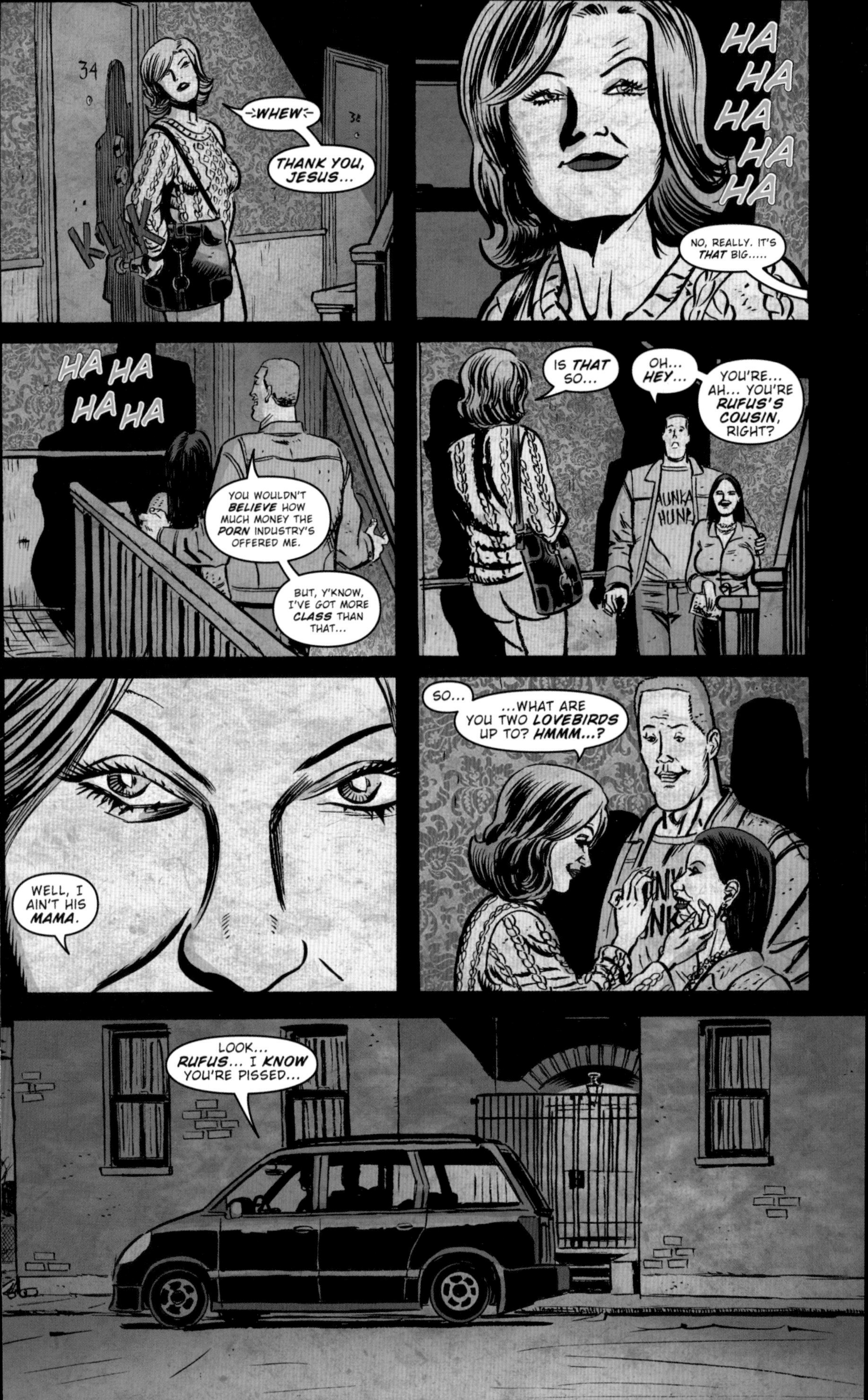
KLIK
-WHEW-
THANK YOU, JESUS...
HA HA HA HA HA
NO, REALLY. IT'S THAT BIG.....
HA HA HA HA
YOU WOULDN'T BELIEVE HOW MUCH MONEY THE PORN INDUSTRY'S OFFERED ME.
BUT, Y'KNOW, I'VE GOT MORE CLASS THAN THAT...
IS THAT SO...
OH... HEY...
YOU'RE... AH... YOU'RE RUFUS'S COUSIN, RIGHT?
WELL, I AIN'T HIS MAMA.
SO...
...WHAT ARE YOU TWO LOVEBIRDS UP TO? HMMM...?
LOOK... RUFUS... I KNOW YOU'RE PISSED...

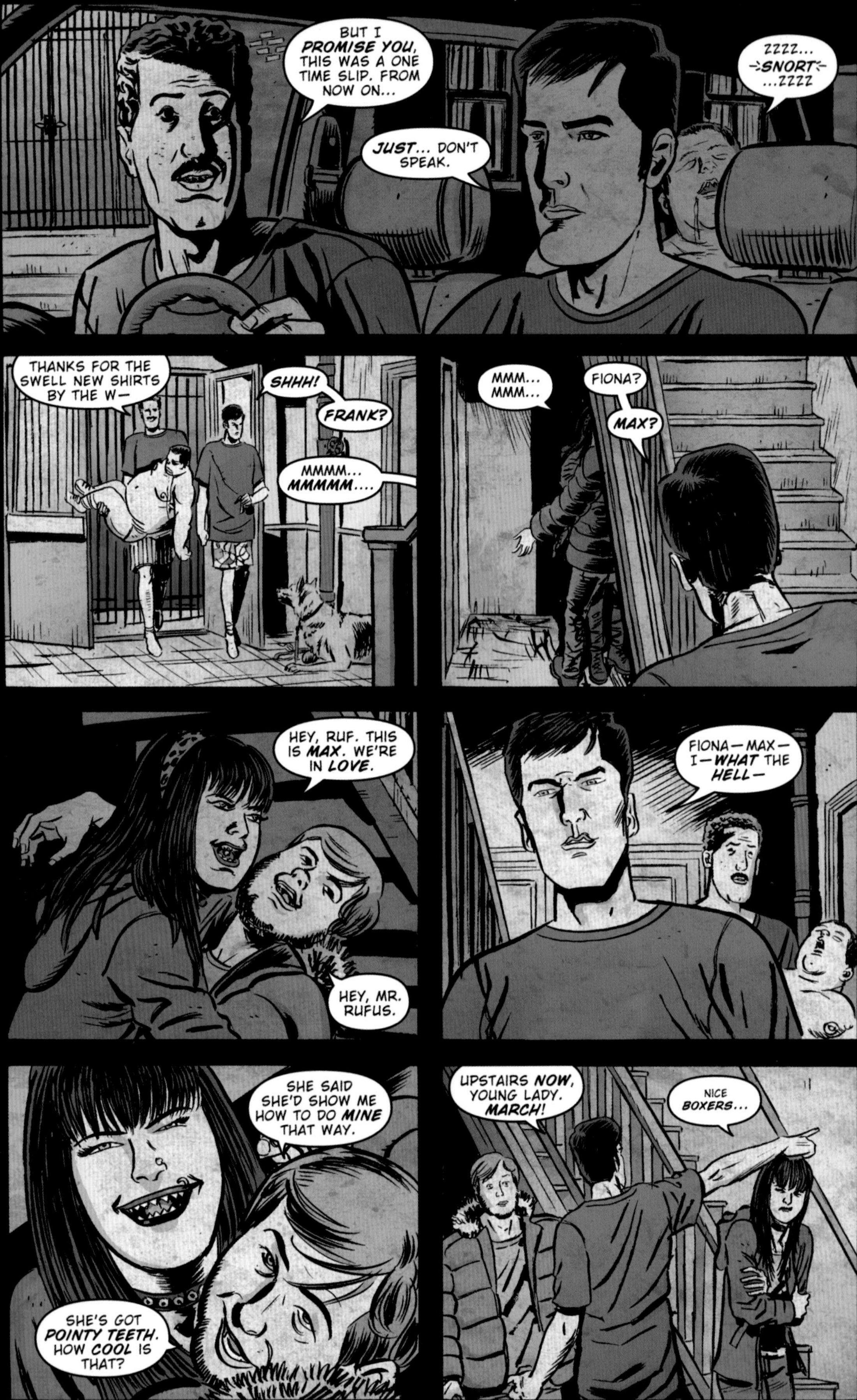
BUT I PROMISE YOU, THIS WAS A ONE TIME SLIP. FROM NOW ON...
ZZZZ... SNORT ...ZZZZ
JUST... DON'T SPEAK.
THANKS FOR THE SWELL NEW SHIRTS BY THE W—
SHHH!
FRANK?
MMMM... MMMMM....
MMM... MMM...
FIONA?
MAX?
HEY, RUF. THIS IS MAX. WE'RE IN LOVE.
HEY, MR. RUFUS.
FIONA—MAX—I—WHAT THE HELL—
SHE SAID SHE'D SHOW ME HOW TO DO MINE THAT WAY.
SHE'S GOT POINTY TEETH. HOW COOL IS THAT?
UPSTAIRS NOW, YOUNG LADY. MARCH!
NICE BOXERS...

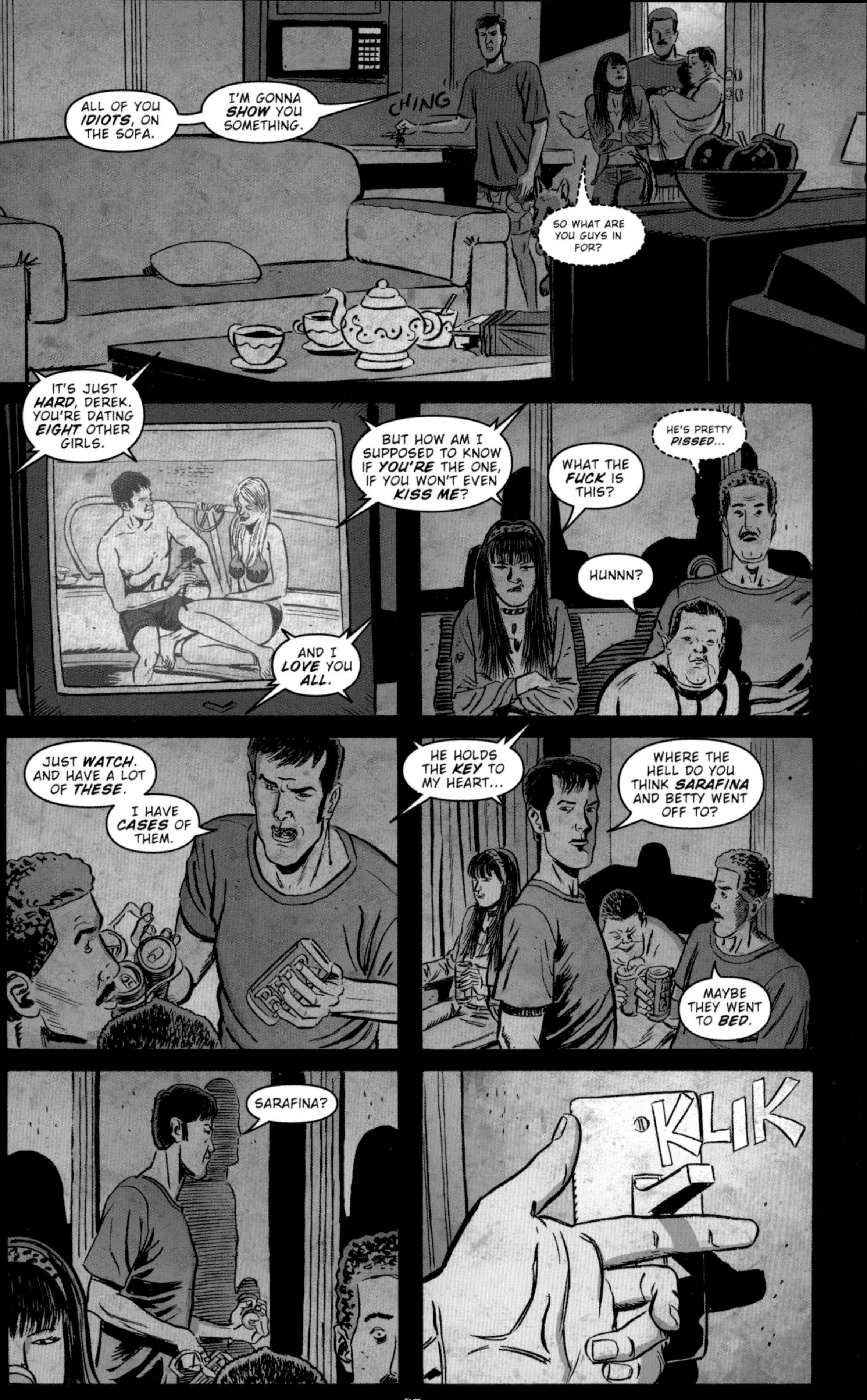

ALL OF YOU IDIOTS, ON THE SOFA.
I'M GONNA SHOW YOU SOMETHING.
CHING
SO WHAT ARE YOU GUYS IN FOR?
IT'S JUST HARD, DEREK. YOU'RE DATING EIGHT OTHER GIRLS.
BUT HOW AM I SUPPOSED TO KNOW IF YOU'RE THE ONE, IF YOU WON'T EVEN KISS ME?
AND I LOVE YOU ALL.
WHAT THE FUCK IS THIS?
HE'S PRETTY PISSED...
HUNNN?
JUST WATCH. AND HAVE A LOT OF THESE.
I HAVE CASES OF THEM.
HE HOLDS THE KEY TO MY HEART...
WHERE THE HELL DO YOU THINK SARAFINA AND BETTY WENT OFF TO?
MAYBE THEY WENT TO BED.
SARAFINA?
KLIK

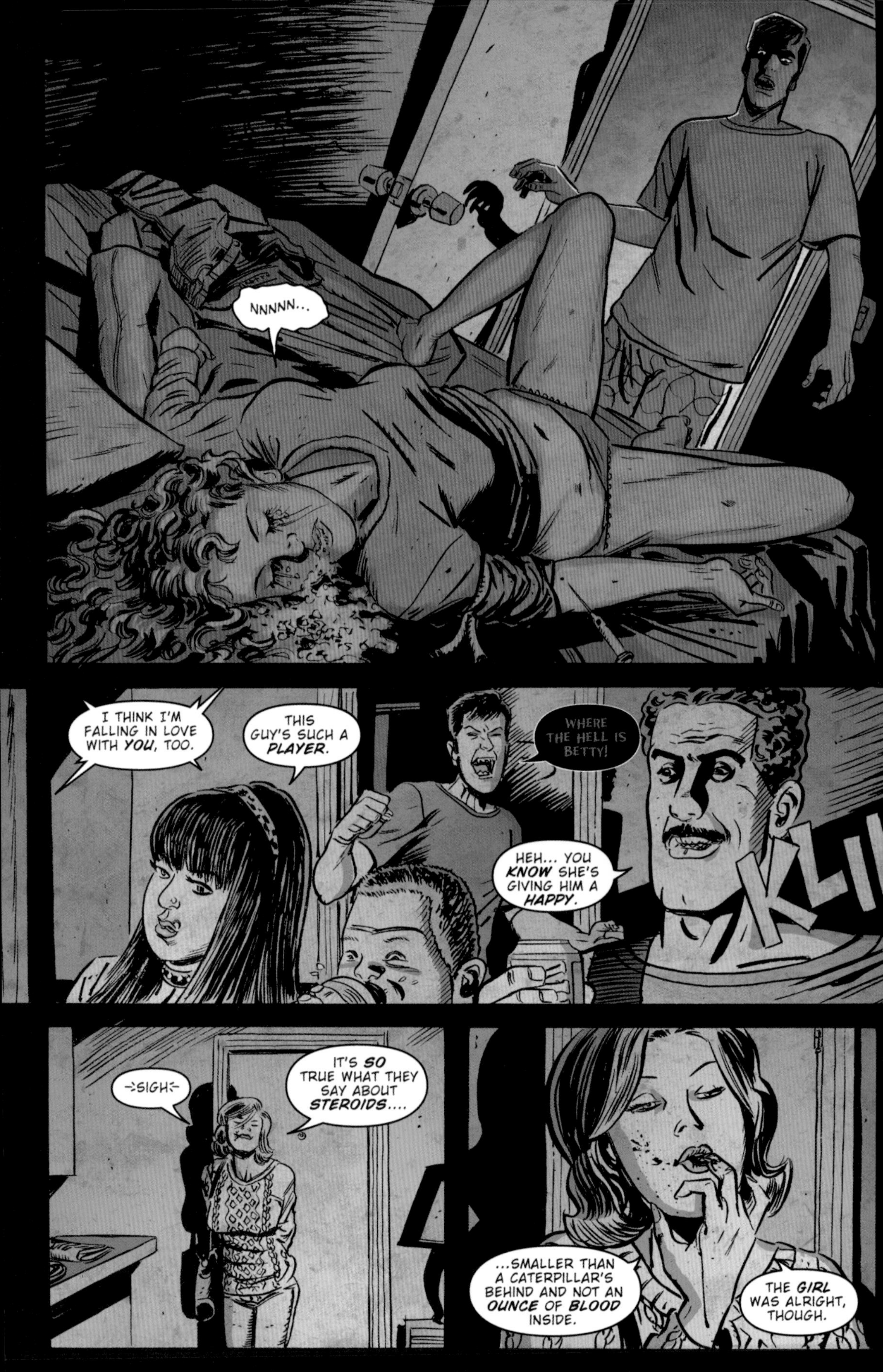
NNNNN...
I THINK I'M FALLING IN LOVE WITH YOU, TOO.
THIS GUY'S SUCH A PLAYER.
WHERE THE HELL IS BETTY!
HEH... YOU KNOW SHE'S GIVING HIM A HAPPY.
KLI
-SIGH-
IT'S SO TRUE WHAT THEY SAY ABOUT STEROIDS....
...SMALLER THAN A CATERPILLAR'S BEHIND AND NOT AN OUNCE OF BLOOD INSIDE.
THE GIRL WAS ALRIGHT, THOUGH.

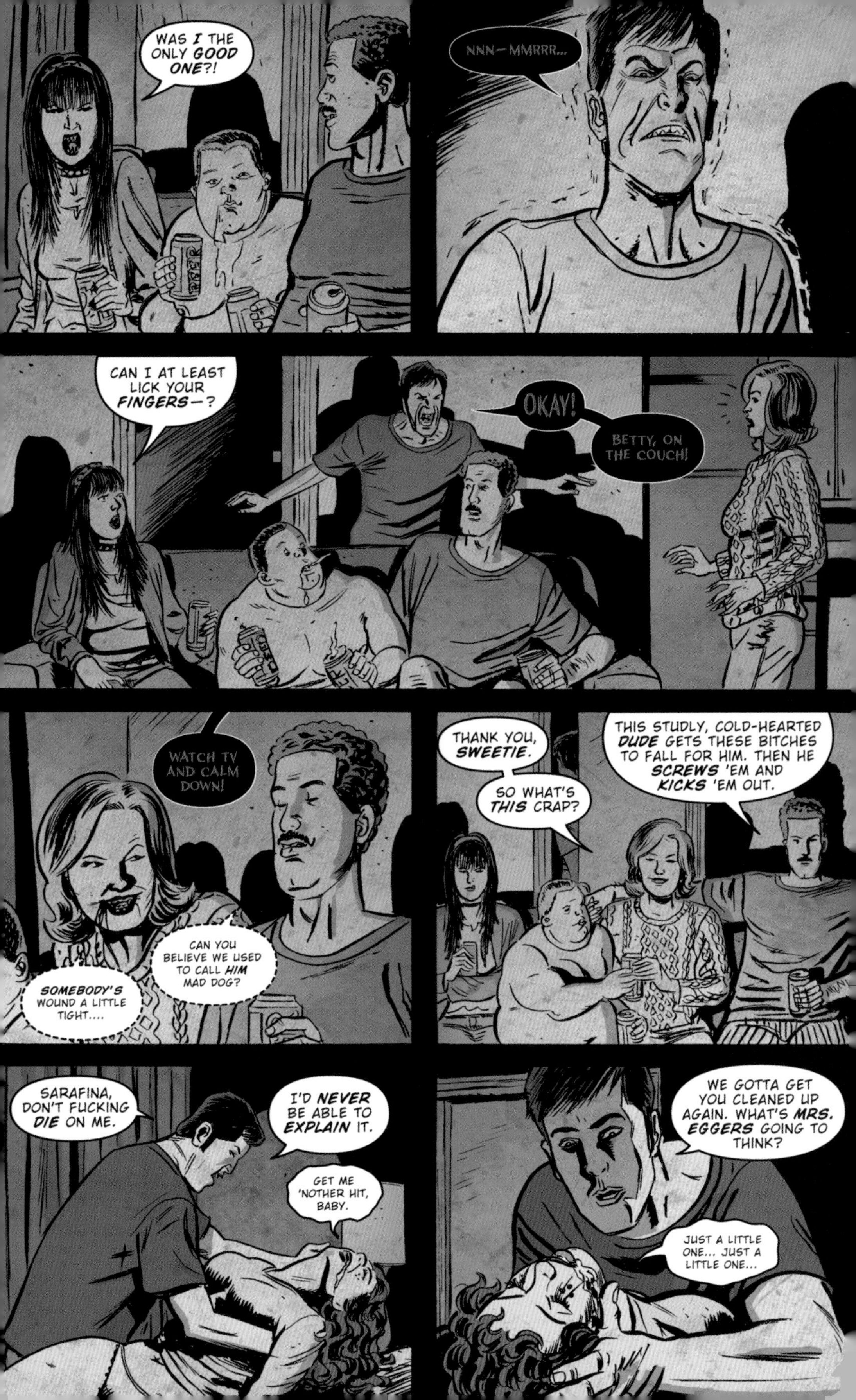
WAS *I* THE ONLY **GOOD ONE**?!
NNN—MMRRR...
CAN I AT LEAST LICK YOUR **FINGERS**—?
OKAY!
BETTY, ON THE COUCH!
WATCH TV AND CALM DOWN!
CAN YOU BELIEVE WE USED TO CALL **HIM** MAD DOG?
SOMEBODY'S WOUND A LITTLE TIGHT....
THANK YOU, **SWEETIE**.
SO WHAT'S **THIS** CRAP?
THIS STUDLY, COLD-HEARTED **DUDE** GETS THESE BITCHES TO FALL FOR HIM. THEN HE **SCREWS** 'EM AND **KICKS** 'EM OUT.
SARAFINA, DON'T FUCKING **DIE** ON ME.
I'D **NEVER** BE ABLE TO **EXPLAIN** IT.
GET ME 'NOTHER HIT, BABY.
WE GOTTA GET YOU CLEANED UP AGAIN. WHAT'S **MRS. EGGERS** GOING TO THINK?
JUST A LITTLE ONE... JUST A LITTLE ONE...

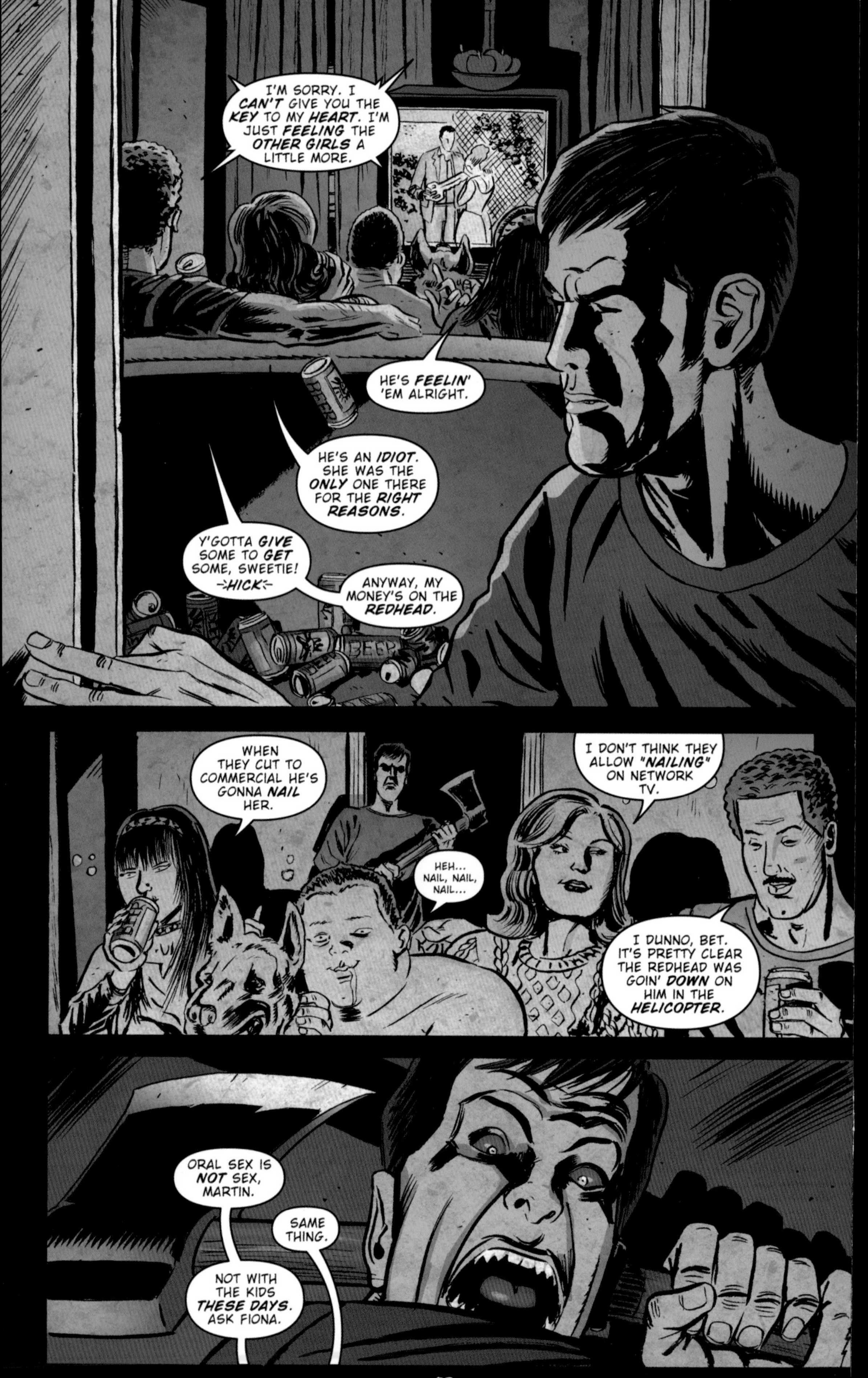
I'M SORRY. I CAN'T GIVE YOU THE KEY TO MY HEART. I'M JUST FEELING THE OTHER GIRLS A LITTLE MORE.
HE'S FEELIN' 'EM ALRIGHT.
HE'S AN IDIOT. SHE WAS THE ONLY ONE THERE FOR THE RIGHT REASONS.
Y'GOTTA GIVE SOME TO GET SOME, SWEETIE!
-HICK-
ANYWAY, MY MONEY'S ON THE REDHEAD.
WHEN THEY CUT TO COMMERCIAL HE'S GONNA NAIL HER.
I DON'T THINK THEY ALLOW "NAILING" ON NETWORK TV.
HEH... NAIL, NAIL, NAIL...
I DUNNO, BET. IT'S PRETTY CLEAR THE REDHEAD WAS GOIN' DOWN ON HIM IN THE HELICOPTER.
ORAL SEX IS NOT SEX, MARTIN.
SAME THING.
NOT WITH THE KIDS THESE DAYS. ASK FIONA.

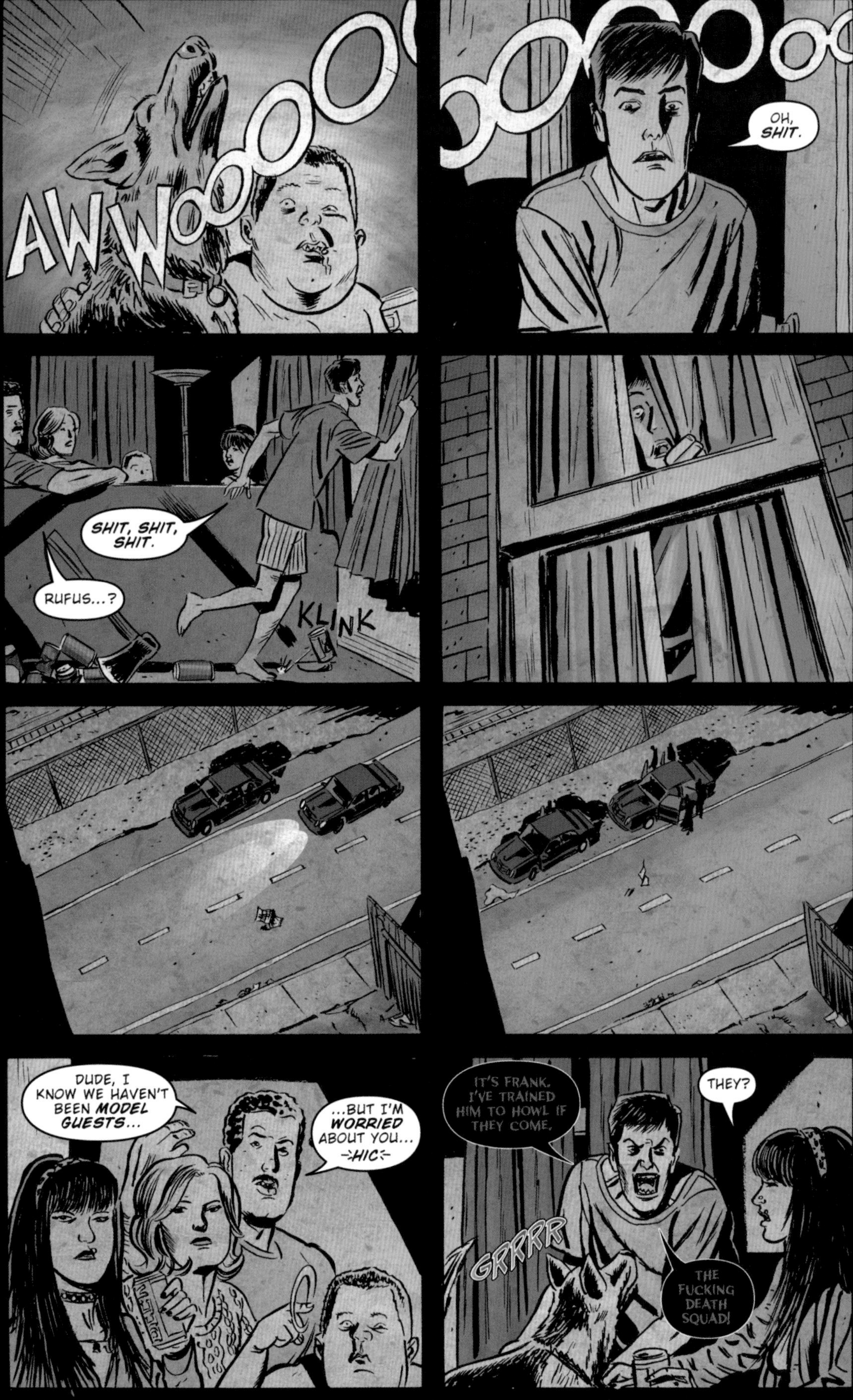
AWWOOOOOOOOOOOO
OH, SHIT.
SHIT, SHIT, SHIT.
RUFUS...?
KLINK
DUDE, I KNOW WE HAVEN'T BEEN MODEL GUESTS...
...BUT I'M WORRIED ABOUT YOU... -HIC-
IT'S FRANK. I'VE TRAINED HIM TO HOWL IF THEY COME.
THEY?
GRRRR
THE FUCKING DEATH SQUAD!

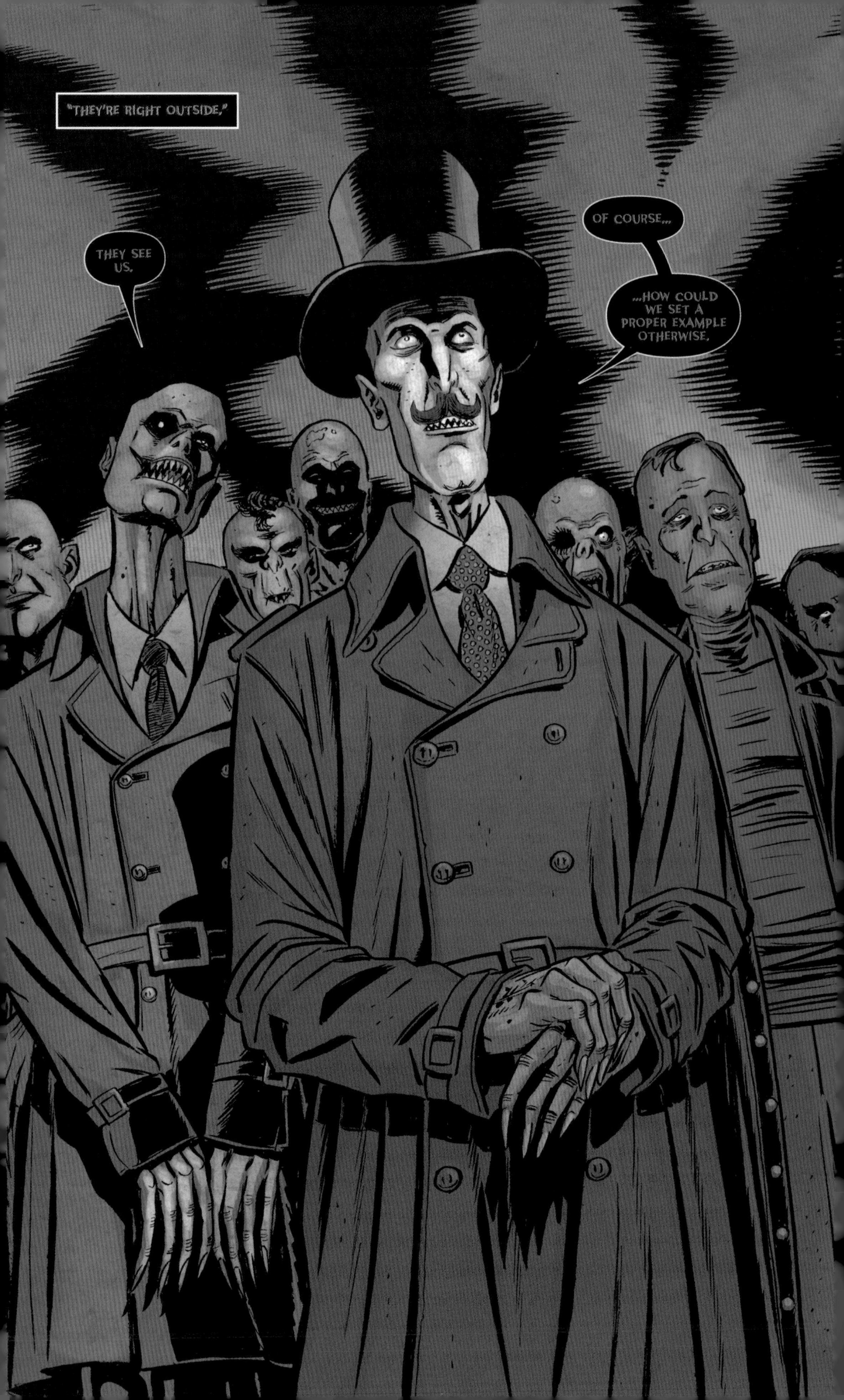
"THEY'RE RIGHT OUTSIDE,"
THEY SEE US.
OF COURSE...
...HOW COULD WE SET A PROPER EXAMPLE OTHERWISE.

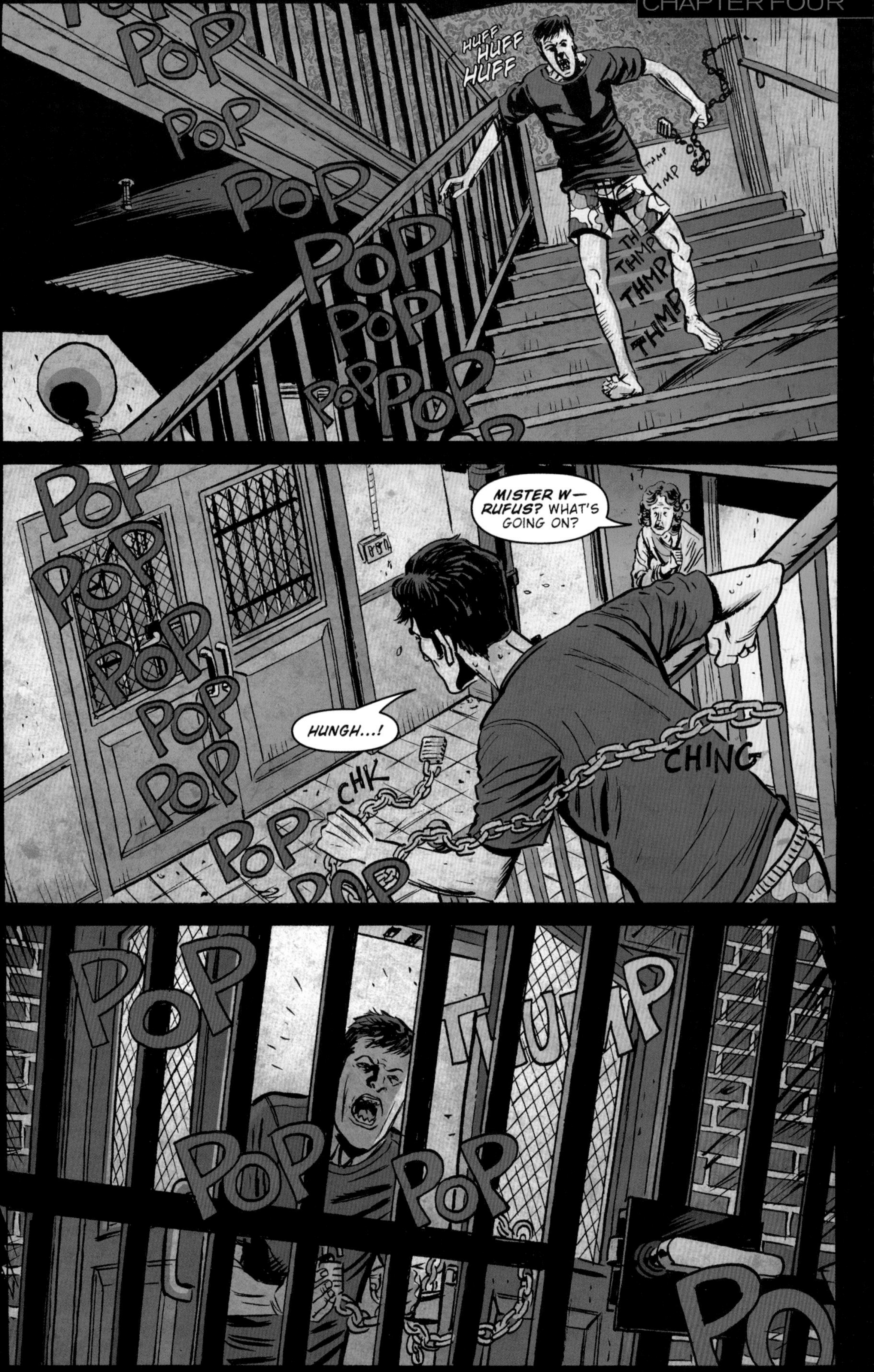
POP
POP
POP
POP
POP
POPPOP
HUFF HUFF HUFF
THMP THMP
THMP THMP THMP THMP
POP POP POP POP POP POP
MISTER W— RUFUS? WHAT'S GOING ON?
HUNGH...!
CHK
CHING
POP
POP POP POP
TWUMP
POP POP
PO

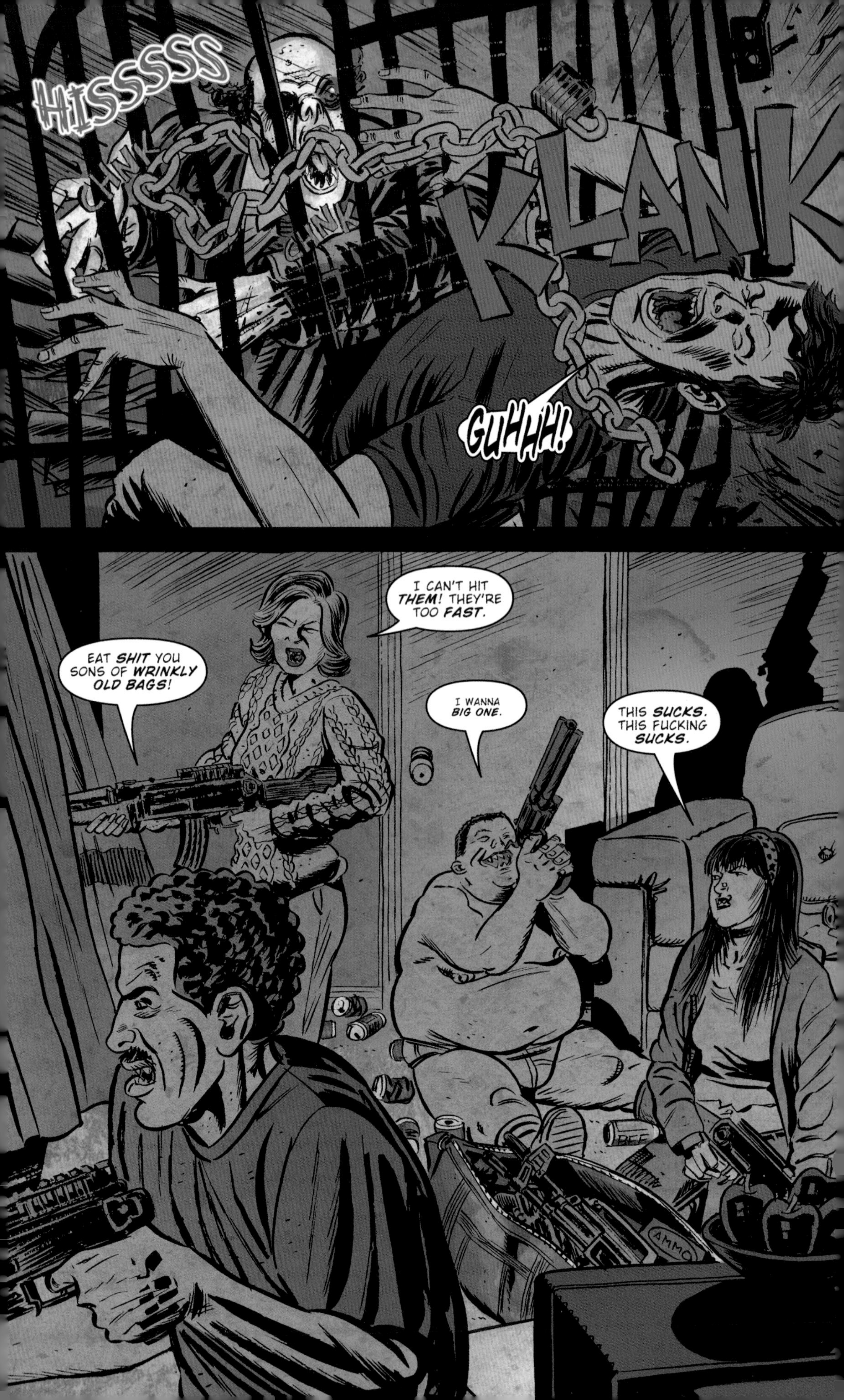
HISSSSS
KLANK
GUHHH!
EAT SHIT YOU SONS OF WRINKLY OLD BAGS!
I CAN'T HIT THEM! THEY'RE TOO FAST.
I WANNA BIG ONE.
THIS SUCKS. THIS FUCKING SUCKS.
AMMO

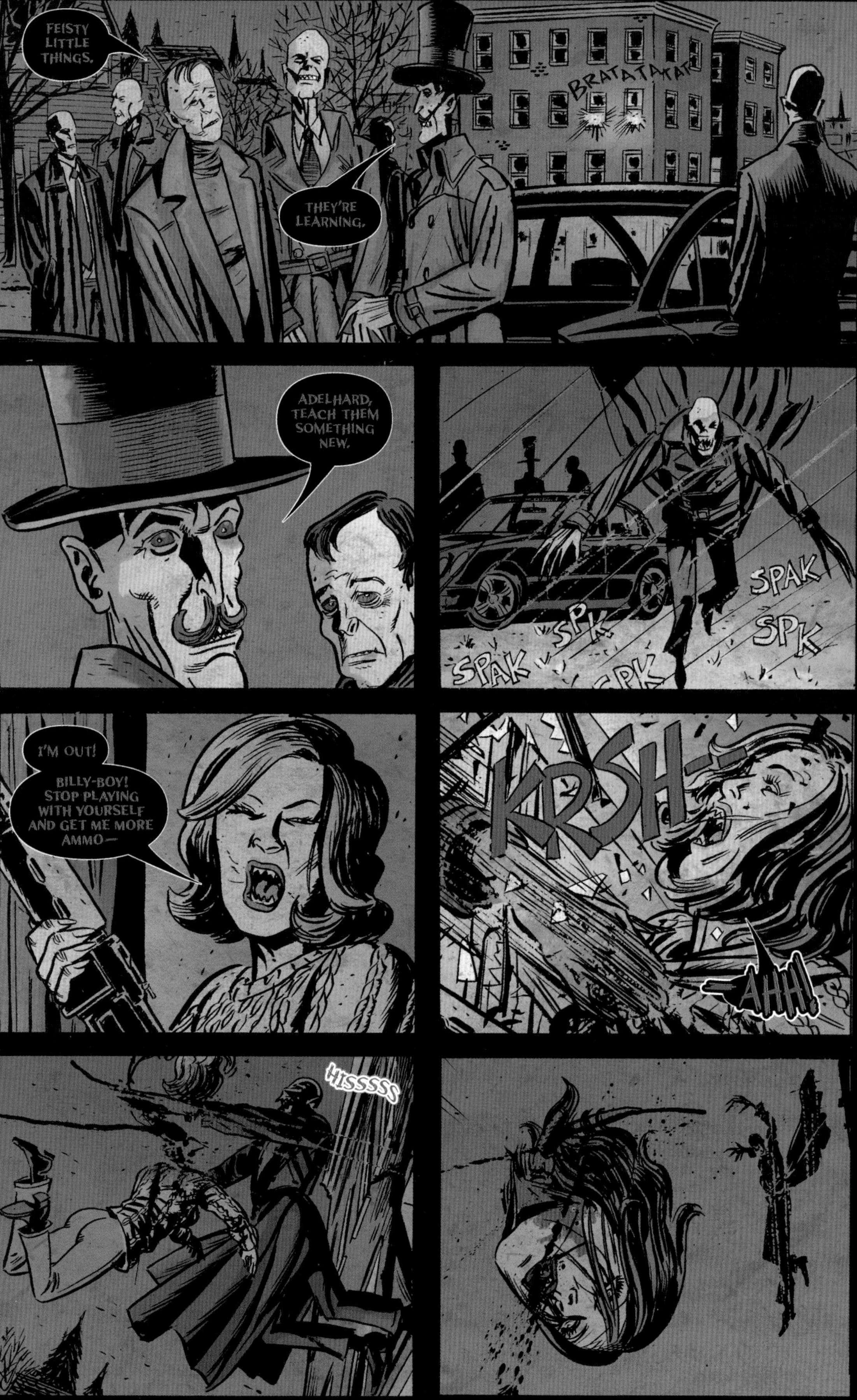
FEISTY LITTLE THINGS.
THEY'RE LEARNING.
BRATATATAT
ADELHARD, TEACH THEM SOMETHING NEW.
SPAK
SPK
SPAK
SPK
SPAK
I'M OUT!
BILLY-BOY! STOP PLAYING WITH YOURSELF AND GET ME MORE AMMO—
KRSH—
—AHH!
HISSSSS

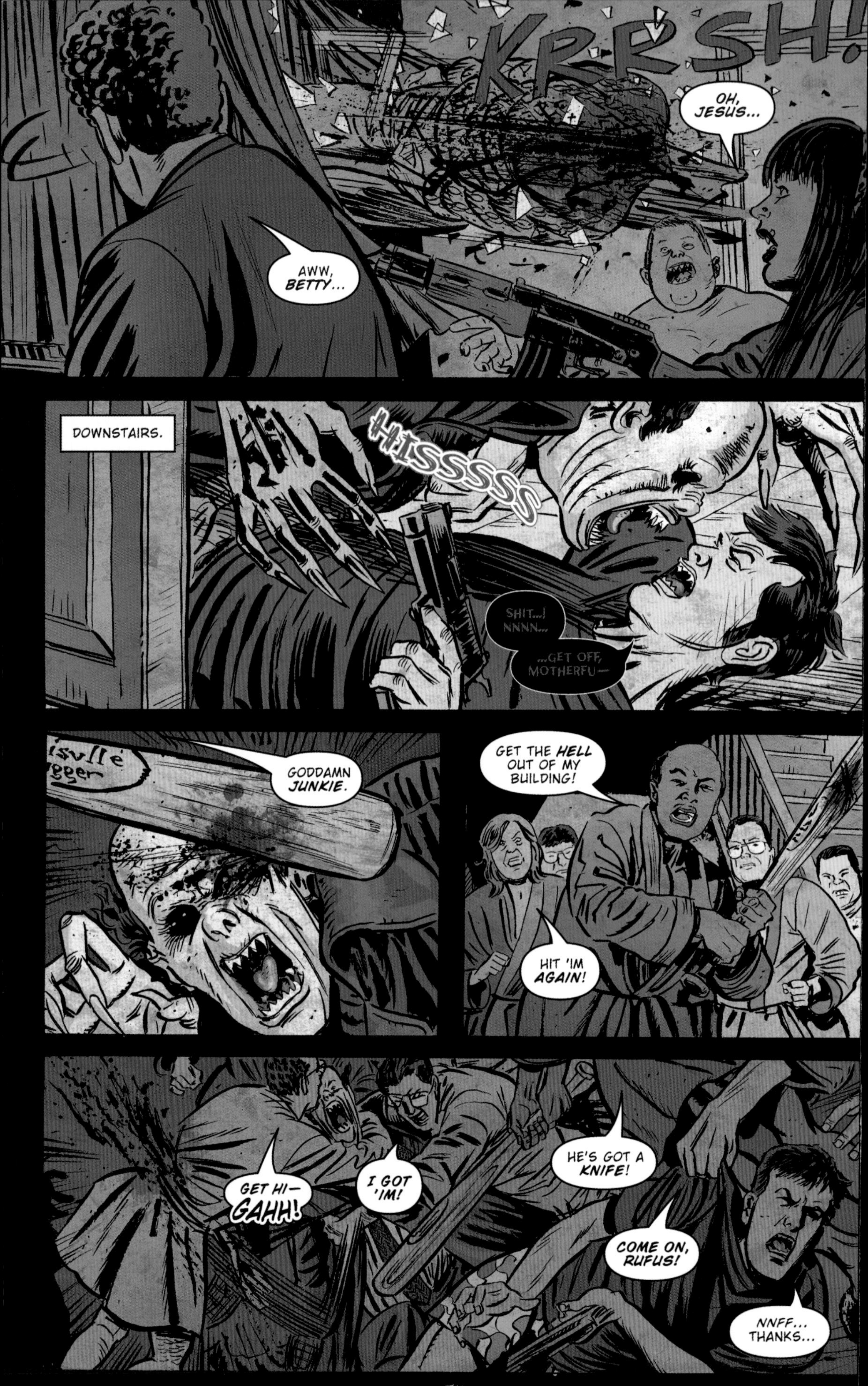
KRRSH!
OH, JESUS...
AWW, BETTY...
DOWNSTAIRS.
HISSSSSS
SHIT...! NNNN...
...GET OFF, MOTHERFU—
GODDAMN JUNKIE.
GET THE HELL OUT OF MY BUILDING!
HIT 'IM AGAIN!
GET HI— GAHH!
I GOT 'IM!
HE'S GOT A KNIFE!
COME ON, RUFUS!
NNFF... THANKS...

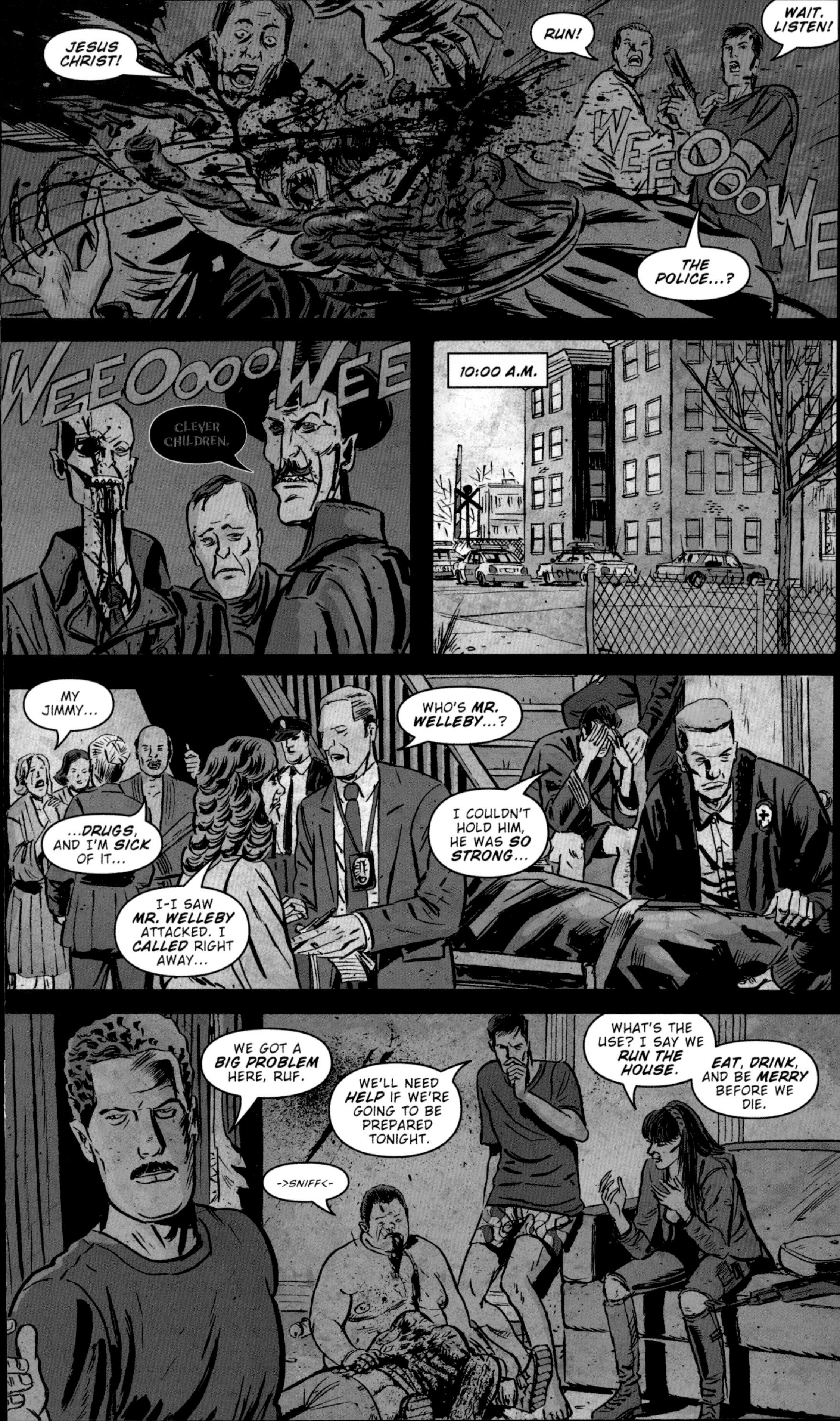
JESUS CHRIST!
RUN!
WAIT. LISTEN!
WEEOOOOWE
THE POLICE...?
WEEOoooWEE
CLEVER CHILDREN.
10:00 A.M.
MY JIMMY...
...DRUGS, AND I'M SICK OF IT...
I-I SAW MR. WELLEBY ATTACKED. I CALLED RIGHT AWAY...
WHO'S MR. WELLEBY...?
I COULDN'T HOLD HIM, HE WAS SO STRONG...
WE GOT A BIG PROBLEM HERE, RUF.
WE'LL NEED HELP IF WE'RE GOING TO BE PREPARED TONIGHT.
->SNIFF<-
WHAT'S THE USE? I SAY WE RUN THE HOUSE.
EAT, DRINK, AND BE MERRY BEFORE WE DIE.

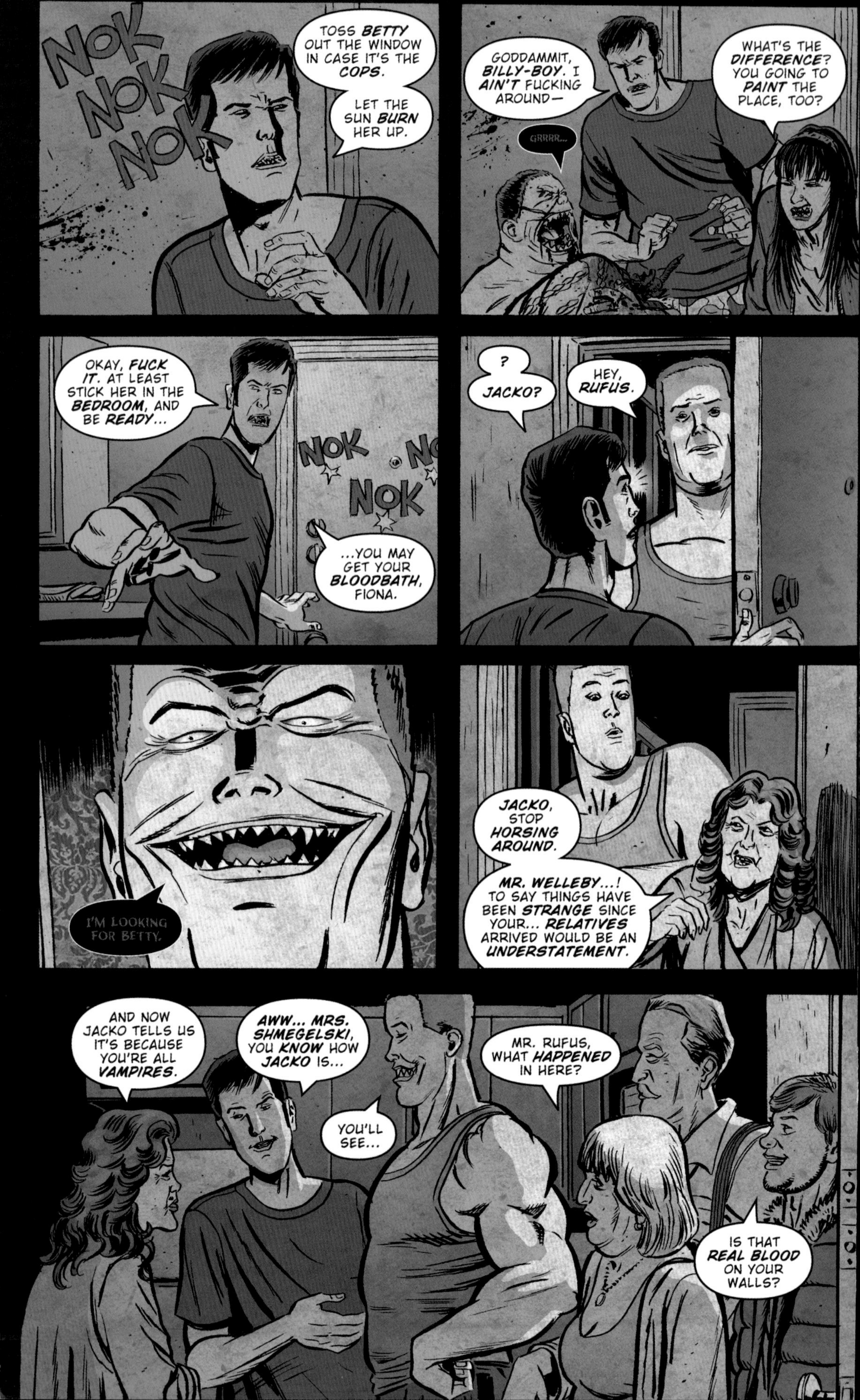

NOK NOK NOK
TOSS BETTY OUT THE WINDOW IN CASE IT'S THE COPS.
LET THE SUN BURN HER UP.
GODDAMMIT, BILLY-BOY. I AIN'T FUCKING AROUND—
WHAT'S THE DIFFERENCE? YOU GOING TO PAINT THE PLACE, TOO?
GRRRR...
OKAY, FUCK IT. AT LEAST STICK HER IN THE BEDROOM, AND BE READY...
NOK NOK
...YOU MAY GET YOUR BLOODBATH, FIONA.
? JACKO?
HEY, RUFUS.
I'M LOOKING FOR BETTY.
JACKO, STOP HORSING AROUND.
MR. WELLEBY...! TO SAY THINGS HAVE BEEN STRANGE SINCE YOUR... RELATIVES ARRIVED WOULD BE AN UNDERSTATEMENT.
AND NOW JACKO TELLS US IT'S BECAUSE YOU'RE ALL VAMPIRES.
AWW... MRS. SHMEGELSKI, YOU KNOW HOW JACKO IS...
YOU'LL SEE...
MR. RUFUS, WHAT HAPPENED IN HERE?
IS THAT REAL BLOOD ON YOUR WALLS?

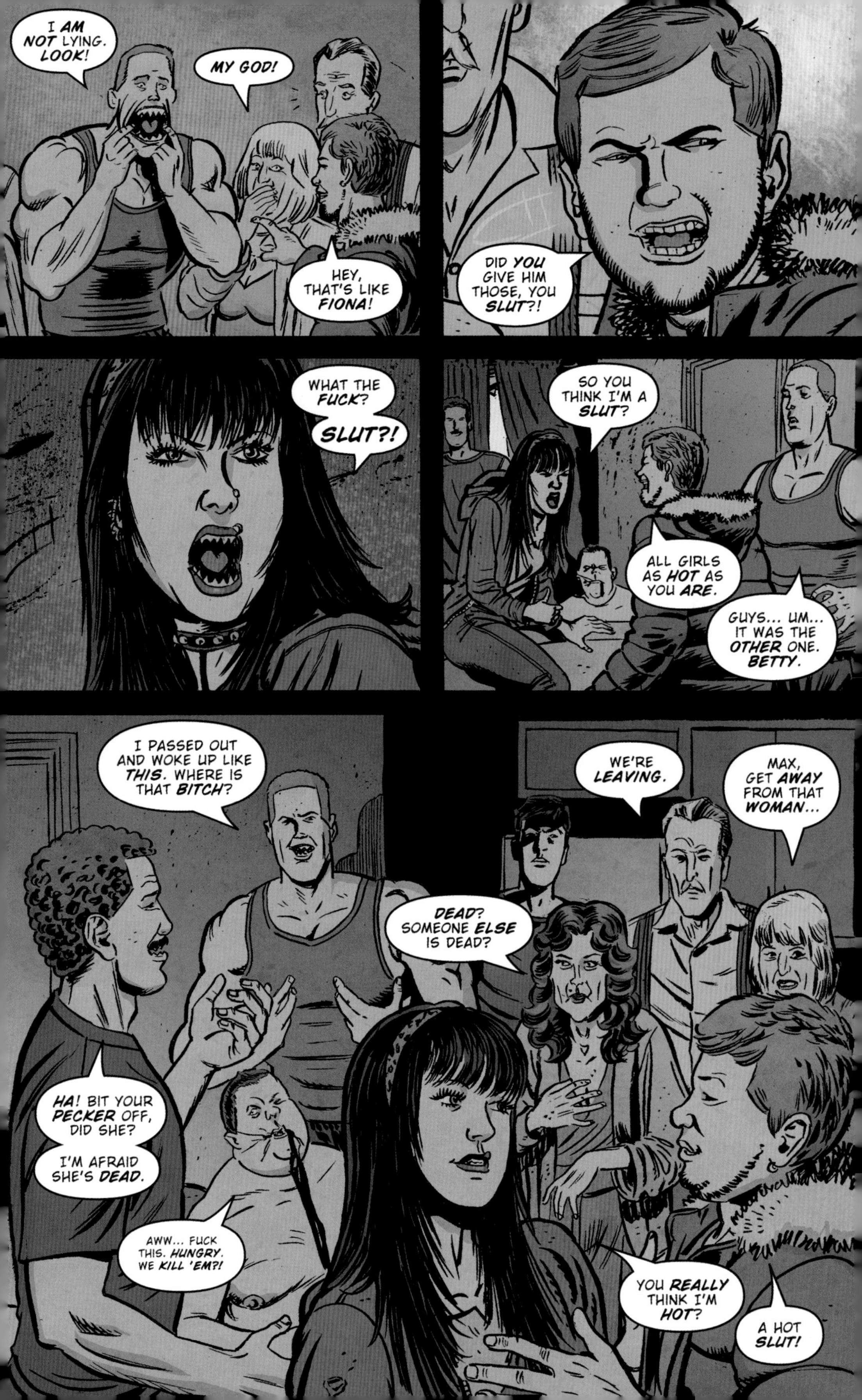
I AM NOT LYING. LOOK!
MY GOD!
HEY, THAT'S LIKE FIONA!
DID YOU GIVE HIM THOSE, YOU SLUT?!
WHAT THE FUCK?
SLUT?!
SO YOU THINK I'M A SLUT?
ALL GIRLS AS HOT AS YOU ARE.
GUYS... UM... IT WAS THE OTHER ONE. BETTY.
I PASSED OUT AND WOKE UP LIKE THIS. WHERE IS THAT BITCH?
HA! BIT YOUR PECKER OFF, DID SHE?
I'M AFRAID SHE'S DEAD.
AWW... FUCK THIS. HUNGRY. WE KILL 'EM?!
DEAD? SOMEONE ELSE IS DEAD?
WE'RE LEAVING.
MAX, GET AWAY FROM THAT WOMAN...
YOU REALLY THINK I'M HOT?
A HOT SLUT!

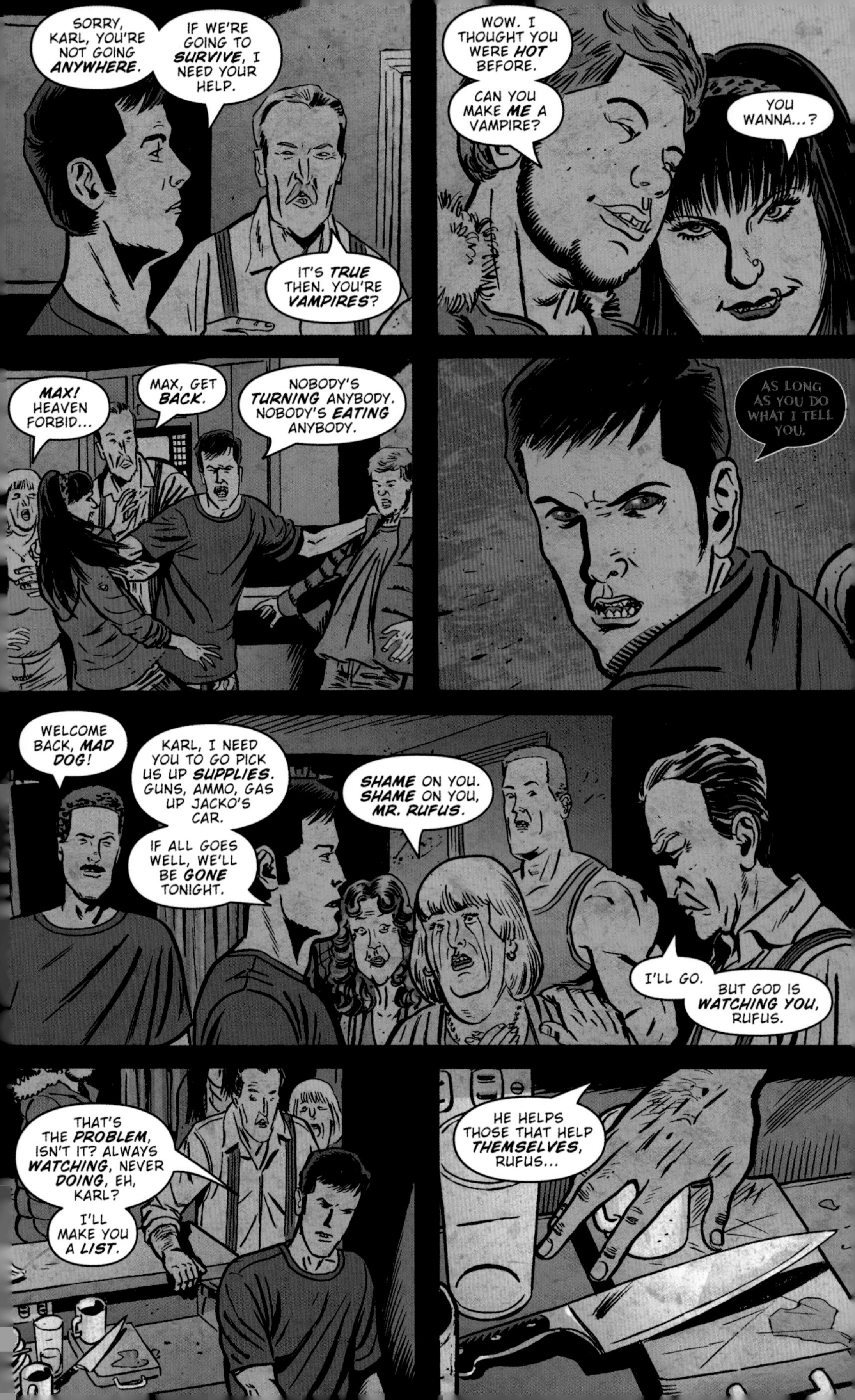
SORRY, KARL, YOU'RE NOT GOING ANYWHERE.
IF WE'RE GOING TO SURVIVE, I NEED YOUR HELP.
IT'S TRUE THEN. YOU'RE VAMPIRES?
WOW. I THOUGHT YOU WERE HOT BEFORE.
CAN YOU MAKE ME A VAMPIRE?
YOU WANNA...?
MAX! HEAVEN FORBID...
MAX, GET BACK.
NOBODY'S TURNING ANYBODY. NOBODY'S EATING ANYBODY.
AS LONG AS YOU DO WHAT I TELL YOU.
WELCOME BACK, MAD DOG!
KARL, I NEED YOU TO GO PICK US UP SUPPLIES. GUNS, AMMO, GAS UP JACKO'S CAR.
IF ALL GOES WELL, WE'LL BE GONE TONIGHT.
SHAME ON YOU. SHAME ON YOU, MR. RUFUS.
I'LL GO.
BUT GOD IS WATCHING YOU, RUFUS.
THAT'S THE PROBLEM, ISN'T IT? ALWAYS WATCHING, NEVER DOING, EH, KARL?
I'LL MAKE YOU A LIST.
HE HELPS THOSE THAT HELP THEMSELVES, RUFUS...

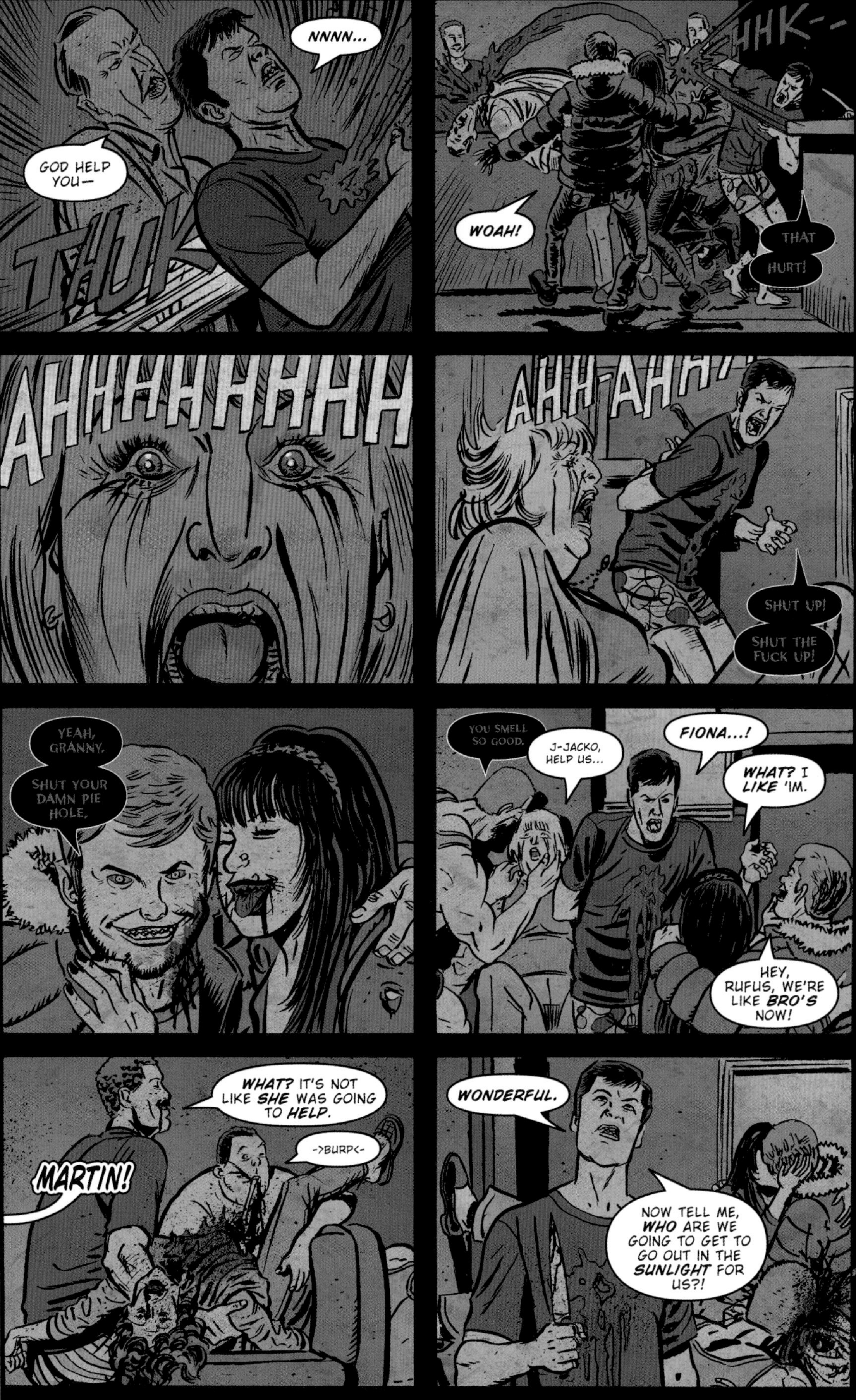

NNNN...
GOD HELP YOU—
THUK
HHK--
WOAH!
THAT HURT!
AHHHHHHHHH
AHH-AHH
SHUT UP!
SHUT THE FUCK UP!
YEAH, GRANNY.
SHUT YOUR DAMN PIE HOLE.
YOU SMELL SO GOOD.
J-JACKO, HELP US...
FIONA...!
WHAT? I LIKE 'IM.
HEY, RUFUS, WE'RE LIKE BRO'S NOW!
WHAT? IT'S NOT LIKE SHE WAS GOING TO HELP.
MARTIN!
->BURP<-
WONDERFUL.
NOW TELL ME, WHO ARE WE GOING TO GET TO GO OUT IN THE SUNLIGHT FOR US?!

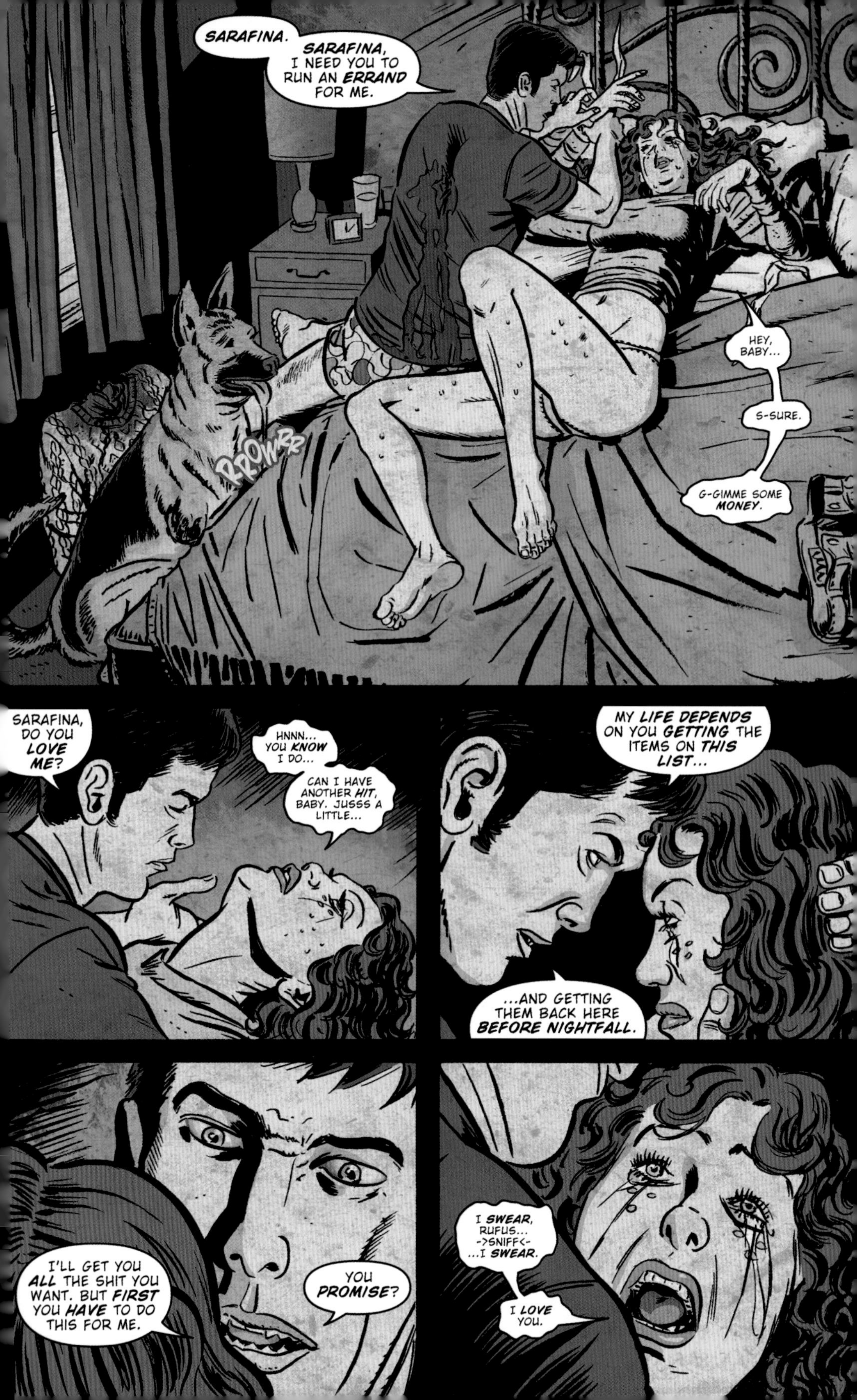
SARAFINA.
SARAFINA, I NEED YOU TO RUN AN ERRAND FOR ME.
RROWRR
HEY, BABY...
S-SURE.
G-GIMME SOME MONEY.
SARAFINA, DO YOU LOVE ME?
HNNN... YOU KNOW I DO...
CAN I HAVE ANOTHER HIT, BABY. JUSSS A LITTLE...
MY LIFE DEPENDS ON YOU GETTING THE ITEMS ON THIS LIST...
...AND GETTING THEM BACK HERE BEFORE NIGHTFALL.
I'LL GET YOU ALL THE SHIT YOU WANT. BUT FIRST YOU HAVE TO DO THIS FOR ME.
YOU PROMISE?
I SWEAR, RUFUS... ->SNIFF<- ...I SWEAR.
I LOVE YOU.

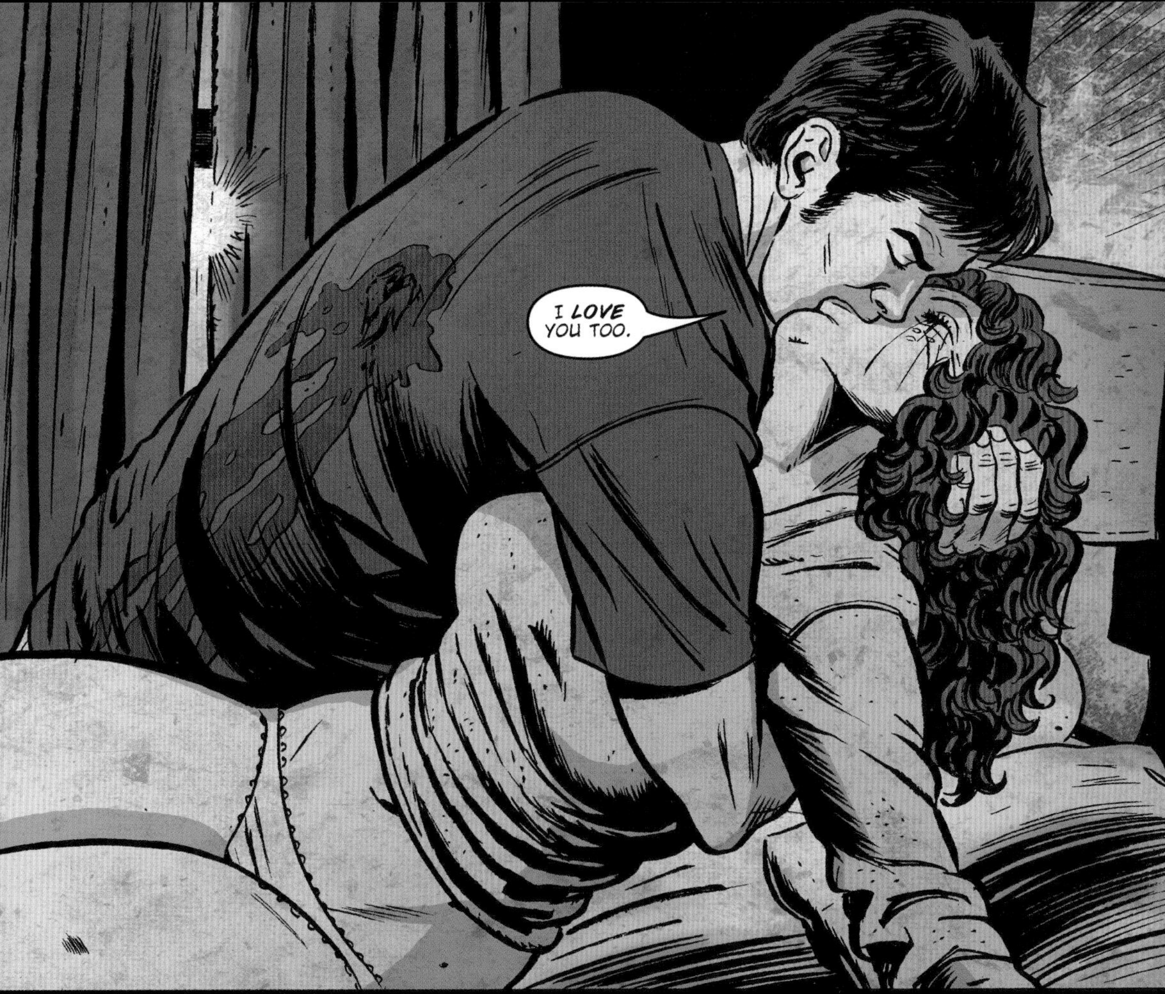
I LOVE YOU TOO.

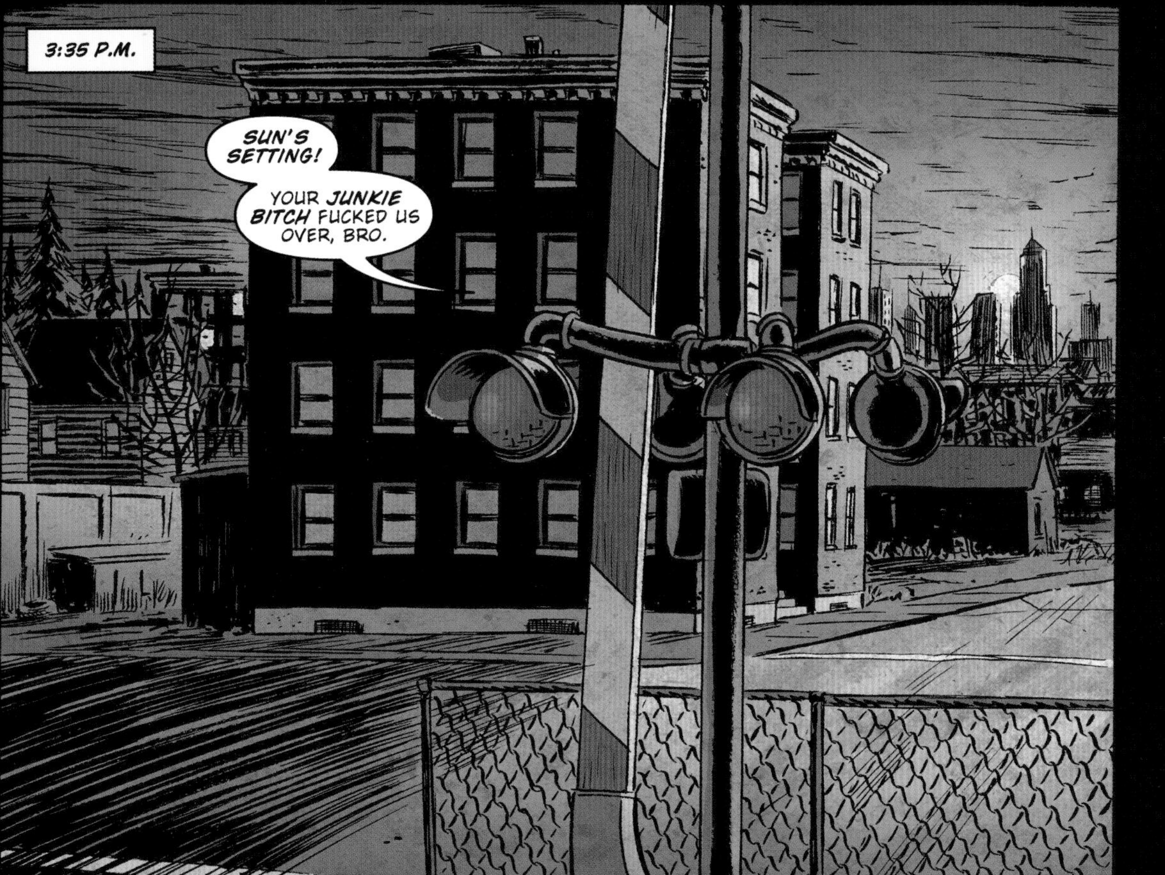
3:35 P.M.
SUN'S SETTING!
YOUR JUNKIE BITCH FUCKED US OVER, BRO.

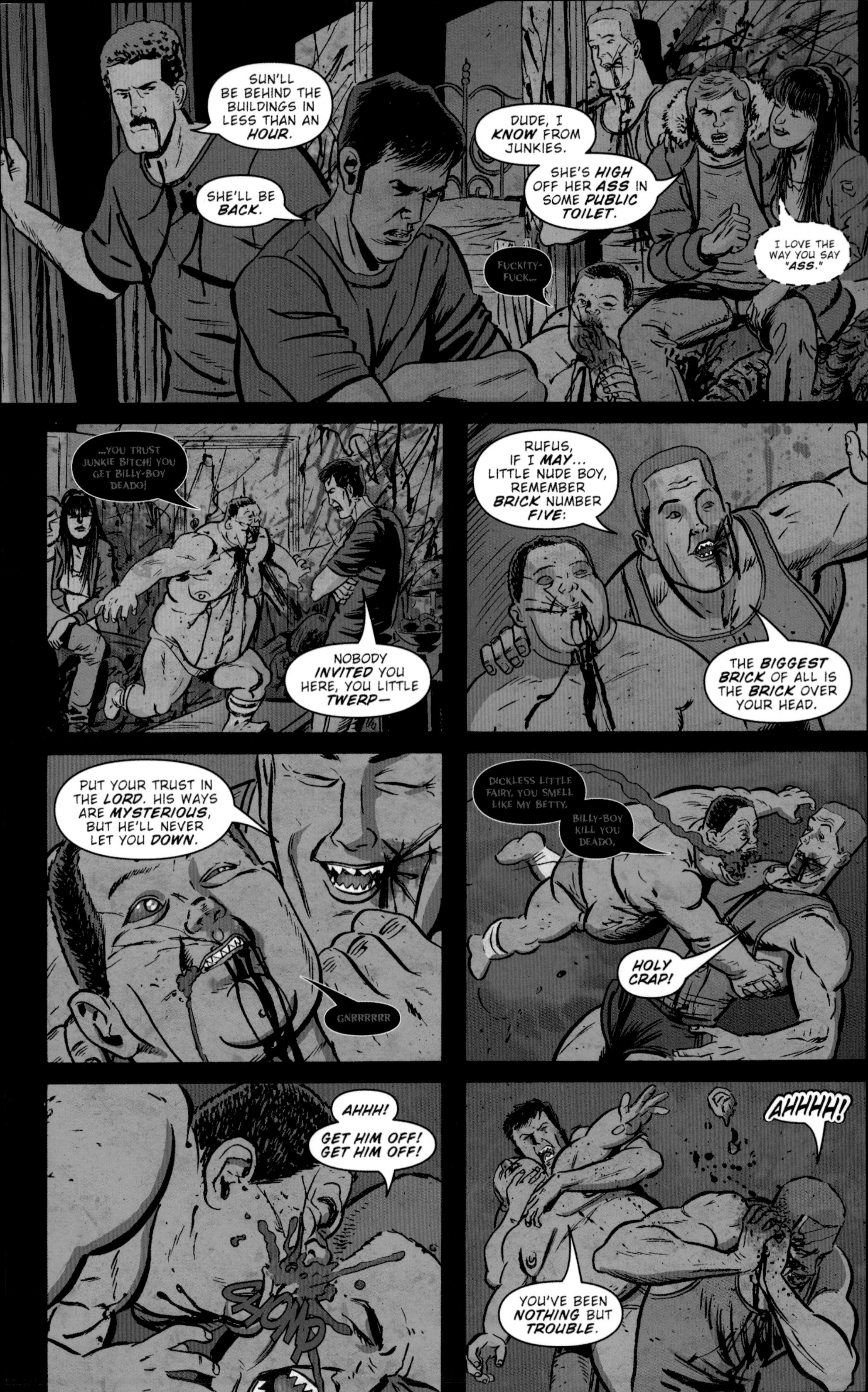
SUN'LL BE BEHIND THE BUILDINGS IN LESS THAN AN HOUR.
SHE'LL BE BACK.
DUDE, I KNOW FROM JUNKIES.
SHE'S HIGH OFF HER ASS IN SOME PUBLIC TOILET.
FUCKITY-FUCK...
I LOVE THE WAY YOU SAY "ASS."
...YOU TRUST JUNKIE BITCH! YOU GET BILLY-BOY DEADO!
NOBODY INVITED YOU HERE, YOU LITTLE TWERP—
RUFUS, IF I MAY... LITTLE NUDE BOY, REMEMBER BRICK NUMBER FIVE:
THE BIGGEST BRICK OF ALL IS THE BRICK OVER YOUR HEAD.
PUT YOUR TRUST IN THE LORD. HIS WAYS ARE MYSTERIOUS, BUT HE'LL NEVER LET YOU DOWN.
GNRRRRRR
DICKLESS LITTLE FAIRY, YOU SMELL LIKE MY BETTY.
BILLY-BOY KILL YOU DEADO.
HOLY CRAP!
AHHH! GET HIM OFF! GET HIM OFF!
AHHHH!
YOU'VE BEEN NOTHING BUT TROUBLE.

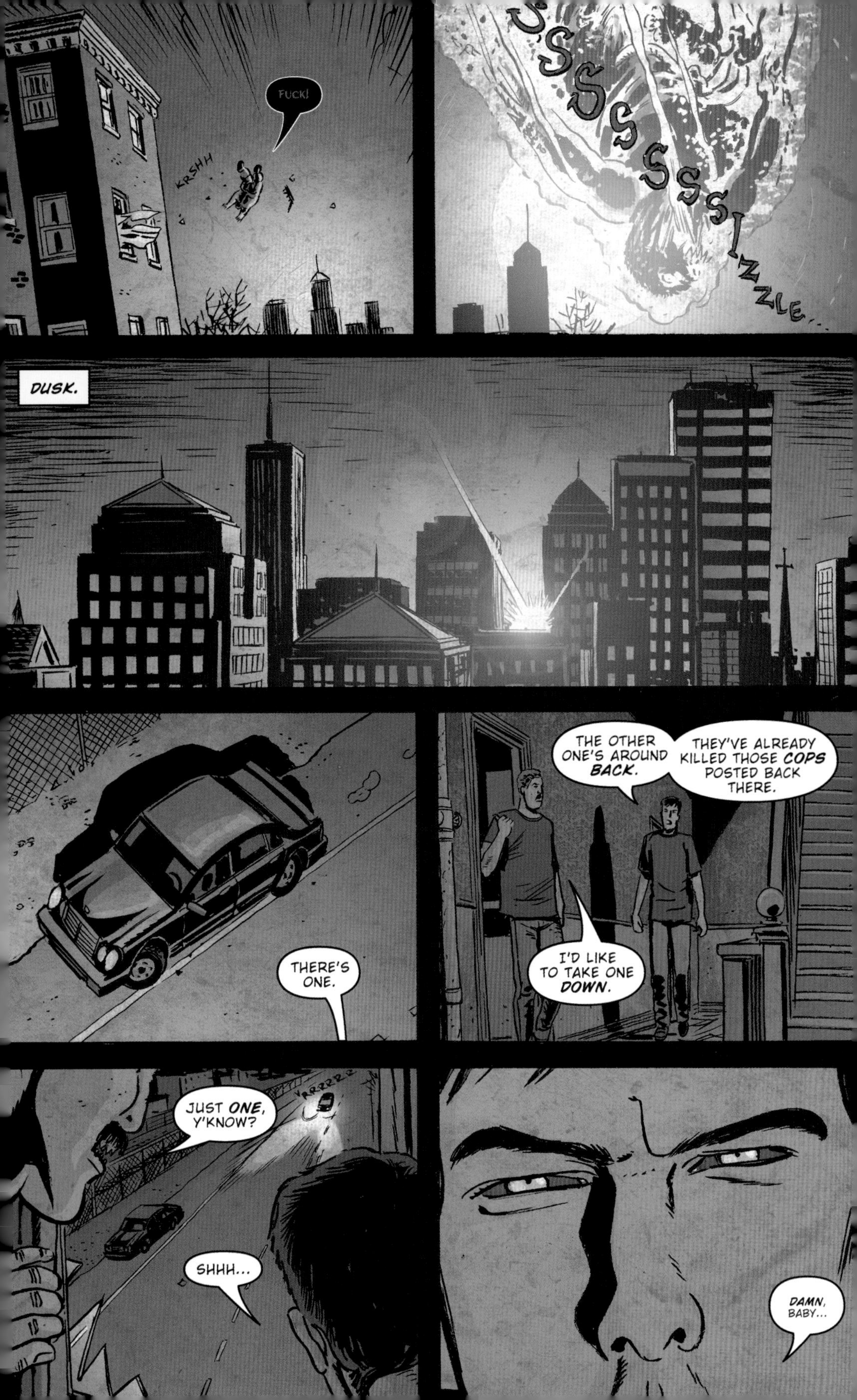
FUCK!
KRSHH
SSSSSSSIZZLE...
DUSK.
THERE'S ONE.
THE OTHER ONE'S AROUND BACK.
THEY'VE ALREADY KILLED THOSE COPS POSTED BACK THERE.
I'D LIKE TO TAKE ONE DOWN.
JUST ONE, Y'KNOW?
SHHH...
DAMN, BABY...

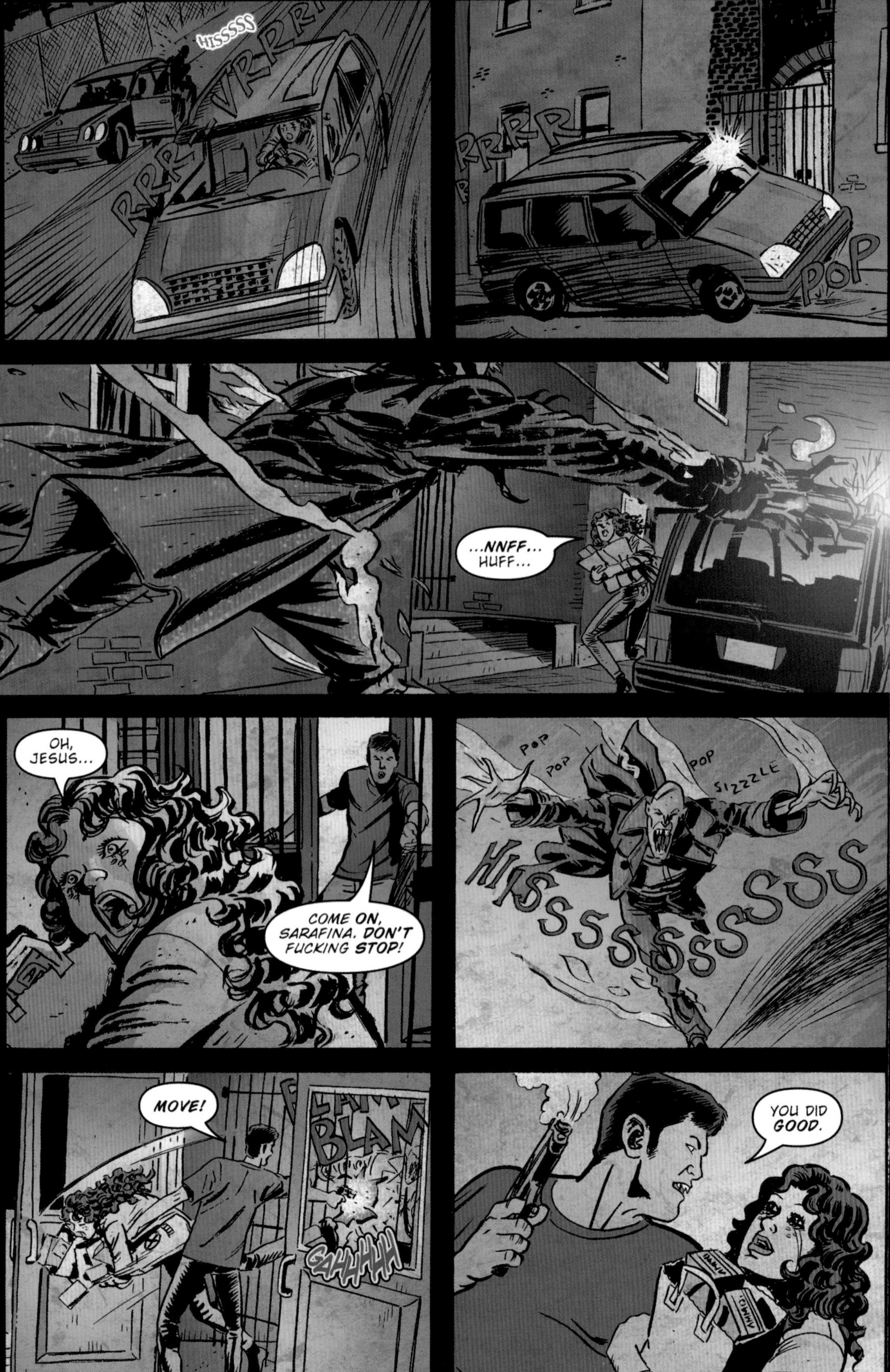
HISSSSS
VRRRR
RRR
RRRR
POP
...NNFF...
HUFF...
OH, JESUS...
COME ON, SARAFINA. DON'T FUCKING STOP!
POP
POP
POP
SIZZZLE
HISSSSSSSSSSSSS
MOVE!
BLAM
GAHHHHH
YOU DID GOOD.

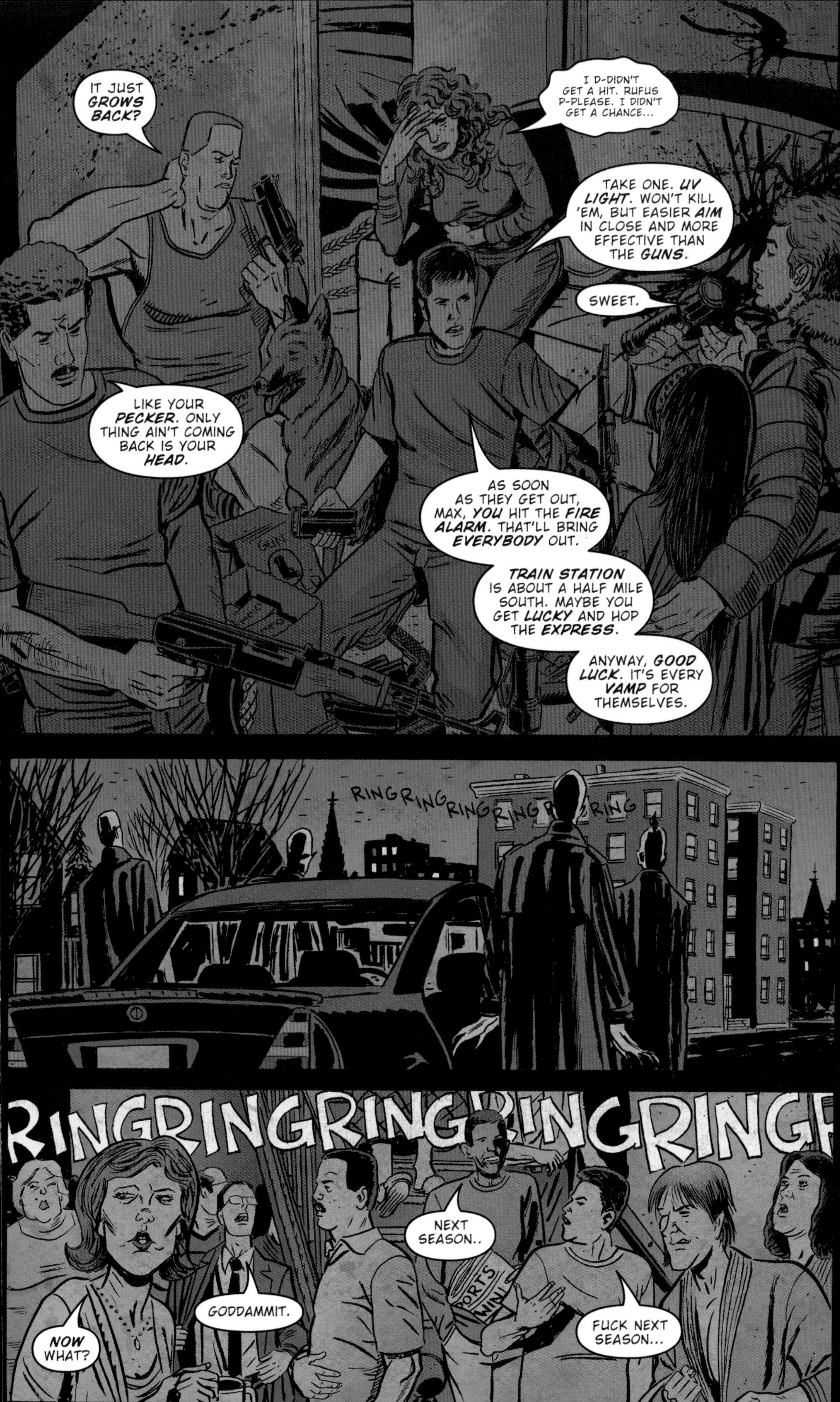
IT JUST GROWS BACK?
I D-DIDN'T GET A HIT. RUFUS P-PLEASE. I DIDN'T GET A CHANCE...
TAKE ONE. UV LIGHT. WON'T KILL 'EM, BUT EASIER AIM IN CLOSE AND MORE EFFECTIVE THAN THE GUNS.
SWEET.
LIKE YOUR PECKER. ONLY THING AIN'T COMING BACK IS YOUR HEAD.
AS SOON AS THEY GET OUT, MAX, YOU HIT THE FIRE ALARM. THAT'LL BRING EVERYBODY OUT.
TRAIN STATION IS ABOUT A HALF MILE SOUTH. MAYBE YOU GET LUCKY AND HOP THE EXPRESS.
ANYWAY, GOOD LUCK. IT'S EVERY VAMP FOR THEMSELVES.
RINGRINGRINGRINGRINGRING
RINGRINGRINGRINGRINGRING
NEXT SEASON..
NOW WHAT?
GODDAMMIT.
FUCK NEXT SEASON...

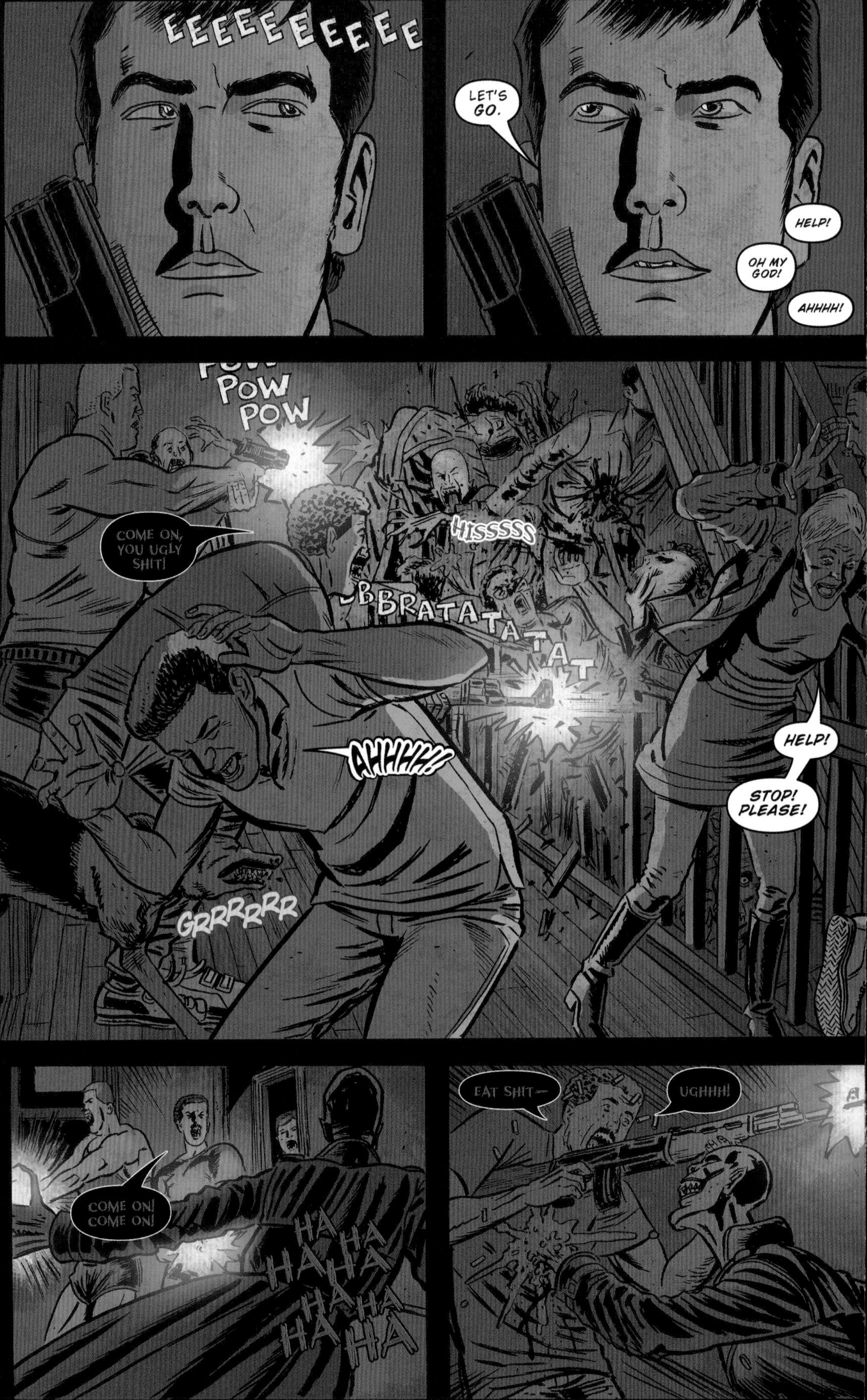
EEEEEEEEEE
LET'S GO.
HELP!
OH MY GOD!
AHHHH!
POW
POW
POW
COME ON, YOU UGLY SHIT!
HISSSSS
BBRATATATATAT
AHHHH!!
HELP!
STOP! PLEASE!
GRRRRRR
COME ON! COME ON!
HA HA HA HA HA HA HA HA HA HA
EAT SHIT—
UGHHH!

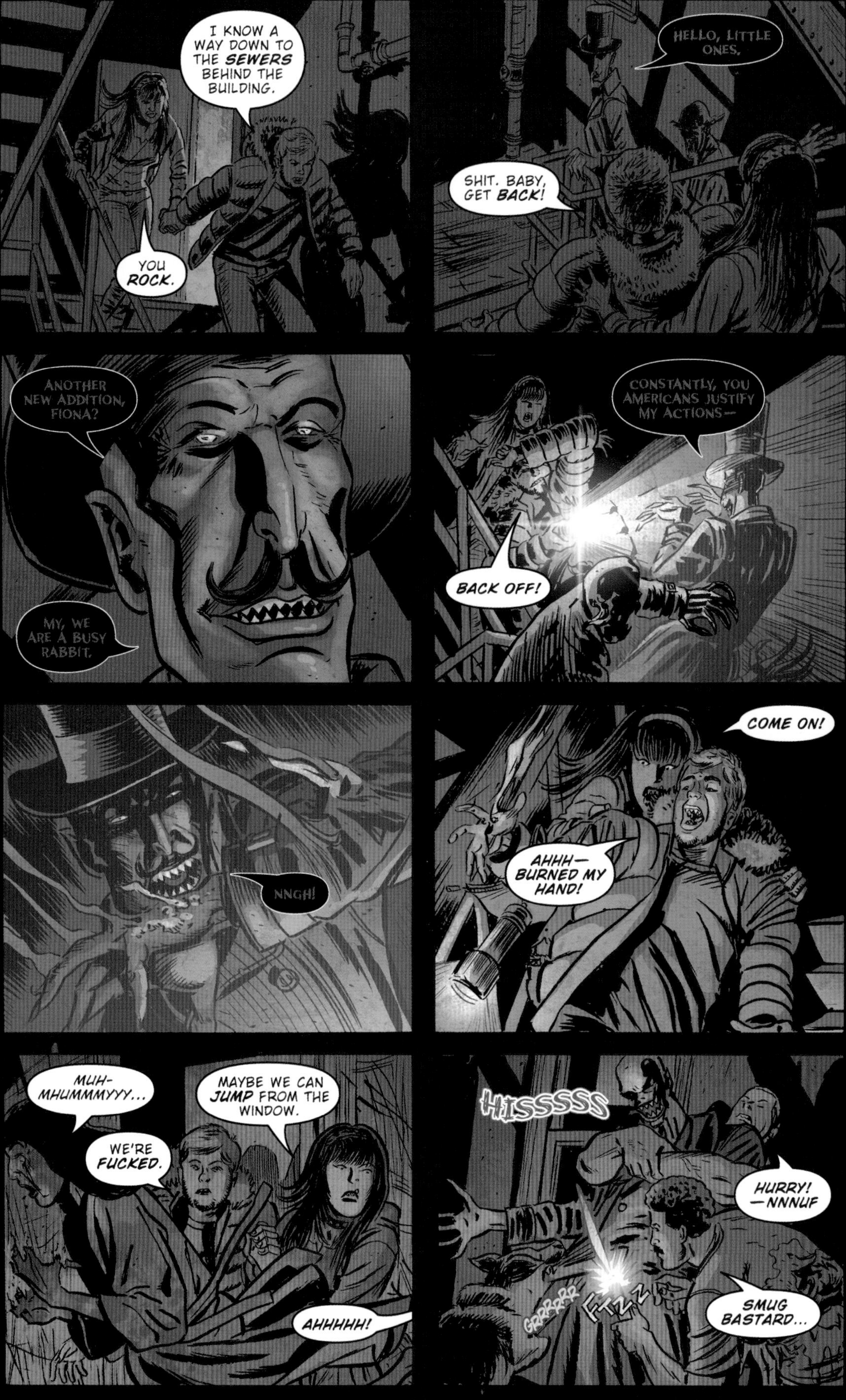
I KNOW A WAY DOWN TO THE SEWERS BEHIND THE BUILDING.
YOU ROCK.
HELLO, LITTLE ONES.
SHIT. BABY, GET BACK!
ANOTHER NEW ADDITION, FIONA?
MY, WE ARE A BUSY RABBIT.
CONSTANTLY, YOU AMERICANS JUSTIFY MY ACTIONS—
BACK OFF!
NNGH!
COME ON!
AHHH— BURNED MY HAND!
MUH- MHUMMMYYY...
WE'RE FUCKED.
MAYBE WE CAN JUMP FROM THE WINDOW.
AHHHHH!
HISSSSS
HURRY! —NNNUF
GRRRRR
FTZZ
SMUG BASTARD...

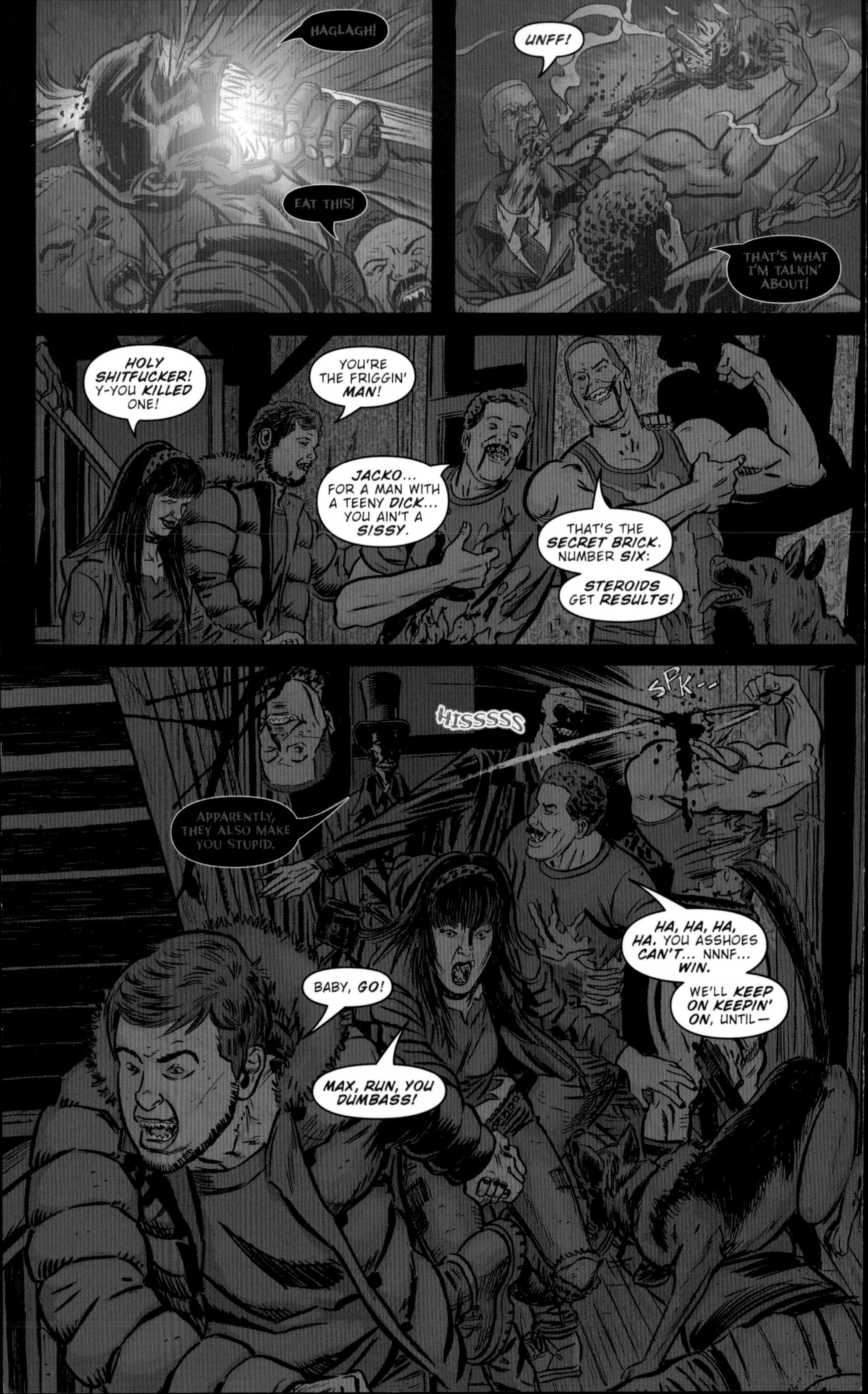
HAGLAGH!
EAT THIS!
UNFF!
THAT'S WHAT I'M TALKIN' ABOUT!
HOLY SHITFUCKER! Y-YOU KILLED ONE!
YOU'RE THE FRIGGIN' MAN!
JACKO... FOR A MAN WITH A TEENY DICK... YOU AIN'T A SISSY.
THAT'S THE SECRET BRICK. NUMBER SIX:
STEROIDS GET RESULTS!
HISSSSS
SPK--
APPARENTLY, THEY ALSO MAKE YOU STUPID.
HA, HA, HA, HA. YOU ASSHOES CAN'T... NNNF... WIN.
WE'LL KEEP ON KEEPIN' ON, UNTIL—
BABY, GO!
MAX, RUN, YOU DUMBASS!

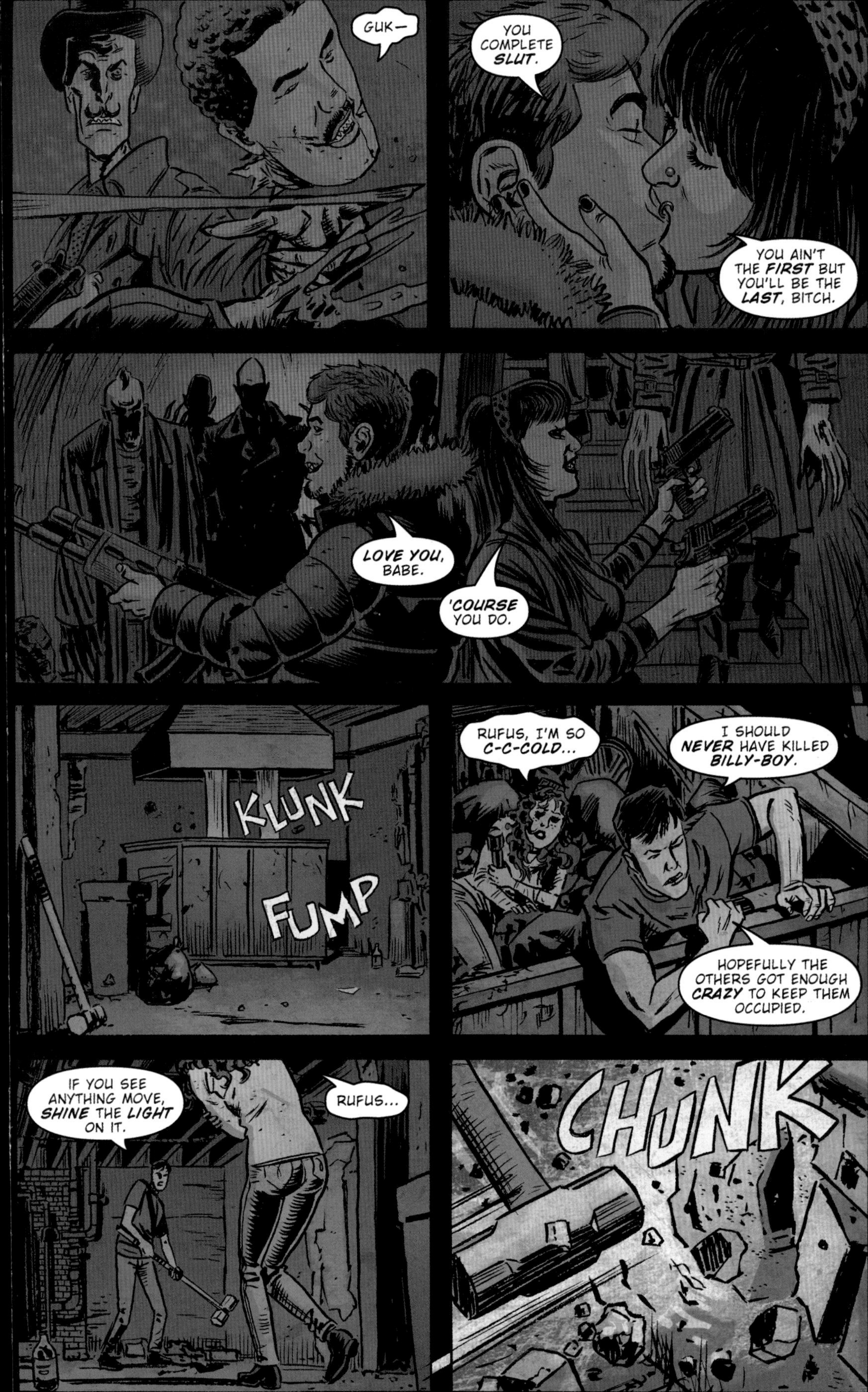
GUK—
YOU COMPLETE SLUT.
YOU AIN'T THE FIRST BUT YOU'LL BE THE LAST, BITCH.
LOVE YOU, BABE.
'COURSE YOU DO.
KLUNK
FUMP
RUFUS, I'M SO C-C-COLD...
I SHOULD NEVER HAVE KILLED BILLY-BOY.
HOPEFULLY THE OTHERS GOT ENOUGH CRAZY TO KEEP THEM OCCUPIED.
IF YOU SEE ANYTHING MOVE, SHINE THE LIGHT ON IT.
RUFUS...
CHUNK

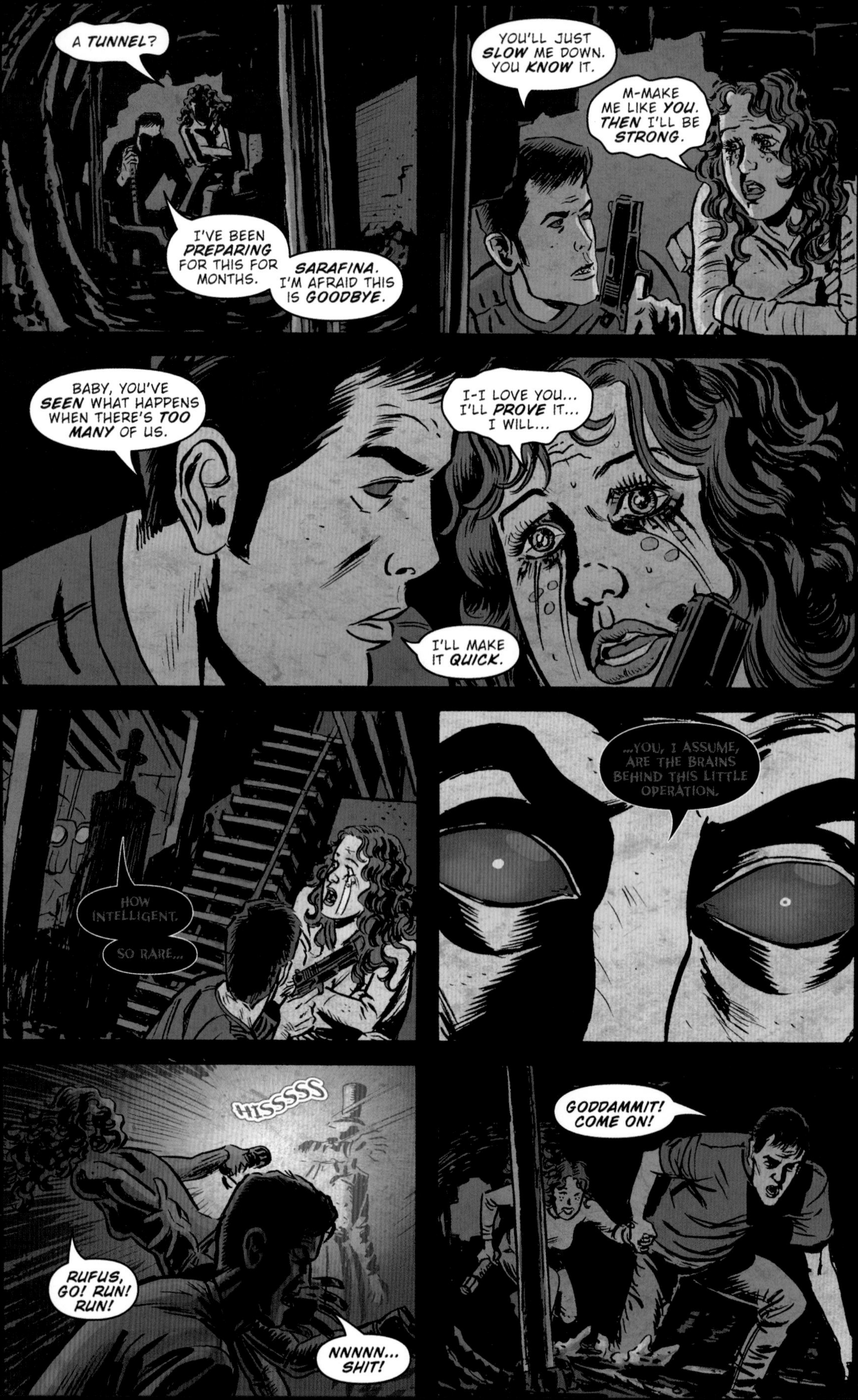
A TUNNEL?
I'VE BEEN PREPARING FOR THIS FOR MONTHS.
SARAFINA. I'M AFRAID THIS IS GOODBYE.
YOU'LL JUST SLOW ME DOWN. YOU KNOW IT.
M-MAKE ME LIKE YOU. THEN I'LL BE STRONG.
BABY, YOU'VE SEEN WHAT HAPPENS WHEN THERE'S TOO MANY OF US.
I-I LOVE YOU... I'LL PROVE IT... I WILL...
I'LL MAKE IT QUICK.
HOW INTELLIGENT.
SO RARE...
...YOU, I ASSUME, ARE THE BRAINS BEHIND THIS LITTLE OPERATION.
HISSSSS
RUFUS, GO! RUN! RUN!
NNNNN... SHIT!
GODDAMMIT! COME ON!

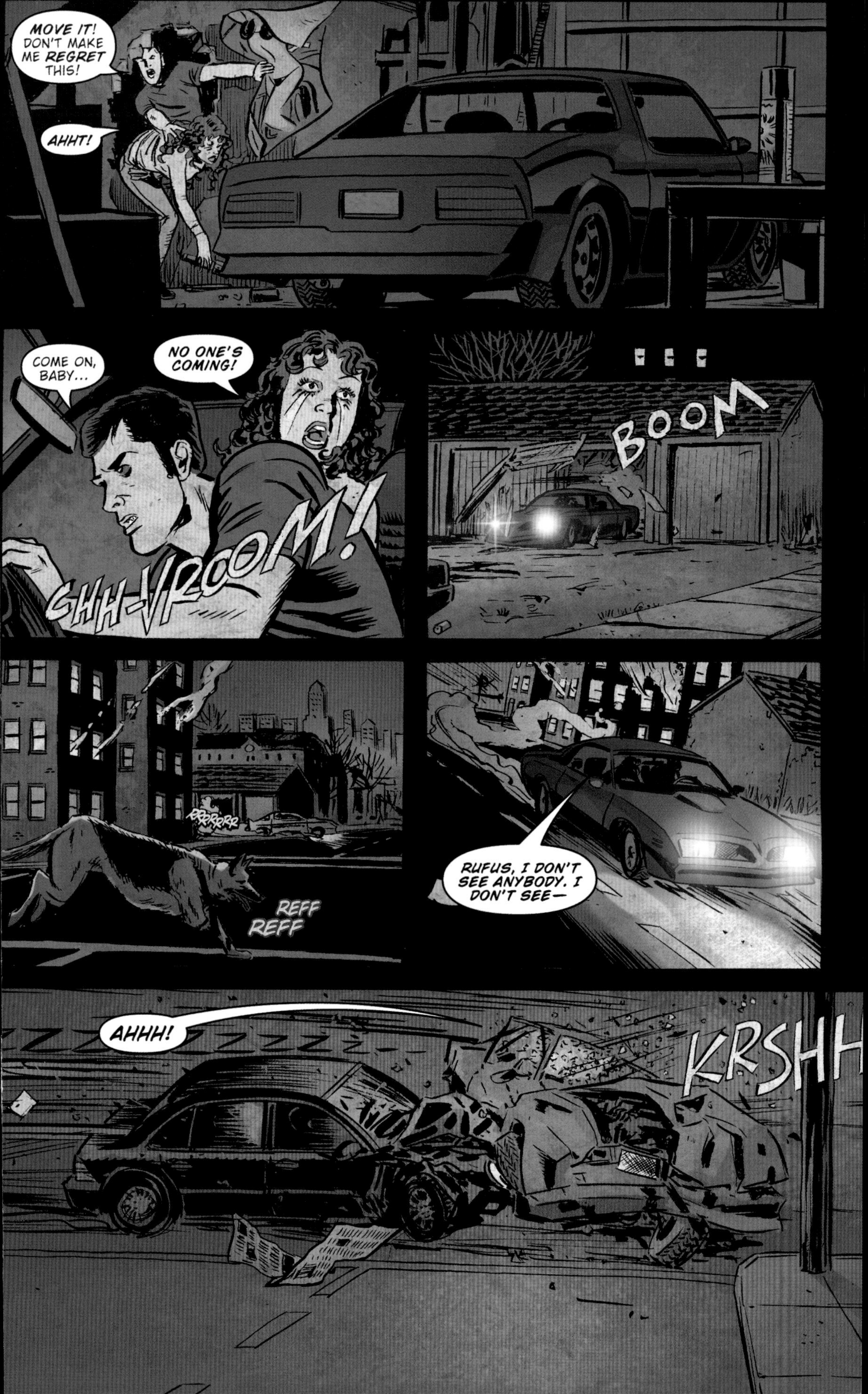
MOVE IT! DON'T MAKE ME REGRET THIS!
AHHT!
COME ON, BABY...
NO ONE'S COMING!
CHH-VROOM!
BOOM
RRRRRRR
REFF REFF
RUFUS, I DON'T SEE ANYBODY. I DON'T SEE—
AHHH!
KRSHH

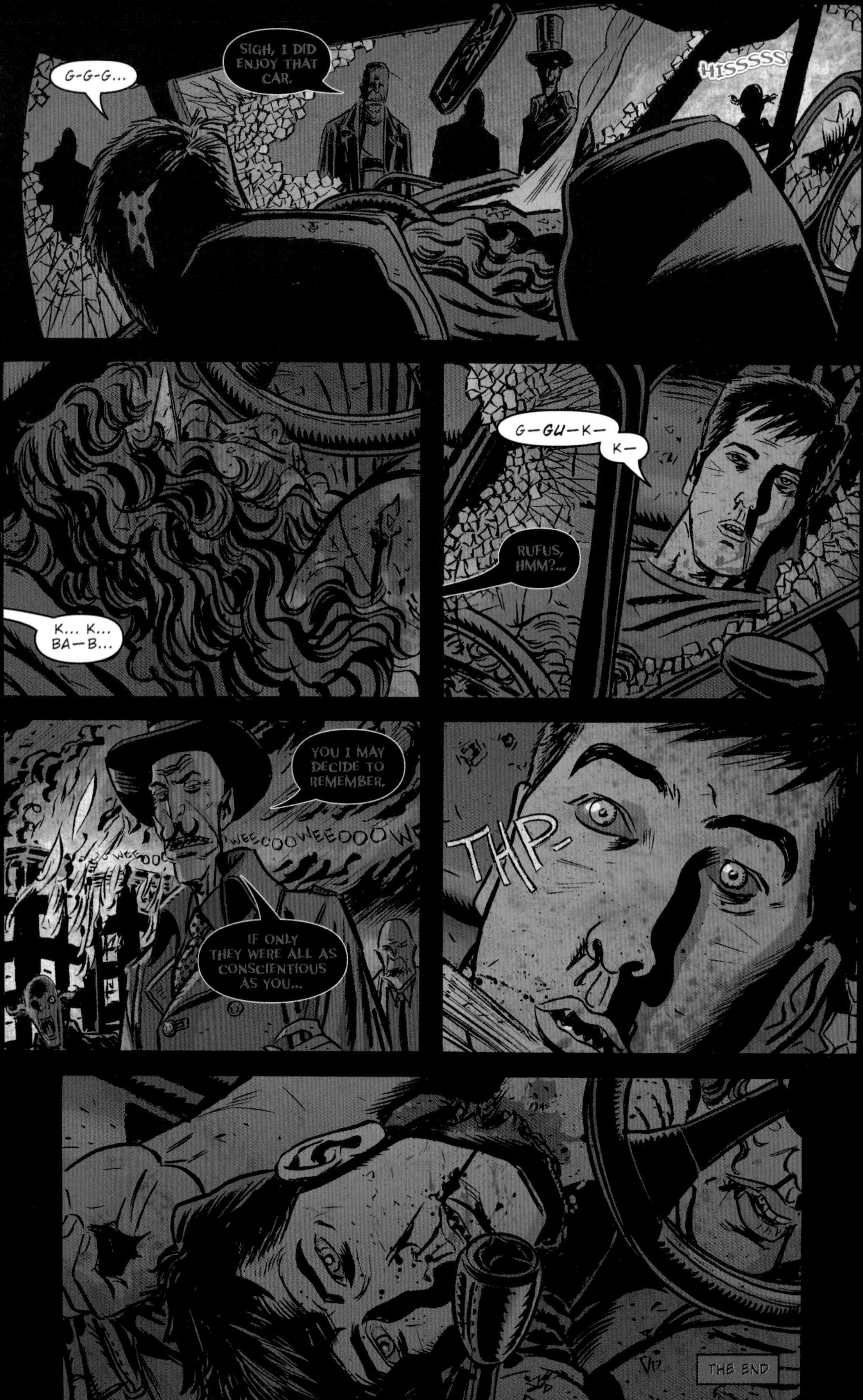
G-G-G...
SIGH, I DID ENJOY THAT CAR.
HISSSSS
K... K... BA—B...
G—GU—K— K—
RUFUS, HMM?...
YOU I MAY DECIDE TO REMEMBER.
WEEOOOWEEOOOW
IF ONLY THEY WERE ALL AS CONSCIENTIOUS AS YOU...
THP-
THE END

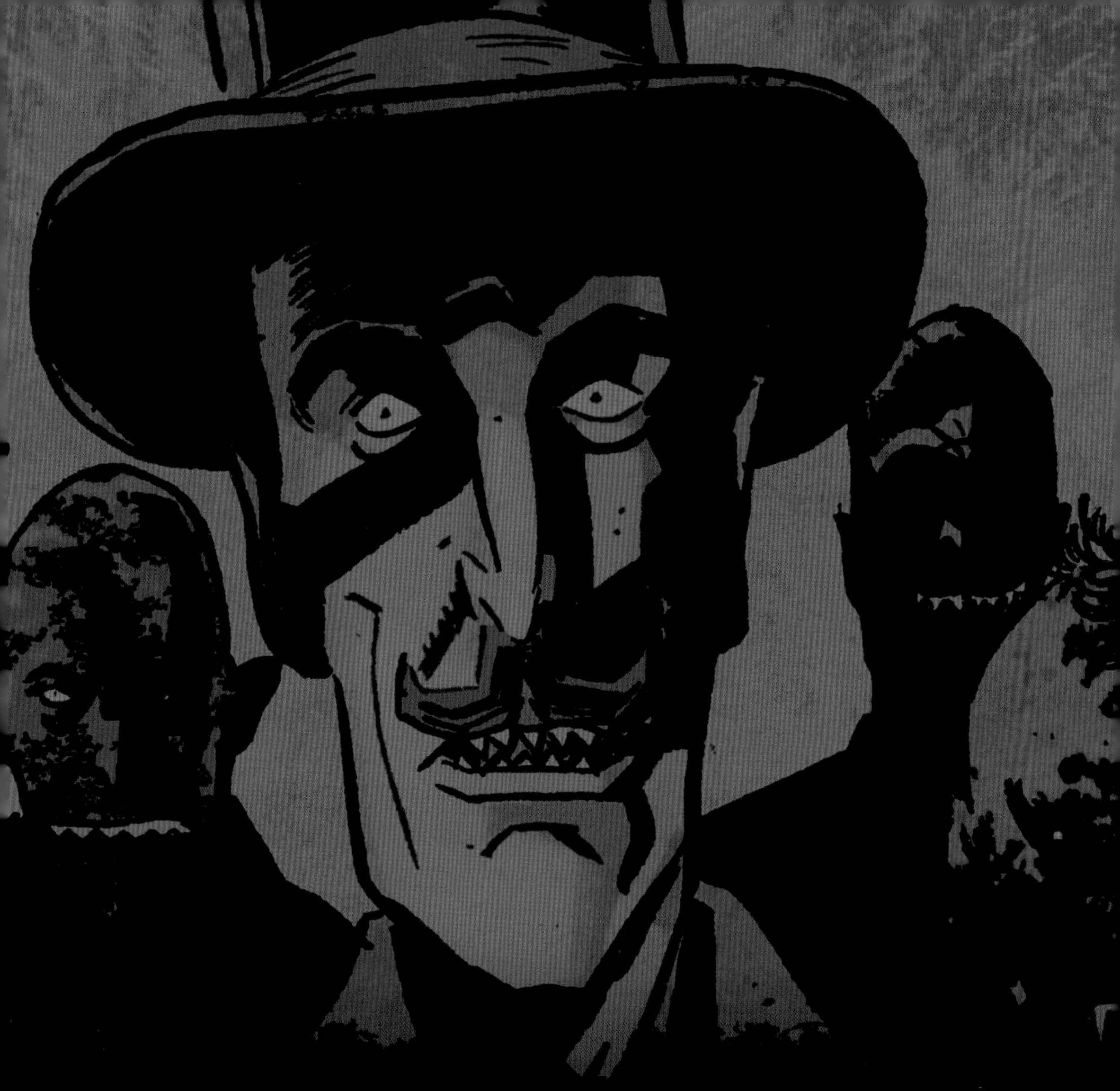

ART GALLERY

Artwork by David Laphar

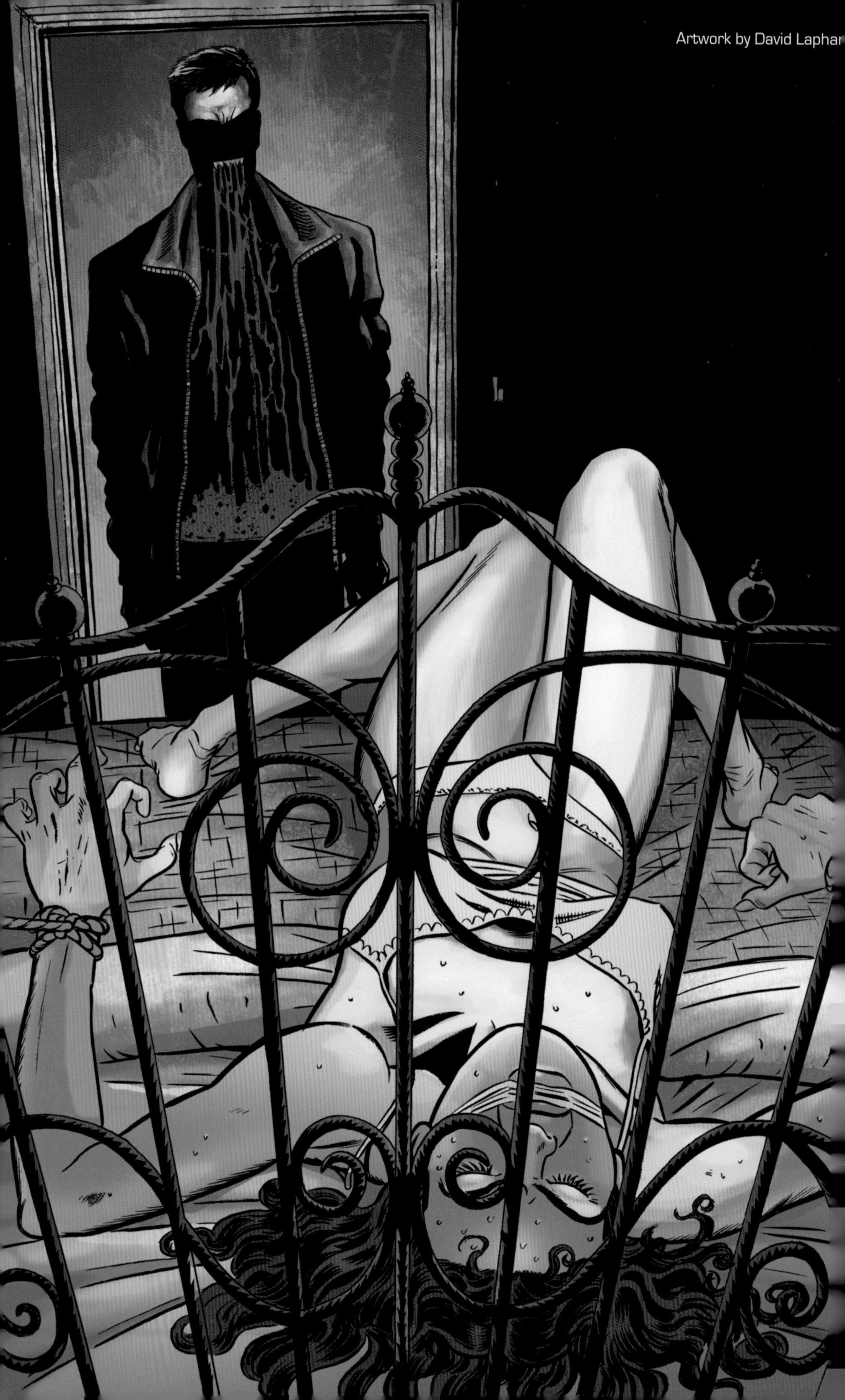

twork by Ben Templesmith

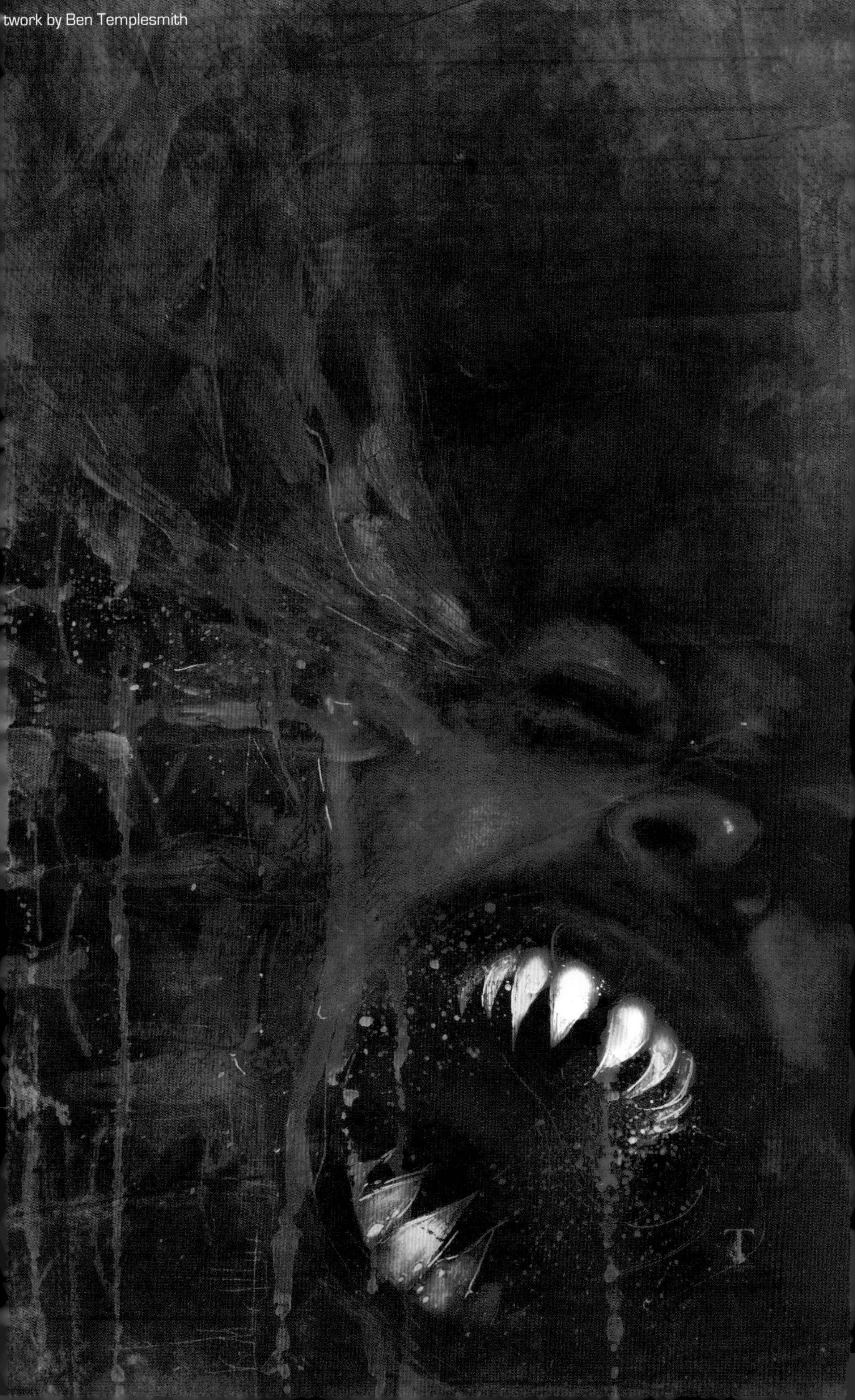

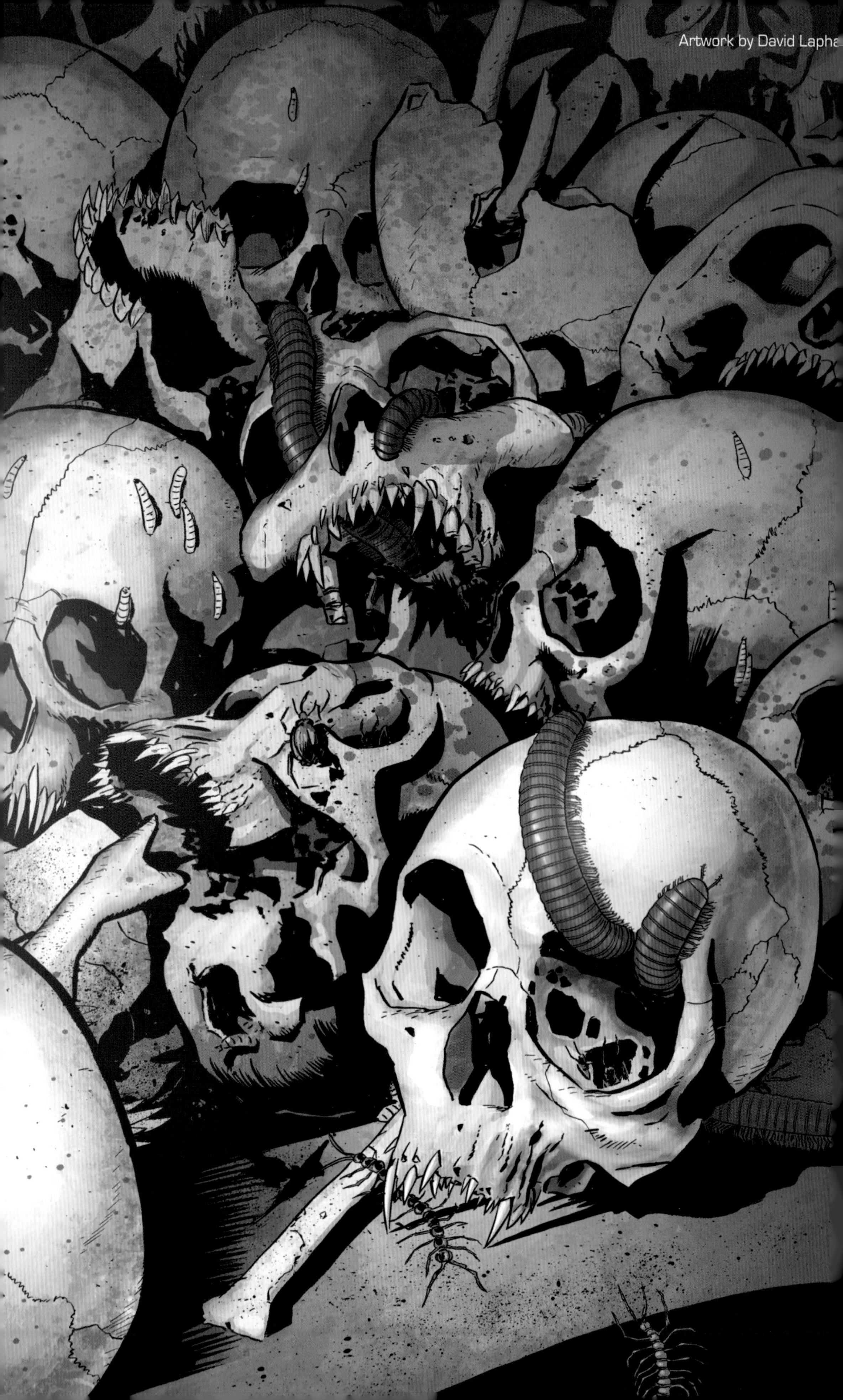

Artwork by David Lapha

rtwork by Ben Templesmith

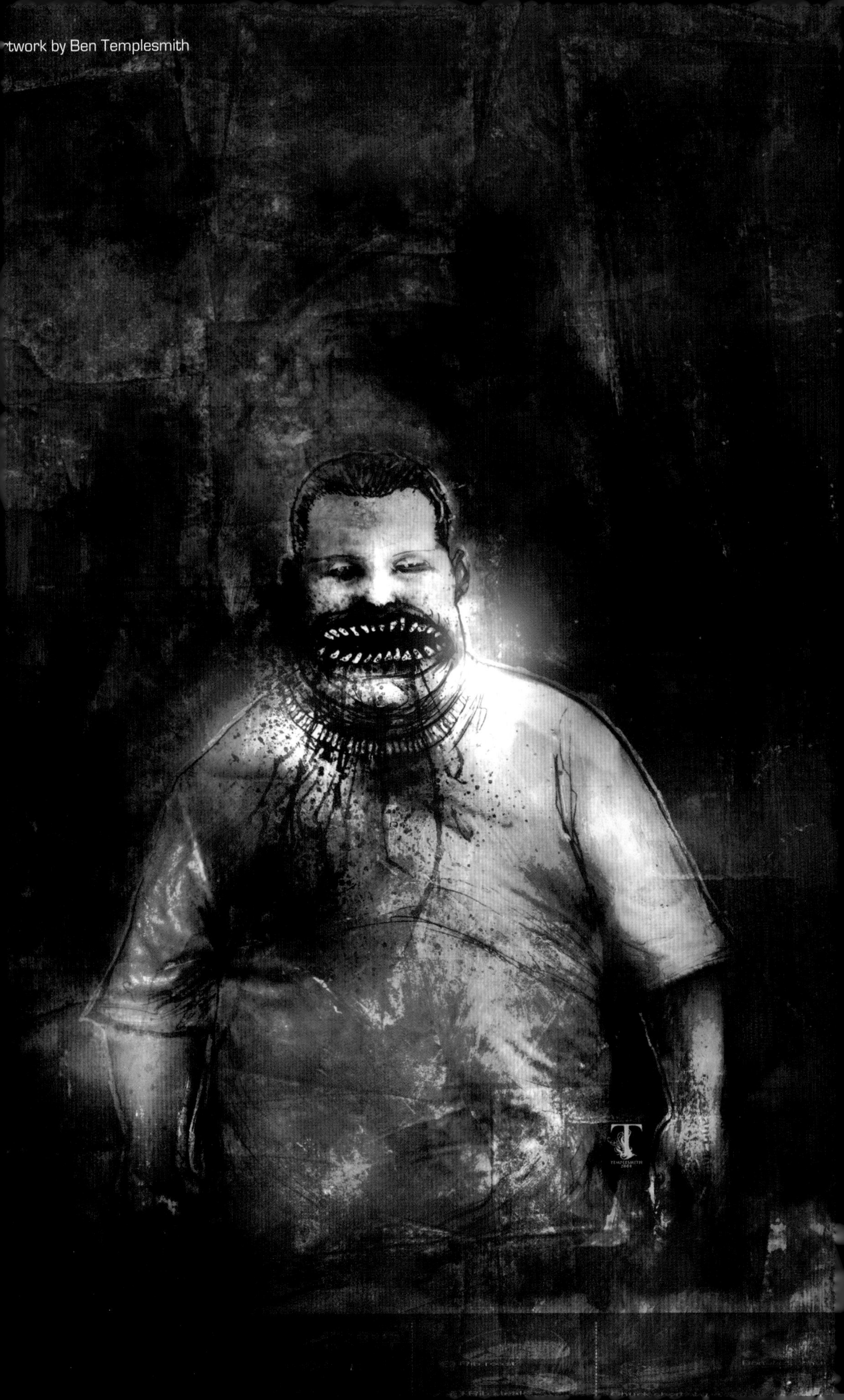

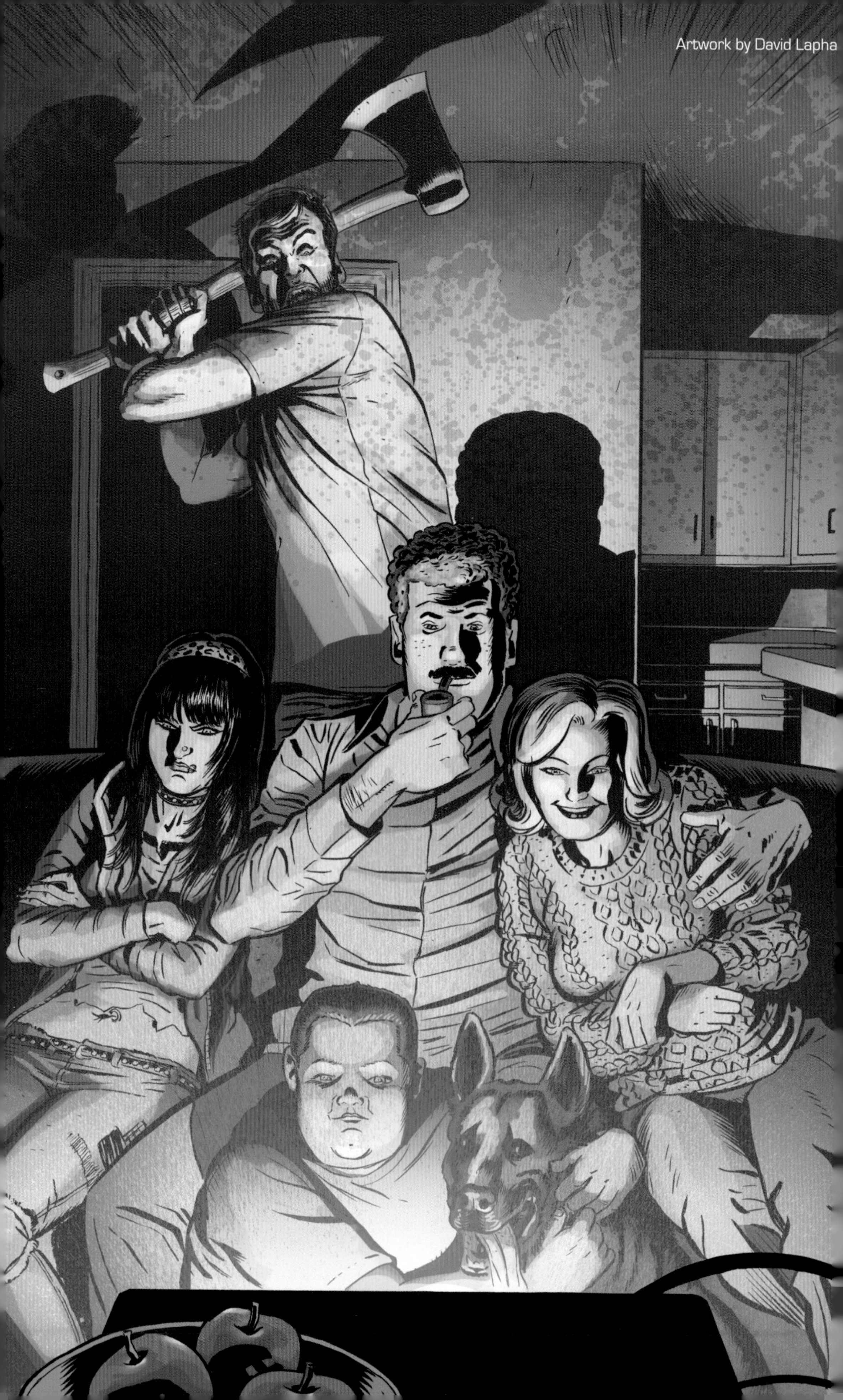

Artwork by David Lapha

Artwork by Ben Templesmith

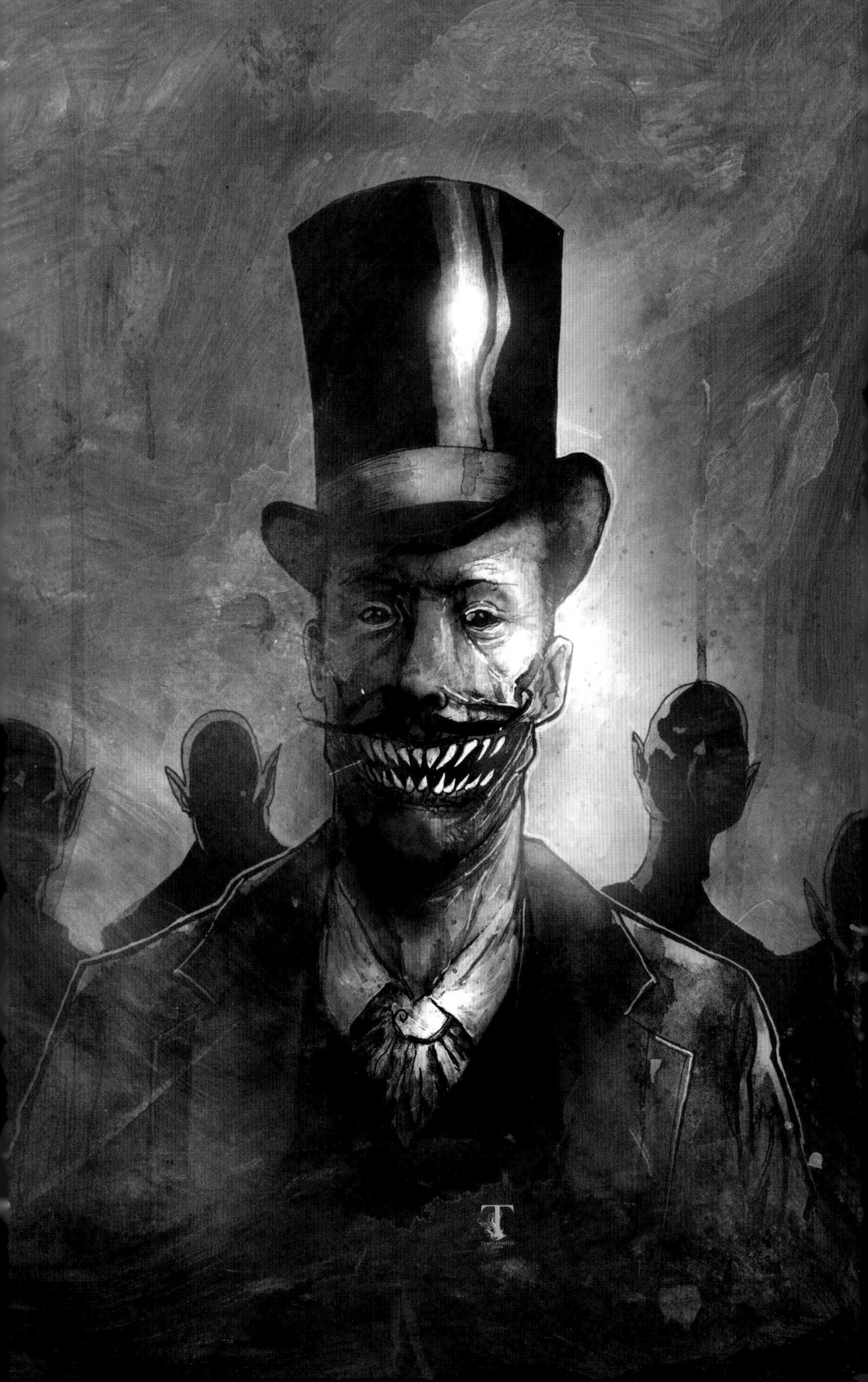

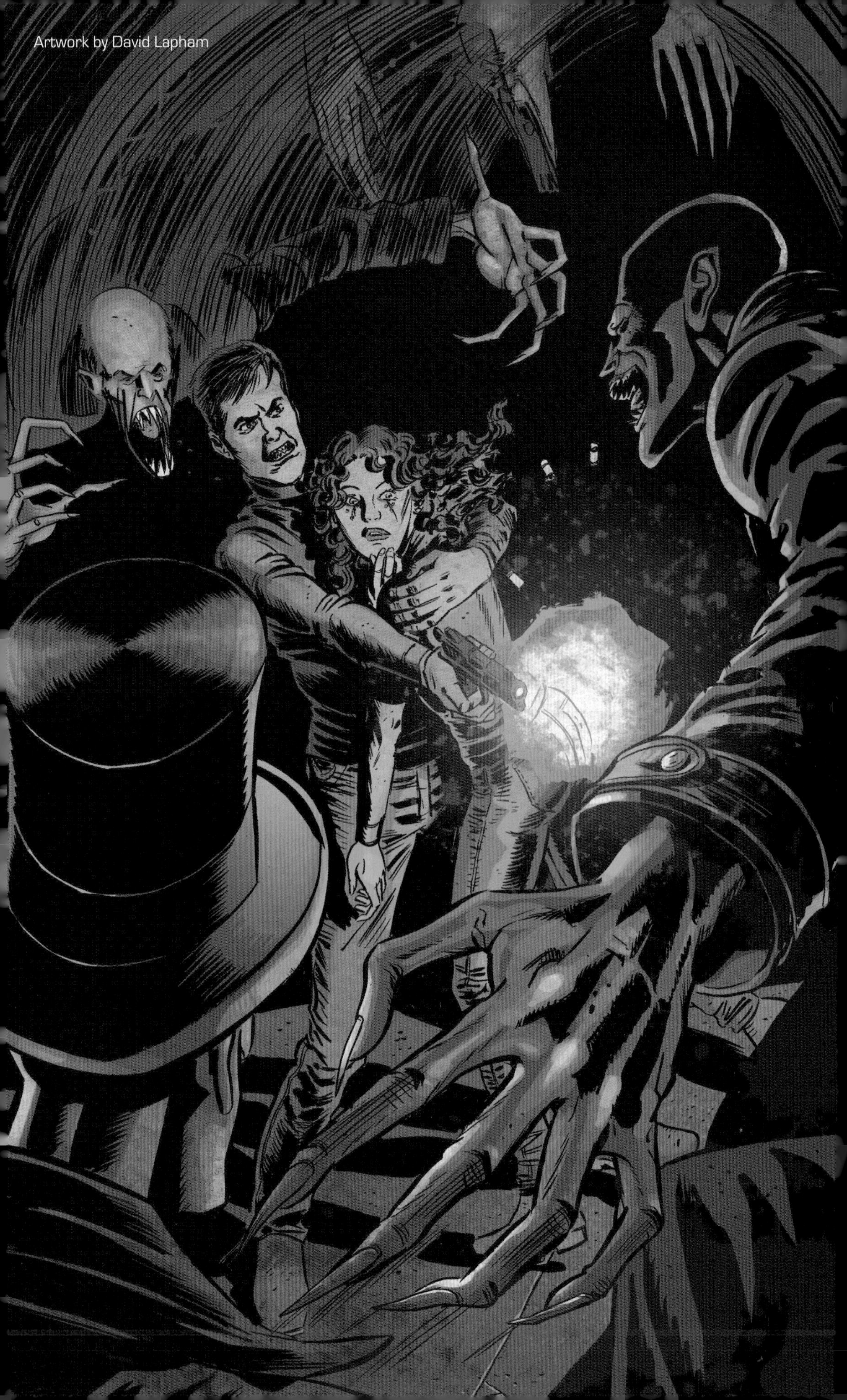
Artwork by David Lapham

Artwork by Ben Templesmith

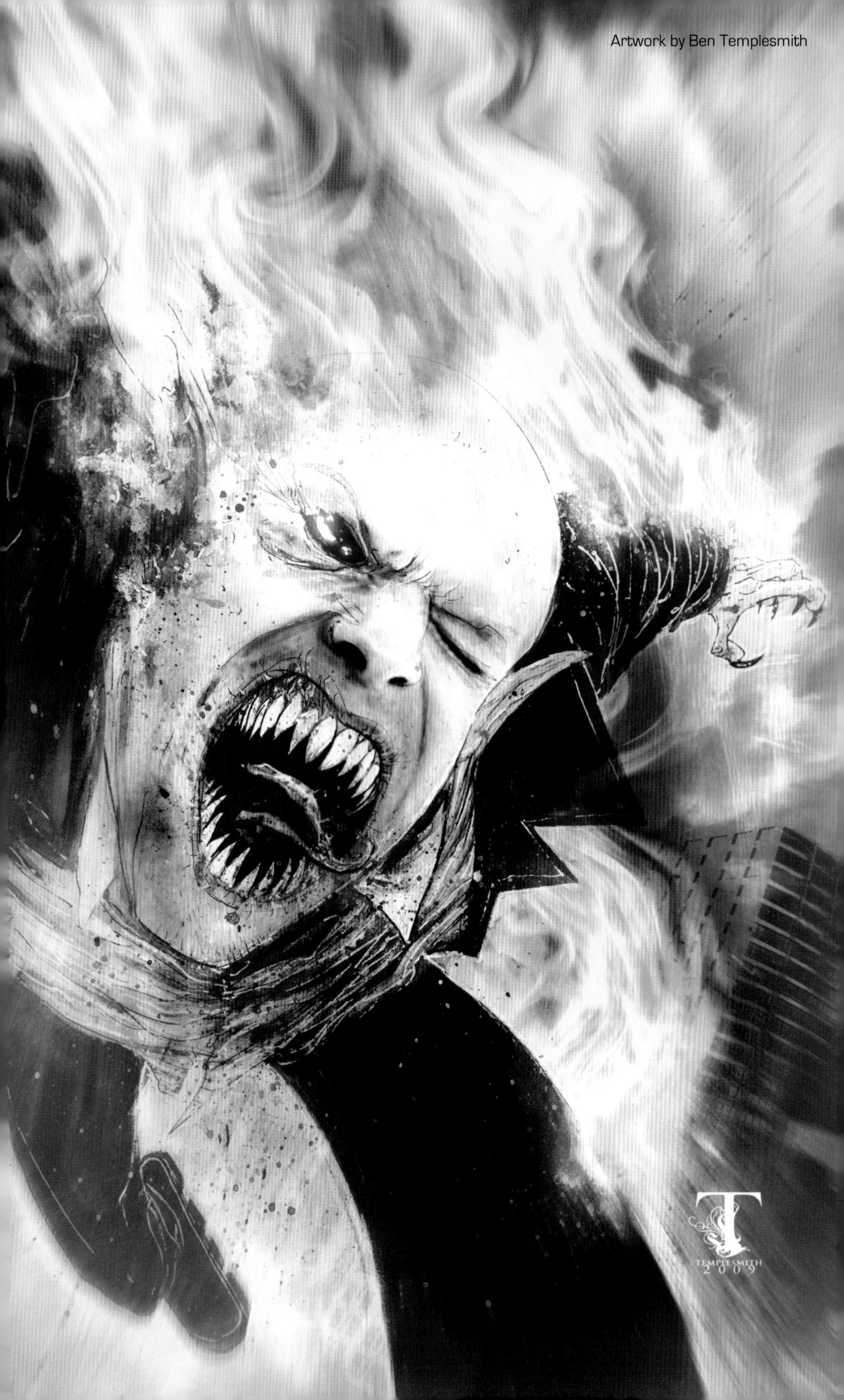
TEMPLESMITH
2009

30 TILL DEATH #2
COVER SKETCHES

A

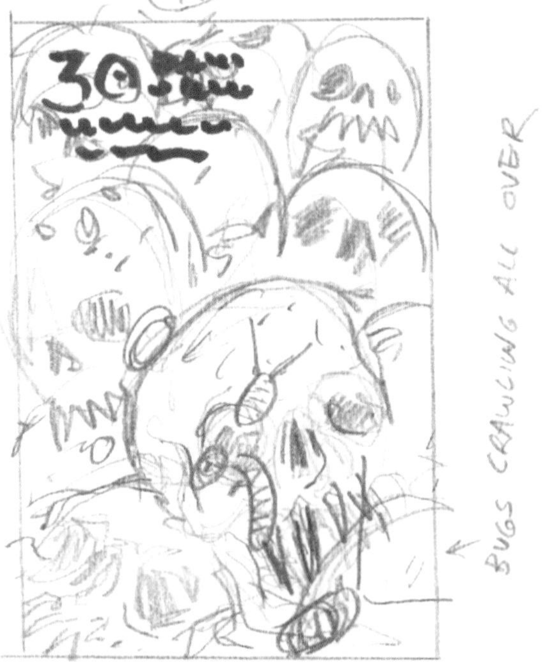
BUGS CRAWLING ALL OVER

PILE OF VAMPIRE SKULLS W/FANGS

B

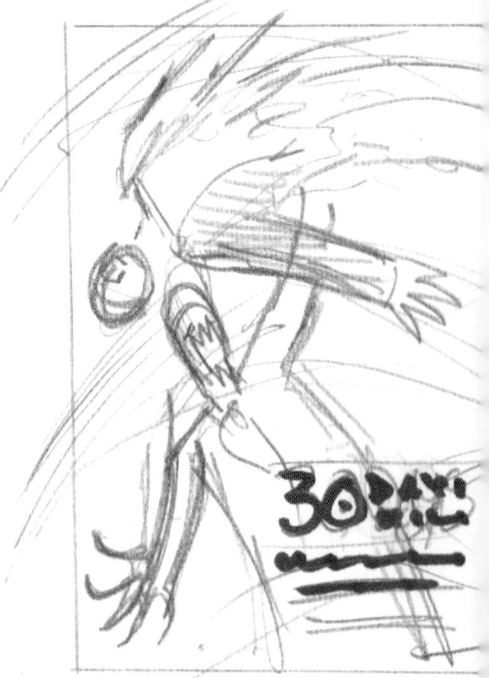

Olbrech of the kill squad holding up Rufus to kill him

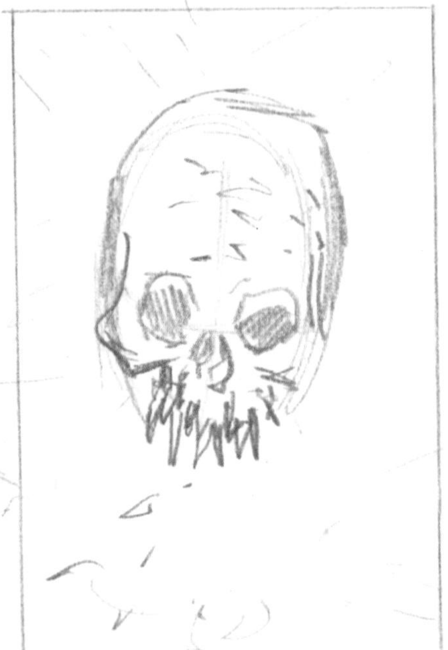

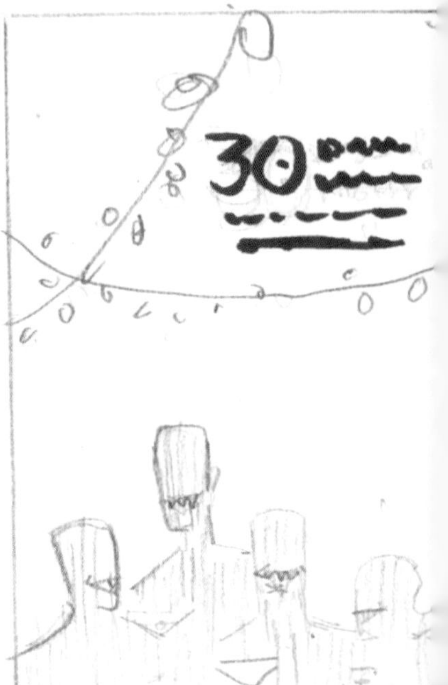

VAMPS AT PARTY